AMERICAN JOURNAL
OF NUMISMATICS
13

Second Series, continuing

The American Numismatic Society Museum Notes

THE AMERICAN NUMISMATIC SOCIETY

NEW YORK

2001

ISSN 1053-8356
ISBN 0-89722-288-1

COMPOSED AND PRINTED IN BELGIUM AT CULTURA, WETTEREN

CONTENTS

AJN Second Series 13 (2001) pp. 1–20

A SMALL FIND OF
SILVER BULLION FROM EGYPT

(PLATE 1)   JOHN H. KROLL*

There is no way of knowing when or under what circumstances this modest group of miscellaneous pieces of silver came into the possession of the American Numismatic Society. It has resided in the Society's Greek vault for probably more than a half century, stored, at least in recent decades, in a tray with a few other minor hoards or parts of hoards. The pieces had once been kept together in a white envelope that was annotated in a nondescript hand: "Hoard from Egypt. . .19".[1]

There are indeed nineteen pieces: three complete round cake ingots; two fifth-century Athenian tetradrachms, of which one had been cut down and the other had been tested with a small gash; one flattened coin-like dump; and thirteen irregular pieces of cut-silver of various sizes. Weights, dimensions, and details are as follows:

* Department of Classics, University of Texas at Austin, Austin TX 78712-1181, USA (jkroll@utxvms.cc.utexas.edu).

[1] I thank Sebastian Heath and Oliver Hoover for bringing the find to my attention, and Peter van Alfen for several crucial references. This paper owes much also to Andrew Meadows of the British Museum Department of Coins and Medals and Henry Kim of the Ashmolean Museum Coin Room for discussion and facilitating my examination of the ingots and cut-silver in their collections in the summer of 2000.

1

Round cake ingots

One side flat and smooth, with two or more irregular extrusions; the other side convex, with a rough surface (except towards the center where the roughness has been abraded through wear). A nick in **2**, flat side, along the rim (at 3 o'clock on Plate 1) was probably cut to expose the metal beneath the surface. Apart from their similar weights **2** and **3** are related by their perpendicular collar-like edge.

1. 92.96 g, 44 x 11 mm (th.).
2. 68.27 g, 38 x 11 mm.
3. 64.30 g, 33 x 13 mm.

Athenian tetradrachms

Obverse: head of Athena r., with frontal eye and three upright olive leaves on the brow of her helmet. Reverse: owl standing r. with olive spray and **AΘE**.

4. 16.99 g, 24 mm, die axis 5 o'clock. Small test-cut beneath the tail of the owl on the reverse.
5. 11.62 g, 24 mm. Segment cut away. The reverse type is entirely obliterated.

Flattened dump

The disk does not appear to be a hammered coin; the suggestion of a possibly obliterated design on the middle of one side is more likely random surface unevenness than traces of an almost completely effaced coin type.

6. 4.29 g, 11 mm.

Pieces of cut-silver

None appear to have been chopped from coins.

7. 12.02 g. Roughly square with a deep test gash in middle. 22 x 20 x 7 mm.
8. 10.70 g. Triangular, cut on all three sides. 25 x 20 x 7 mm.
9. 10.73 g. Edge fragment of cake ingot; cut on two sides. 18 x 20 x 10 mm.

10. 12.89 g. Amorphous lump composed of six or more small pieces fused together by heat.

11. 6.43 g. Amorphous lump composed of several small pieces fused together by heat.

12–19. Irregular cut chunks: 8.56 g, 5.52 g, 5.97 g, 3.48 g, 2.86 g, 2.27 g, 2.24 g, 1.11 g.

Despite the poor preservation of the Athenian tetradrachms, the visible details indicate that both coins date roughly to the third quarter of the fifth century.[2] Since the coins are damaged, we should probably date the find to the later fifth or the earlier fourth century.

COMPARABLE HOARDS FROM EGYPT

There can be no doubt that the find comes from Egypt, as it replicates the contents of a number of fifth- and fourth- century Egyptian hoards, which typically include cake ingots and chopped ingot fragments along with Greek coins, both whole (though frequently gashed) and in chopped pieces. For purpose of comparison, I here list ten such hoards which were recorded with some attention to their uncoined silver, along with three silver hoards (cited and reviewed by Dressel and Regling 1927: 6) in which there were no coins. The three hoards without coins were most likely secreted before Greek coins began to flood into Egypt in the last quarter of the sixth century.

---

[2] Stylistically both pieces belong after Starr (1970) Group V.A but before the full-blown mechanical standardization of the later fifth-century owls. No. **4**, with its tidy, unevenly-sized letters (small omicron) and owl with a two-part wing articulated in high relief, has parallels in Starr (1970: pls. XX.195 [Group V.B] and XXII.1′-3′ [early "post-449"]). To judge from the helmet palmette, **5** is later, definitely after Group V. Now that Starr's terminus of 449 has been adjusted upwards to c. 454 (Kroll 1993: 6), **4** should belong around the middle of the fifth century, **5** somewhere in or soon after the third quarter—unless it is actually one of the many imitations of later fifth-century owls manufactured in Egypt in the fourth century and perhaps in the late fifth (see below); given its poor preservation it is impossible to tell. No. **4**, on the other hand, is almost certainly Athenian since Egyptian imitations did not copy owls of pre-standardized type with layered wings and smallish omicrons.

No Coins

a. Samanoud (ancient Sebennytos, in the Delta), 1890s (Dutilh 1899: 287–88; Dressel and Regling 1927: 6 no. 1), gift to the Greco-Roman Museum, Alexandria: 470 pieces of chopped silver, including pieces of jewelry.

b. Mit Rahineh (ancient Memphis), February 1906, from excavations at Kom el-Qala (Brugsch 1906: 16[3]; Dressel and Regling 1927: 6 no. 2): 4 whole cake ingots (92 g, 142 g, 147 g, 149 g), of which two had been gashed across with a chisel, and the half of a fifth cake ingot (107 g). The silver tested at 95% fine.

c. Tel el-Athrib, near Benha (Delta), excavated on September 27, 1924 (Engelbach 1924; Dressel and Regling 1927: 6 no. 3): 50 kg of silver in the form of lumps, ingots, amulets, rings and other small, mostly fragmentary objects in two broken pottery jars. Engelbach lists and illustrates many of the inscribed and figured objects, and states that "[t]hey all seem to date between the XXVIth dynasty [c. 672–525 BC] and Ptolemaic times, but none of them permit us to date them more precisely." Cairo Museum inv. no. 48859.[4]

With coins

d. Mit Rahineh (ancient Memphis) 1869 (*IGCH* 1636; c. 500 BC [Jenkins]): 23+ coins; 73 kilograms of ingots and cut-silver. See note 3 above.

---

[3] Brugsch lists a second lot of cake ingots from Mit Rahineh that came from an earlier find and had been deposited in the Cairo Museum. These ingots, however, may have been part of hoard "d" below, Mit Rahineh 1860. Weights are 80 g, 98 g, 133 g, 158 g, and 257 g; the third ingot was test-cut with a chisel.

[4] Regling mentions that the Berlin cabinet acquired a lot of 233 g of small to minuscule pieces of silver lumps, wire, sheet, and foil that were alleged to be part of the same find. He was surely right to reject as modern additions three coins from northern Greece (fourth and second centuries BC), which were included with the silver.

e. Demanhur (Delta) 1900–01 (*IGCH* 1637; c. 500 BC [Kraay]): 164 coins; 2 cake ingots ("Silberkuchen" [Dressel and Regling 1927: 9]).

f. Sakha (Delta) 1897, (*IGCH* 1639; early fifth c. BC [Jenkins]): 72+ coins; 3 pieces of silver ingots and an uncertain number of coin fragments, all of which were melted down as worthless (Dressel 1900: 250).[5]

g. Benha el-Asl (Delta) 1929 (*IGCH* 1640; c. 485 BC [Robinson]): 77+ coins, most gashed or fragments; 13 small cake ingots (weighing from 48 g [diam. 35 mm] down to 9 g [diam. 20 mm]); 2 cut-silver fragments. The British Museum acquired all of the unminted silver. Robinson (1930, 1931) gives the weight and dimension of each piece and illustrates one of the larger ingots (1930: pl. IX, no. 33). Some of the smaller ingots may be fused or partially melted coins.

h. Asyut (Middle Egypt) 1968 or 1969 (*IGCH* 1644; c. 475 BC [Price]): 631+ coins, many gashed or fragments; 5 fragments of cake ingots, and one roughly hemispherical dump (Price and Waggoner 1975: 115, with photos of two of these pieces, pl. xxxi).

i. Naucratis (Delta) 1885 ("silversmith's hoard") (*IGCH* 1647; 450–425 BC [Barron]): 15 coins (of which 6 are Athens of mid to late fifth-century style), with 42 oz of roughly cast and cut-up lumps of silver.

j. Zagazig (Delta) 1901 (*IGCH* 1645; c. 470 [Barron], but a much later date, probably in the fourth century BC, is called for): 84 coins, of which the latest are 5 Athenian tetradrachms, 4

---

[5] In the hoard publication, Dressel (1900: 250) writes in addition that about forty squarish, stamped lead pieces were associated with the hoard. He illustrates two, one with the obverse, the other with a reverse stamp of a post-480 Athenian drachm, both apparently trial pieces for the production of imitation Athenian drachms in Egypt. If these remnants from an Egyptian mint were truly found with the silver (one can only say that it is at least not beyond the realm of possibility and is reminiscent of the bronze reverse die that was allegedly found with the coins of the Tel el-Athrib hoard [see note 14 below]), the burial date of the assemblage would have to be lowered considerably.

of the second half of the fifth century and one apparently of the fourth[6]; 16 cake ingots, and two cut halves of ingots, all of which are preserved in Berlin. Six of the ingots, of which one has the fourth-century-looking Athenian tetradrachm corroded onto it, are illustrated in Dressel and Regling (1927: pl. IV).

k. Delta 1940 (*IGCH* 1650; 375–350 BC [Robinson]): 9 coins, including Sidon, some gashed; 2 coins (?) with fused, obliterated types; 1 small cast disk ingot (Robinson 1960: pl. II.12), now in the Ashmolean Museum—8.33 g, diam. 27 mm, th. 5 mm even.

l. Beni Hasan (Middle Egypt) 1903 (*IGCH* 1651; c. 360 BC [Jenkins]): 77 coins (of which 55 are Athens, fifth-century type; with Sidon, Tyre, Gaza); 1 small cake ingot (22 g; diam. 28 mm) and 6 irregularly cut ingot fragments. Robinson (1937) gives weights and dimensions of the uncoined silver pieces, which are in the British Museum.

m. Naucratis (Delta) 1905 (*IGCH* 1652; c. 360 BC [Jenkins]): 83 coins (of which 70 are Athens: 68 of fifth-century type, 2 of

---

[6] Three of the five later Athenian tetradrachms (Dressel and Regling 1927: nos. 219–221) were illustrated for the first time in Kraay (1975: plate, nos. 1–3). They, together with the fourth (no. 222) that Kraay did not illustrate, are of the standardized type of the second half or last third of the fifth century and led Kraay to suggest a closing date of c. 440 BC for the hoard. But at least one of these tetradrachms, the wide-flan no. 220 (Kraay 1975: no. 3) is surely an Egyptian imitation of the fourth century, and none of the others are above suspicion of being fourth-century Egyptian imitations as well (see below).

In order to check the accuracy of the published drawing of the tetradrachm (no. 223) corroded onto Ingot b (Dressel and Regling 1927: pl. IV), Dr. B. Weisser of the Berlin Cabinet kindly sent me a cast and photograph, which tend to confirm that the Athena of this tetradrachm does indeed appear to have a profile eye, fully opened at the front, in keeping with standard Athenian owl silver of the fourth century. But since there are some particles of redeposited silver over the outline of the eye, one cannot be sure, and it may be that the front of the eye was only partially open, as on Athens' silver-plated and gold coinages of the last decade of the fifth century. Unfortunately, the tetradrachm's reverse, which otherwise might decide the matter, is affixed to the ingot and cannot be inspected. For all one can tell, this coin too may be Egyptian in origin.

fourth-century type); "a few silver ingots and probably also coin fragments" (Dressel and Regling 1927: 4).

Could the ANS assemblage be a small parcel from one of these later hoards? It is not impossible, but differences in the character of the unminted silver make it unlikely. For instance the very small bits of cut-silver, like our **15–19**, have not been reported from any of these later finds; nor are any of the better preserved hoards known to have produced lumps of silver, like our **10** and **11**, composed of smaller pieces that had been partially melted together, although Robinson (1960: 35) notes that "[h]alf melted coins and lumps of fused metal are regularly found in hoards from the Persian empire and especially Egypt."

Probably the most intriguing piece in the ANS material is the flattened dump (**6**) that has the exact weight of an Attic drachm and a nearly exact counterpart in the great early fifth-century mixed hoard of bullion and archaic coins from Taranto, Italy (*IGCH* 1874). The disk from Taranto, slightly ovoid and flatter, weighs 4.31 g.[7] A third but lighter flattened silver dump (test-cut with a chisel) showed up in the late sixth-century mixed coin/bullion hoard from Selinus, Sicily in 1985 (Arnold-Biucchi, Beer-Tobey, Waggoner 1988: 26, pl. 12 A); at 2.45 g, affiliation, if any, with a standard weight system is not obvious. Together, these "flans" form a class of anonymous, typeless, but still coin-like pieces, produced in some cases as standard-weight drachms, that circulated in areas where silver was transacted by weight. There are no sure indications that any of these flattened disks had once been a struck coin.

Any distinctiveness of the ANS Egyptian find is thus to be found in its smaller pieces. The two Athenian tetradrachms, on the other hand, are entirely typical of Egyptian silver assemblages of the fifth century and most of the fourth, as are the three ingots of bun or cake type. Other kinds of ancient silver ingots are known from finds outside of Egypt—like the rectangular slab or brick ingots recovered in Western

---

[7] There is a photograph with some of the cut-silver from the Taranto hoard in Price (1980: fig. 60).

Greek contexts[8] or the flat pancake ingots that came to light in the Antilebanon 1981 hoard (Hurter and Paszthory 1984: 121, pls. 16–17 nos. b–i)[9]—but in Egypt the round, plano-convex cake type of ingot recurs without exception and is the prevalent ingot type in contemporary mixed hoards from the Levant as well.[10]

Such ingots owe their shield-like shape to having been cast in open, saucer-like crucibles. One face (the upper, open side at time of casting) is regularly flat and smooth; the other side, shaped by the concave mould, is convex and normally has a rough, pitted surface caused by the gritty texture of the mould (which was probably made of coarse ceramic). Often protruding from the smooth, upper surface are one or more irregular knobs or extrusions of silver formed by solidification of highly viscous bubbles of metal when highly purified molten silver cools. In a discussion of these extrusions, C. Conophagos (1980: 329–30) states that they form only on silver with a purity of 98.5% or higher and therefore served as a guarantee of an ingot's fineness.

In shape and size, the ANS specimens are fairly typical, and compare closely to the ingots from the Zagazig hoard illustrated by Dressel and Regling (1927: pl. VI). The largest of the Zagazig specimens is considerably bigger than any of the ANS ingots, weighing 156 g and having a diameter of 57 mm; the smallest, with a 22-mm diameter and weighing a mere 15.5 g, is very much smaller. In some Egyptian hoards, like Benha el-Asl and the Delta hoards, nearly all of the round ingots are small, not much or not any larger than a Greek

---

[8] See the end of an brick ingot from the Taranto hoard pictured in Babelon (1912: 335) and the complete brick ingot (725 g) with an inscribed dedication to Zeus, from Sicily, in the British Museum (Hirschfeld 1893–1916: no. 423 = *IG* XIV no. 597). Lead isotopic analysis of the piece of a flat slab ingot in the Selinus hoard (Arnold-Biucchi et al. 1988, ingot B) has provisionally identified its silver as probably coming from Spain (Beer-Tobey et al. 1998) or Iran (Stos-Gale 2001: 66–67). It and the other Selinus ingots, now in a private collection, have been on deposit at the Ashmolean Museum.

[9] Most of these ingots are now in the British Museum (inv. 1988-4-12-1 to 6).

[10] See, for example, the fine specimens, all with extrusions, in the Ras Shamra 1936 hoard (*IGCH* 1478; Schaeffer 1939: 485–86, fig. 11). The earliest known ingots of silver in cake form are the three inscribed with the name of the Neo-Hittite king Barrakkab, 733–732 BC, from a hoard (now see Gitin and Golani 2001: 38) excavated at Zinjirli in western Syria.

silver tetradrachm; such smaller ingots tend to be disk-like, with relatively even thicknesses, but since they were cast in round moulds with
one side rough and the other side smooth (and may sometimes have an
silver extrusion on their flat side), it seems reasonable to associate
them with the normally larger plano-convex ingots.

Some cake ingots were very large indeed, although the evidence for
them comes from outside of Egypt. At 420.8 g, the complete cake
ingot (diam. 80 mm) from the Selinus hoard (Arnold-Biucchi, Beer-
Tobey, Waggoner, 1988: 26, pl. 12, ingot E) weighs very close to a
Attic/Aeginetan mina (433 g); and the very thick, cut quarter of
another cake ingot in the same hoard (ingot D, 597.4 g) comes from an
ingot that must have originally weighed in the neighborhood of 2400 g.
The 140-plus "cakes" (*phthoides*) of unminted silver stored in the
Parthenon on the Athenian Acropolis in 344/3 BC and listed in an
Athenian treasury inscription of that year were much larger still, each
weighing 12 minas (5196 g) or one-fifth of a talent.[11]

Apart from documenting the great size of these Athenian ingots,
their itemization in the inscription serves to remind us that the conven-
tional modern term, cake or bun ingot, mirrors good ancient practice,[12]

[11] See *IG* II^2.1443 lines 12–88; text and translation in Harris (1995: 123–27),
where (as in *LSJ*) the word *phthois* is misleadingly translated "bar" instead of
"ingot". The ingots were stored and inventoried in groups of five, i.e., by talents. It
is interesting that very few of these cakes weighed an exact 1200 drachms, most
being a drachm or more off one way or the other, in a deviation from ideal weight
that is reminiscent of Greek coins. The heaviest of the ingots weighed 1208 drachms,
the lightest 1184.

[12] In an inscribed account of late fifth-century Athens (*IG* I^3.376 lines 57, 105,
111, 1170), the same word for cake (*phthois*) is used for smaller ingots of gold,
which collectively weighed 300 drachms, from Skaptesyle in coastal Thrace.
Since a unit of the Spartans' primitive iron currency was known as a *pelanor,* or
sacrificial cake, it would seem that this Spartan money was effectively a money of
iron cake ingots. Plutarch (*Moralia* 226D) writes that a *pelanor* weighed a mina; and
as iron is about 30% less dense than silver, a Spartan iron *pelanor* would have been
somewhat larger than the Selinus ingot E, i.e., about large enough to entirely fill the
hand. Bronze was another metal that was commonly traded in cake or bun form.
Cake ingots of bronze go back to the second millennium; for bibliography and an
informative discussion of the 24 bronze cake ingots recovered from the Late Bronze
Age shipwreck off the SW coast of Turkey in the late 1950s, see Bass (1967: 78–81).
A very large disk ingot of bronze (so Boardman 1985: no. 158) is depicted on the

and also how inaccurate it is to refer to the cake ingot as a "Syro-Egyptian" type (cf. Price and Waggoner 1975: 115), despite its common appearance in Egyptian and Levantine hoard contexts. Lead isotopic analyses of the cake ingot and ingot quarter from the Selinus hoard have in fact revealed that the silver of both came from Aegean sources; in the case of the complete Selinus ingot (E), the silver is almost certainly from Laurion (Beer-Tobey, Gale, Kim, Stos-Gale 1998; Stos-Gale 2001: 66). It is to be hoped that in time the ANS and other ingots can be likewise sourced by identifying their lead isotope "fingerprints". Meanwhile, the most suggestive evidence for the origin of most ingots in Egyptian (and Levantine) bullion hoards is provided by the Greek coins that were found with them; for if most of the coined silver in Egypt came as it did from the mining districts of the northern and central Aegean basin, these should also be the sources that in the sixth and fifth centuries were supplying most of the unminted silver to Egypt as well.

It is generally recognized that authorities in Egypt began to mint and make payments in silver coin in the first half of the fourth century, in large part (scholars have assumed) for compensating the foreign mercenaries who were recruited for Egypt's struggles for independence from Persia. The silver coinage of choice was the fifth-century Athenian tetradrachm, the supply of which, once Athens ceased minting silver near the end of the Peloponnesian War, was hugely augmented by Egyptian imitations, some occasionally with Aramaic or demotic inscriptions (Kraay 1976: 294–295; Lipinski 1982; Buttrey 1982, 1984; Jones and Jones 1988: 107–110; Price 1993; further bibliography in Stroud 1974: 169–71 and Figueira 1998: 530–534).[13] The great Egyptian hoards of such Athenian and pseudo-

---

fourth-century grave stele of the bronze-smelter Sosinos in the Louvre (Clairmont 1970: no. 10); the still larger, smooth round object behind it is probably the mould in which it was cast.

[13] To the various types of Egyptian imitations that have been identified and discussed over time, it has been recently proposed (Nicolet-Pierre 2000b) to add a well-defined group of Athenian tetradrachms of the first third of the fourth century; these tetradrachms were the first to depict the head of Athena with a profile eye and the first to display a newly proportioned owl with an enlarged and heavily-fringed head. According to Nicolet-Pierre, these coins are to be recognized as free and highly

Athenian tetradrachms date to the fourth century.[14] As we have seen, however, in the fifth century and also for much of the fourth, silver was hoarded in Egypt in the form of bullion, and to this day scholars are not entirely in agreement as to the significance of these earlier hoards: whether the bullion in them was assembled for monetary purposes or merely as a commodity, valuable primarily as raw material for the manufacture of jewelry and fine metal vessels. Early commentators regularly dubbed the hoards "silversmiths' hoards" (cf. the Naucratis hoard, "g" above; Engelbach 1924) or interpreted them as remains of a jeweler's workshop (Brugsch 1906) or of a mint (Dutilh 1899). But early in the last century Dressel (1900: 257–58) and Dressel and Regling (1927: 12) insisted on the currency interpretation, explaining that the frequency and character of such finds, which regularly included coins and ingots that had been chopped into smaller pieces, point to a monetary convention, well known, for example, from medieval northern and eastern Europe (cf. Williams 1997: frontispiece [silver bullion hoard from Viking England, eighth c. AD] and fig. 117 [Russian cut-silver ingot of the twelfth or thirteenth c. AD]),[15] in

creative Egyptian imitations of fifth-century owls. But the profile eye and the stubby, shaggy-headed owl happen also to be characteristic of the voluminous Athenian pi-style silver of the second half of the fourth century; and since it is unthinkable that the Athenians would have modeled the latter coinage on foreign imitations, the tetradrachms in question may be safely removed from suspicion as pseudo-Athenian. Although the only such tetradrachms with recorded findspots come from hoards in Sicily and one hoard in Egypt (Tel el-Athrib, see note 14), their unmistakable style is to be seen very clearly in the tribols and diobols in the small lamp hoard from Ag. Ioannis Rentis in Attica (*IGCH* 89; Kroll 1993: 8 n. 25).

[14] Tel el-Athrib 1905 (*IGCH* 1663): 700 tetradrachms (together, according to the vendor, with the bronze reverse die for a fifth-century Athenian owl tetradrachm). Tell el-Maskhouta (Delta) 1947–48 (*IGCH* 1649): 6000+ tetradrachms. Reports of the latter find and the Aramaic inscriptions on the relatively intact silver bowls found with the coins clearly indicate that the find (which also included gold-set agate inlays) was a treasure of a temple dedicated to the foreign goddess Alat, and not a currency hoard. The inscribed bowls had been dedicated around 410 BC by chieftains of some Qedarite Arabs, another alien group settled in Egypt under Persian auspices (Rabinowitz 1956, 1959; Brooklyn Museum 1956: 43–44). It is worth noting that the Athenian coins in these and other fourth-century hoards, like hoards l and m above, are rarely gashed and were apparently never chopped into pieces.

[15] The word *ruble* comes from the Russian verb "to cut (off)". For an important survey of such historical comparanda, see Regling (1926: 225–236).

which exchange was transacted through the cutting and weighing out of silver bullion on the scale. E.S.G. Robinson (1930: 94) accepted this interpretation as conclusive. Yet in the new *Oxford Encyclopedia of Ancient Egypt,* P. F O'Rourke (2001: 288) comes dangerously close to reviving the old silversmith interpretation by writing, with reference to the coins in the bullion hoards, that "[i]t is highly doubtful, however, that these coins were considered of any intrinsic value by native Egyptians, other than the artisans who worked in gold and silver. To the metalworkers, such coins were desirable as a source of bullion..." and that "beyond their value as metal, coins appear to have played next to no role in the Egyptian economy of the sixth and fifth centuries BCE."[16] However true this last statement may be, O'Rourke's attention to metalworkers shows that he was unaware that silver *bullion* played a very significant role in the Egyptian economy during those centuries.

That it did has been understood for some time from the great papyrus archive of the Jewish military settlement at Elephantine near Aswan in upper Egypt. The records, written in Aramaic, began around 500, after the Persian king established the military colony, and continued to the beginning of the fourth century. In the many documents that deal with economic matters—marriage contracts, bills of sale, loan agreements, receipts of payment, deeds of ownership, and the like—prices and means of transaction are expressed in weights of silver.[17] There being no state silver coinage at this time, it is clear that the community employed a currency of silver that was weighed out on

---

[16] Möller (2000: 209) suggests an alternative non-currency use, declaring that "[s]ilver was a prestige object in Egypt, circulating only among the elite, who utilized it either for gift exchange or to demonstrate their wealth". For explicit mention of the use of a balance in the payment of this silver, see the Elephantine marriage contract (Kraeling 1953: Papyrus 7), c. 420 BC: "If Yehoyishma divorces her husband...she shall become liable for divorce money. She shall sit by the scales and shall give to her husband 7 silver shekels and 2 quarters" (lines 24–26). The harbor taxes in silver and gold listed in an Egyptian customs record of the first half of the fifth century must similarly have been weighed out (Yardeni 1994; Briant and Descat 1998).

[17] The weights, most commonly the shekel and the Persian *karsh*, are non-Egyptian.

the balance, similar to that which was employed throughout the Persian empire at the time (Porten 1968: 62–72; Naster 1970), and which of course had been independently implied by the contemporary Egyptian hoards of silver bullion, as Dressel and Regling had deduced. Thus, just as in Mesopotamia and the Levant, where over two dozen hoards of silver bullion, some as early as the second millennium, have come to light, and where the textual evidence for the use of silver as an important monetary instrument is older and much more abundant than in Egypt, texts and hoards readily supplement each other and allow us to identify such hoards confidently as monetary in nature.[18] Marriage contracts on papyri from the Persian era attest further to the widespread monetary use of silver in Egypt at this time; the formulaic contracts are written in demotic and record penalty payments in weights of silver, the weights being the traditional Egyptian *deben* and *kite*. (Porten 1968: 68; Chauveau 1998: 140–141).

In Egypt the exchange use of silver can be traced back to the New Kingdom, when prices were notationally expressed in weight-units (*debens*) of copper—unlike silver, a metal native to Egypt—and payments could be made in any goods, including livestock, in a fixed-value type of barter-exchange arrangement (Kemp 1989: 248–250). Hence silver and gold might both be used, and it is worth noting that the great fourteenth-century hoard from Amarna (Kemp 1989: 244–45, fig. 82; Williams 1997: fig. 11) consisted of bullion in both metals.[19] Yet even within this context of heterogeneous exchange, written documents from the craftsmen's village of Deir el-Medina near Thebes reveal that by the twelfth century the word for silver (*hedj*) had acquired a broader, colloquial meaning as a kind of generic term for "money" (Janssen 1975: 9; Kemp 1989: 248–250; Williams 1997: 20–21).

If this marks an early stage in the recognition of silver as the preferred metal in economic exchange, by the Persian period silver

---

[18] On Near Eastern texts, see the overview in Williams (1997: 16–19). On Near Eastern hoards (and texts), see most recently Le Rider (2001: 1–17), Gitin and Golani (2001), and Stern (2001).

[19] As did the earlier and larger Tod Treasure of the twentieth century BC (Bisson de la Roque 1950).

had become monetarily so dominant that copper was no longer used
notationally, fines and payments were expressed in terms of and
routinely transacted in silver, and the hoarding of silver bullion, as
finds indicate, had became commonplace. Clearly, by the sixth and
fifth centuries, silver was far more abundant in Egypt than earlier,
the result, one assumes, of large-scale importation of the metal from
the Aegean, at first probably through Levantine middlemen and then,
after the establishment of Naucratis as a Greek emporium in the later
seventh century, from trade directly with Greek suppliers. In the
second half of the seventh century also, Egypt began to receive an
unprecedented influx of foreigners from the Aegean and the Levant,
who came as merchants and mercenary soldiers and established their
own, separate ethnic communities (Ray 2001: II.269–271). Since most
of them, like the Jewish soldiers garrisoned at Elephantine, came from
regions where weighed silver bullion had long served as currency, the
presence and special economic importance of these communities could
only have intensified the wide-spread use of this practice in Egypt.

A major modification within this currency emerged over the course
of the fifth century as Egyptians came increasingly to prefer silver in
the form of the Athenian tetradrachm. Fifth-century hoards reveal
that after c. 480 the Athenian tetradrachm was virtually the only
specie of Greek coinage that continued to enter Egypt[20] and, as noted
above, the demand for these coins eventually became so heavy that the
Egyptians resorted to minting great quantities of them themselves.
Apparently, in certain transactional circumstances payment in any
other kind of silver was no longer acceptable. The earliest written
evidence specifying payment in this coinage (or in its unit of weight)
dates from the last decade of the fifth century and the first decade of
the fourth. In the Aramaic dossier from Elephantine, documents of the
years 408, 401, 400, and 399 specify payments of a "stater" or a "stater

---

[20] The heavy and exclusive importation of the Athenian tetradrachm, especially
after c. 450, is a phenomenon well documented in the Levant as well as Egypt.
Now see Nicolet-Pierre (2000a), who notes also the large numbers of Egyptian
pseudo-Athenian tetradrachms that are found in the Levant in the fourth century
and suggests that the popularity of Athenian owl silver there might be due largely
to Egyptian influence.

of Greek silver" ("silver of *Yawan*," i.e., of Ionia, the place name Near Eastern peoples used for Greece at large) (Porten 1968: 64, 69; Naster 1970: 34–35; Lipinski 1982: 23–24; with Grelot 1972: nos. 6, 7, and 63). Similarly, among the demotic contracts recorded on ostraca from the oasis site of Manâwir in Egypt's western desert, five, which date from 410 to 400, stipulate penalty payments in "staters" or "staters of Ionia", and a sixth, dating to 393 or 387, concerns a loan deposit of one stater (Chauveau 2000: 138–139). There can be no doubt that these staters are Athenian tetradrachms, not only because of the latter's exclusive ubiquity at this time in Egypt, but also since several of the contracts define the Greek stater in traditional Elephantine or Egyptian silver weight units, informing that it was a coin (and weight unit) of 17+ g.

In the main administrative and population centers of Egypt, preference for the transactional use of the Athenian tetradrachm ought to have taken hold earlier than we find at Elephantine and at an oasis in the Western Desert. But as the mixed character of some of the fourth-century hoards implies, silver continued to circulate and be transacted in bullion form as earlier, even as payments in Athenian tetradrachms might be increasingly preferred or required, with or without weighing, in particular economic contexts. For every one of the late fifth- and early fourth-century ostraca from Manâwir that gives a penalty in staters, there is another that specifies payment in traditional weights of silver (*deben*) (Chauveau 2000: 140–141). One assumes that coin use, normally without weighing, must have steadily advanced over bullion use as the fourth century wore on, but it may not have been until the advent of the Ptolemaic economy that the long transition was finally completed.

Among the several stages of the evolution of silver currency in Egypt, the nineteen-piece ANS find survives as a modest witness to the intermediate and long-lived bullion phase when even Athenian tetradrachms were still regarded as pieces of silver to be transacted by weight. However prized they may have been for their familiarity and reputation for fineness, one of the two hoard tetradrachms (5) had been cut down and could have never passed at face value, without weighing. As for the find itself, as it had been assembled from small pieces of silver as well as large, it implies, perhaps more palpably

than any of the other recorded hoards, that weighed silver in Persian-
era Egypt was employed not only for major transactions, but also in
many that must have been quite humble.

REFERENCES

Arnold-Biucchi, C., L. Beer-Tobey, and N. M. Waggoner. 1988. A
    Greek archaic silver hoard from Selinus. *ANS Museum Notes*
    33:1–35.
Babelon, E. 1912. Trouvaille de Tarente. *Revue Numismatique* (4th
    ser.) 16:1–40.
Bass, G. F. 1967. *Cape Gelidonya: a Bronze Age shipwreck*. Transactions
    of the American Philosophical Society (n.s.) 57, part 8. Philadel-
    phia: American Philosophical Society.
Beer-Tobey, L., N. H. Gale, H. S. Kim, and Z. A. Stos-Gale. 1998.
    Lead isotope analysis of four late archaic silver ingots from the
    Selinus hoard. In: A. Oddy and M. Cowell, eds., *Metallurgy in
    numismatics 4*, pp. 385–390. London: Royal Numismatic Society.
Bisson de la Roque, F. 1950. *Trésor de Tôd*. Cairo: Institut Français
    d'Archéologie Orientale.
Boardman, J. 1985. *Greek sculpture: the classical period*. London and
    New York: Thames and Hudson.
Briant, P. and R. Descat. 1998. Un registre douanier de la satrape
    d'Égypte à l'époque achéménide. In: N. Grimal and B. Menu, eds.,
    Le commerce en Égypte ancienne, pp. 59–104. Cairo: Institute
    Française d'Archéologie Orientale du Caire.
Brooklyn Museum of Art. 1956. *Five years of collecting Egyptian art,
    1951–1956*. Brooklyn: Brooklyn Museum.
Brugsch, E. 1906. Sur deux trouvailles de culots d'argent provenant de
    Mit-Rahineh. *Annales du service des antiquités de l'Égypte* 7:16.
Buttrey, T. V. 1982. Pharaonic imitations of Athenian tetradrachms.
    In: T. Hackens and R. Weiller, eds., *Proceedings of the 9th Interna-
    tional Congress of Numismatics, Berne, September 1979*, pp. 137–139.
    Louvain-la-Neuve and Luxembourg: Association Internationale des
    Numismates Professionels.
—. 1984. Seldom what they seem—the case of the Athenian tetra-

drachm. In: W. Heckel and R. Sullivan, eds., *Ancient coins of the Greco-Roman world: the Nickle numismatic papers*, pp. 292–294. Waterloo, Ontario: Wilfred Laurier University Press.

Chauveau, M. 2000. La première mention du statère d'argent en Égypte. *Transeuphratène* 20:137–143.

Clairmont, C. W. 1970. *Gravestone and epigram*. Mainz on Rhine: Verlag Philipp von Zabern.

Conophagos, C. E. 1980. *Le Laurium antique et la technique grecque de la production de l'argent*. Athens: Ekdotiki Hellados.

Dressel, H. 1900. Altgriechischer Münzfund aus Ägypten. *Zeitschrift für Numismatik* 22:231–258.

Dressel, H. and K. Regling. 1927. Zwei ägyptische Funde altgriechischer Silbermünzen. *Zeitschrift für Numismatik* 37:1–138.

Dutilh, E. D. J. 1899. Vestiges d'atelier monétaire. *Journal Internationale d'Archéologie Numismatique* 2:283–288.

Engelbach, R. 1924. The treasure of Athribis (Benha). *Annales du service des antiquités de l'Égypt* 24:181–185, pls. II–V.

Figueira, T. 1998. *The power of money: coinage and politics in the Athenian empire*. Philadelphia: University of Pennsylvania Press.

Gitin, S. and A. Golani. 2001. The Tel Miqne-Ekron silver hoards: the Assyrian and Phoenician connections. In: M. Balmuth, ed., *Hacksilber to coinage: new insights into the monetary history of the Near East and Greece*, pp. 27–48. ANS Numismatic Studies 24. New York: American Numismatic Society.

Grelot, P. 1972. *Documents araméens d'Égypte*. Paris: Éditions du Cerf.

Harris, D. 1995. *The treasures of the Parthenon and Erechtheion*. Oxford and New York: Oxford University Press.

Hirschfeld, G. 1893–1916. *Collection of ancient Greek inscriptions in the British Museum IV*. London: British Museum.

Hurter, S. and E. Paszthory. 1984. Archaischer Silberfund aus dem Antilibanon. In: A. Houghton et al., eds., *Studies in honor of Leo Mildenberg*, pp. 111–125. Wetteren: Editions NR.

Janssen, J. J. 1975. *Commodity prices from the Ramessid period*. Leiden: E. J. Brill.

Jones, M. and M. J. Jones. 1988. The Apis house project at Mit Rahineh: preliminary report of the sixth season, 1986. *Journal of the American Research Center in Egypt* 25:105–120.

Kemp, B. J. 1989. *Ancient Egypt: anatomy of a civilization*. London and New York: Routledge.

Kraay, C. M. 1975. Archaic owls of Athens: new evidence for chronology. In: H. Mussche et al., eds., *Thorikos and the Laurion in archaic and classical times*, pp. 145–160. Miscellanea Graeca 1. Ghent: Belgian Archaeological Mission in Greece.

—. 1976. *Archaic and classical Greek coins*. Berkeley and Los Angeles: University of California Press.

Kraeling, E. G. 1953. *The Brooklyn Museum Aramaic papyri: new documents of the fifth century B.C. from the Jewish colony at Elephantine*. New Haven: Yale University Press.

Kroll, J. H. 1993. *The Greek coins*. The Athenian Agora, vol. 26. Princeton: American School of Classical Studies at Athens.

Le Rider, G. 2001. *La naissance de la monnaie*. Paris: Presses Universitaires de France.

Lipinski, E. 1982. Egyptian Aramaic coins from the fifth and fourth centuries B.C. In: S. Scheers, ed., *Studia Paulo Naster oblata I: numismatica antiqua*, pp. 23–33. Louvain: Departement Oriëntalistiek.

Möller, A. 2000. *Naukratis: trade in archaic Greece*. Oxford: Oxford University Press.

Naster, P. 1970. *Karsha* et *sheqel* dans les documents araméens d'Eléphantine. *Revue Belge de Numismatique* 116:31–35.

Nicolet-Pierre, H. 2000a. Tétradrachmes athéniennes en Transeuphratène. *Transeuphratène* 20:107–119.

—. 2000b. In H. Nicolet-Pierre and C. Arnold-Biucchi, Le trésor de Lentini (Sicile) 1957 (*IGCH* 2117). In: S.H. Hurter and C. Arnold-Biucchi, eds., *Pour Denyse: divertissements numismatiques,* pp. 165–171. Bern: [n. p.].

O'Rourke, P. F. 2001. Coinage. In: D. B. Redford, ed., *The Oxford encyclopedia of ancient Egypt*, vol. 1, pp. 288–291. Oxford and New York: Oxford University Press.

Porten, B. 1968. *Archives from Elephantine*. Berkeley and Los Angeles: University of California Press.

Price, M. J., ed. 1980. *Coins: an illustrated survey, 650 BC to the present day*. London: Hamlyn Publishing Group.

—. 1993. More from Memphis and the Syria 1989 hoard. In: M. Price, A. Burnett, and R. Bland, eds., *Essays in honour of Robert Carson and Kenneth Jenkins,* pp. 30–35. London: Spink.

Price, M. J. and N. Waggoner. 1975. *Archaic Greek coinage: the Asyut hoard*. London: V. C. Vecchi.

Rabinowitz, I. 1956. Aramaic inscriptions of the fifth century B.C.E. from a North-Arab shrine in Egypt. *Journal of Near Eastern Studies* 15:1–9.

—. 1959. Another Aramaic record of the North Arabian goddess Han-Ilat. *Journal of Near Eastern Studies* 18:154–155.

Ray, J. D. 2001. Late period: an overview. In: D. B. Redford, ed., *The Oxford encyclopedia of ancient Egypt*, vol. 2, pp. 267–271. Oxford and New York: Oxford University Press.

Regling, K. 1926. Geld. In: M. Ebert, ed., *Realllexikon der Vorgeschichte*, vol. 4, pp. 204–238. Berlin: W. de Gruyter.

Robinson, E. S. G. 1930. A find of archaic Greek coins from the Delta. *Numismatic Chronicle* (5th ser.) 10:91–105.

—. 1931. Further notes on the Delta (Benha el-Asl) hoard. *Numismatic Chronicle* (5th ser.) 11:68–71.

—. 1937. A hoard from "Sidon" [Beni-Hassan]. *Numismatic Chronicle* (5th ser.) 17:197–199.

—. 1960. Two Greek coin hoards. *Numismatic Chronicle* (6th ser.) 20:29–36, pl. II.

Schaeffer, C. F. A. 1939. Une trouvaille de monnaies archaïques grecques à Ras Shamra. In: *Mélanges syriens offerts à M. René Dussaud*, pp. 461–478. Paris: Librairie Orientaliste Paul Geuthner.

Starr, C. G. 1970. *Athenian coinage, 480–449 B.C.* Oxford: Clarendon Press.

Stern, E. 2001. The silver hoard from Tel Dor. In: M. Balmuth, ed., *Hacksilber to coinage: new insights into the monetary history of the Near East and Greece*, pp. 19–26. ANS Numismatic Studies 24. New York: American Numismatic Society.

Stos-Gale, Z. A. 2001. The impact of the natural sciences on studies of *Hacksilber* and early silver coinage. In: M. Balmuth, ed., *Hacksilber to coinage: new insights into the monetary history of the Near East and Greece*, pp. 53–76. ANS Numismatic Studies 24. New York: American Numismatic Society.

Stroud, R. S. 1974. An Athenian law on silver coinage. *Hesperia* 43:157–188.

Williams, J., ed. 1997. *Money, a history.* London: British Museum Press.

Yardeni, A. 1994. Maritime trade and royal accountancy in an erased customs account from 475 BCE on the Ahiquar scroll from Elephantine. *Bulletin of the American Schools of Oriental Research* 293:67–78.

AJN Second Series 13 (2001) pp. 21–34
© 2002 The American Numismatic Society

SCYTHIANS IN THE WEST PONTIC AREA:
NEW NUMISMATIC EVIDENCE

(PLATES 2–3)   ELENA STOLYARIK*

The history of the Scythian migration from the North Pontic steppes to the western coasts of the Pontus Euxinus, one of the farthest edges of the ancient *oikoumene*, has many aspects. This article discusses some of the relevant numismatic evidence, mainly two groups of Scythian coins. The first group, in the name of King Ateas, contributes to our understanding of the Scythian strategic position just prior to the rise of Macedonian power. The second group, anonymous bronzes probably struck by a Greek polis in the Dobrudja, shows that the Scythians remained an important political factor in the region.

The Scythians first entered the Dobrudja (the West Pontic region around the delta at the mouth of the Danube) when they defeated the Persian king Darius in 515–512 BC. This victory increased Scythian hegemony over the North Black Sea steppes. During the reign of King Ariapeithes (490–470 BC), the nomadic Scythian tribes consolidated and settled down, thereby altering the political balance in the Northwest Pontic region. By the beginning of the second quarter of the fifth century BC, Scyths not only controlled the steppe regions

* The American Numismatic Society, Broadway at 155 Street, New York, NY 10032, USA (elena@amnumsoc.org).

21

but also exercised a so-called "barbarian protectorate" (Vinogradov 1989) over nearly all the Greek poleis of the region, including Olbia, Tyra, and Nikonion. At the end of the fifth century BC the growth of the nomad population in a limited territory led to active expansion. In the first half of the fourth century BC, an independent group of Scythian tribes under King Ateas invaded the Dobrudjan region.

THE COINAGE OF KING ATEAS, 360–339 BC

Nine silver coins are known with the name of Ateas, of which four came to light between 1997 and 2000. They form two typological groups with two sub-groups:

Group 1

Obv.: Herakles head wearing a lion's skin to left
Rev.: **ΑΤΑΙΑΣ**; Horseman, bearded, with long hair, wearing Scythian costume, shooting a bow, galloping to left.

1.1. Plate 2 no. 1. Didrachm: 19.5 mm, 6.83 g. State Historical Museum collection (Moscow). (Anokhin 1965: 3-15).
1.2. Plate 2 no. 2. Didrachm: 19 mm, 5.78 g. Same dies as **1.1**. Hermitage collection, St. Petersburg (Anokhin 1965: 3-15).
1.3. Plate 2 no. 3. Didrachm: 20 mm, 6.93 g. Same type as **1.1** and **1.2** but different dies. On obv.: beneath the Herakles head, monogram **ΤΙ**. Athens, the Numismatic Museum. = Gorny 1997. Auction 82, #55

Subgroup 1a

Obv.: same as Group 1
Rev.: **ΑΤΑΙΑΣ**; Horse galloping left

1a.1. Plate 2 no. 4. Drachm: 15 mm, 3.35 g. Numismatik Lanz Auction 92, no. 165 (1999).
1a.2. Plate 2 no. 5. Drachm: 16mm, 3.29g. Classical Numismatic Group Auction 54, no. 501 (2000) = Collection of Jonathan Kagan (New York)

Group 2

Obv.: Artemis head with bow and quiver over her shoulder right.
Rev.: **ATAIA** same type as Group 1, but different die. Under the horse-man, **ΚΑΛ**.

2.1. Plate 2 no. 6. Drachm: 19 mm, 5.75 g. Münzkabinett der Museen der Stadt Gotha. (Imhoof-Blumer 1908: 168, Taf. X no. 22).
Plate 2 no. 7. Drachm: 18 mm, 5.74 g. Same dies on obverse and reverse as **2.1**. British Museum collection. (Hill 1912: 137, pl. VI no. 5; *SNG BM* no. 200).
Plate 2 no. 8. Drachm: 15 mm, 5.23 g. Same as **2.1**, but different dies. Varna Museum collection (Rogalski 1956: 119).

Subgroup 2a

Obv.: same type as Group 2, but different die
Rev.: same type as Group 2, but different die. Monogram **TE** under the horseman.

2a.1. Plate 2 no. 9. Hemidrachm: 14 mm, 2.93 g. Gorny, Auction 96, nos. 68, 97, 148 (1999).

None of these coins has an archaeological context that could contribute to the dating. It is, however, possible to combine evidence from iconography, metrology, and written sources to build a firm basis for further discussion.

The attribution, chronology, and even the authenticity of the coins of Ateas were discussed extensively during 1960s and 1970s (Anokhin 1965, 1973; Brabich 1977; Gerasimov 1967, 1972: 3–16; Karishkovskii 1962, 1971; Rogalski 1961, 1970, 1974; Shelov 1965, 1967, 1971). They can be divided into two clear groups on the basis of iconography and metrology. The coins with Heracles' Head and Horseman resemble the type used by Philip II of Macedon between 359 and 336 BC (Le Rider 1977; *SNG ANS 8* Group A.2 nos. 396, 397). These coins of Group 1 (didrachms: 6.93 g, 6.83 g, 5.78 g) and Subgroup 1a (drachms: 3.35 g, 3.29 g) appear to be struck on a light Thraco-Macedonian standard (Le Rider 1977: 354; Kraay 1976: 330; Troxell 1997: 17–18).

The Ateas coins with Artemis on the obverse (Group 2 and Subgroup 2a) resemble the types used by the Macedonian city Orthagoria around

350 BC or later (*SNG ANS 7* no. 562). However, the Artemis drachms (5.75 g, 5.74 g, 5.23 g) and the hemidrachm (2.93 g) are struck to a lower weight standard than the Heracles coins: the Persian standard (Kraay 1976: 330; Zograph 1951: 42). The Artemis coins bear the mark **ΚΑΛ** and should therefore have been struck at Callatis. A similar image of Artemis was used a century later for the counterstamps of Callatis on autonomous bronzes (Rogalski 1956: 119–123).

The coins with Heracles' head bear no mintmark. Stylistic resemblance to the coins of Heraclea Pontica (*SNG BM* 1595–1602; *SNG Stancomb* 815, 816) struck under the tyranny of Satyros (352–345 BC) has led to the suggestion that the coins were struck there (Anokhin 1973: 38). The publication of a new example of the coin, which bears the monogram **ΤΙ**, in an auction catalog of Dieter Gorny (Gorny, Auktion 82, no. 55, 1997), has led to the new speculation that **ΤΙ** is a monogram of Satyros' nephew and successor in the tyranny, Timotheus (345–337 BC). The problem with this theory is that by the reign of Timotheus and Dionysius, the coins of Heraclea Pontica no longer bore Heracles on the obverse, but rather Dionysus (*SNG BM* 1605–1609; *SNG Stancomb* 817, 816). So the Ateas coin issues with Heracles' head are unlikely to have been struck at Heraclea Pontica during the reign of Timotheus. The monograms **ΤΙ** on Plate 2 no. 3 and **ΤΕ** on Plate 2 no. 9 are probably magistrates' names or control marks.

It is improbable that Heraclea Pontica, quite some distance from the Dobrudja, struck the Ateas coins. Heraclea Pontica was, however, the mother-city of Callatis, and it is possible that the iconographic resemblances of the Heracles obverse are the result of artistic transfer—and possibly even the transfer of engravers—between the mother-city and its colony. Moreover, Heracles was popular both among the Greek colonies of the West Pontus and among the Scythians. The Scythians regarded Heracles as the progenitor of their race. Scythes, the eponymous founder of the Scythians and the son of Heracles, became his father's heir by bending his bow (Herodotus 4.9.10). The image of Heracles bending his bow appeared on the first silver coin of Olbia on the northwestern Black Sea littoral in 460–440 BC (Karishkovskii 1960, 1984, 1988: 48–52). A century later, the representation of Heracles and the Scythian horseman shooting a bow was used again, as a symbol of Greek-Scythian syncretism in the West Pontus. The head of the horseman on the Ateas coins is also found on a Cyzicene stater from the Orlovka hoard buried in the lower Danube region (burial date 340–330 BC; *IGCH* 726) (Plate 2 no. 10). This has been identified as the head of a Scythian, dated to the second quarter of the fourth century BC (Bulatovich 1970: 82). Electrum cyzicenes at that time performed the function of an international coinage on the Pontic shores. The appearance of images of Scythians on Black Sea currency supports the historical evidence for the growing political power of Scythian tribes in this region during the fourth century BC. The image of the horse-archer on the reverse finds parallels in the artworks from Solokha, Kul-Oba, and Chertomlik, the Scythian barrows of the late fifth and fourth centuries BC (Artamonov 1969: pls. 201, 202, 272; Mantsevich 1987: 88–92, cat. 61; Grakov 1971: 81; Kopeikina 1986: 38–40); for examples see Plate 3 nos. 1 and 2.

The types of the first group of Ateas coins were probably inspired by Macedonian royal iconography and can be neatly fitted into the historical record. Relations between the Scythians and the Macedonians were friendly at first. The Scythians had promises from the Macedonians of aid against the king of the Histriani, a ruler of the native tribes of the lower Danube (Pompeius Trogus in Justinus 9.1–2). Philip, despite his siege of Byzantium and his efforts to assimilate Odrysian Thrace, sent troops to Ateas. But when the Macedonians came, Ateas felt no need of them, because the king of the Histriani had died. The troops were sent back without payment and with an insulting message. Philip then made war on Ateas. The battle that followed in 339 BC ended in the death of Ateas and a crushing defeat of the Scythians (Just. 9.2.1–16; Clem. Alex., *Strom.* 5.31.3; Lucian, *Macrob.* 10). It is clear that the Ateas coins could have been struck no later than 339 BC, the year of Ateas' demise. To set the earlier limit, we must determine when the Scythians under Ateas first ruled the Dobrudja region. Ateas at one point threatened that if Byzantium continued to damage his "revenues", his horses would drink their water (Clem. Alex. 5.31.3). This would have to have occurred between 364 BC, when Byzantium left the second Athenian empire and pursued an independent policy, and the siege by Philip II in 340 BC. But Ateas' threat to move his cavalry to the Propontis, an area patrolled by the Thracians, was only possible after the final disintegration of the Odrysian state. This happened after

the death of Cotys I in 359 BC and during Philip II's war with the
Thracian kings in the late 350s and 340s BC. Macedon's war against
the Thracians created a power vacuum that allowed Ateas and his Scythians to dominate the Dobrudja (Shelov 1971: 57–58; Melukova 1979:
241; Iliescu 1975; Blavatskaya 1952: 80).

The coins of Group 1 and Subgroup 1a probably were struck on the
Thraco-Macedonian, or rather Rhodian, standard. This standard, based
upon a drachma weighing about 3.85–3.95 g has often been called
"Phoenician", but the place of its origin was Chios. During the last
decades of the fifth century and the beginning of the fourth it became
known as the Rhodian standard. The primary weight of the tetradrachm (around 15.6–15.8 g) was soon replaced by a weight of about
14.5–14.7 g, later even 13.2–13.6 g, and the drachma fluctuated over a
broad range: from 3.9–3.95 g to 3.3–3.4 g (Segre 1928: 231–235; Zograph 1951: 44–45). This standard was used by the Macedonian rulers,
some Thraco-Macedonian tribes, and the Greek mercantile *poleis* of the
Pontus, the Propontis, and Thrace: Abdera, Maroneia, Ainos, Byzantium, Thasos, Amisos, Mesembria, Apollonia (Karishkovskii 1961: 11;
Jurukova 1976: 9). The coinages of these active trade centers form
the bulk of most of the hoards from the Thracian-West Pontic region
between 400 and 325 BC (*IGCH* pp. 96–104). The Greek cities of the
Pontus and the Propontis used the Rhodian standard until 350–340
BC, when they adopted the Persian weight system. It is only with
Alexander III that the Attic standard was adopted (Le Rider 1963,
1971; Thompson 1966; Iliescu 1973).

This metrological evidence, combined with iconography and the historical record, helps to determine the chronology of the Ateas coinage.
Ateas moved into Dobrudja in the 350s BC. Around that time he
struck the first issue of his coinage (Group 1 and Subgroup 1a) on the
Rhodian standard and used Macedonian types, indicating his friendship
with Macedon. Sometime between 350 and 340 the mint of Callatis
started to produce an autonomous coinage on the Persian weight system (Iliescu 1973). At the same time the new Ateas coinage (Group 2
and Subgroup 2a) was created on a similar lighter standard. It is important to emphasize that while the reverse type of both groups remained the same (Scythian horseman shooting a bow), the obverse
type changed: Heracles was replaced by Artemis. A double motive

probably led Ateas to this change of type: first, to distinguish the new, lighter coins from the older ones, and secondly, because of the break with Macedon. The latest issues of the 340s would have been struck for military payment as Ateas prepared for what proved to be the final showdown with the Macedonians.

ANONYMOUS ISSUES WITH SCYTHIAN TYPE

New numismatic evidence of the relations between Scythians and the West Pontic Greek cities appeared several years ago. Bronze coins bearing the type of Dionysus head/galloping horseman but without indication of a ruler's name or mint were found near Dionysopolis (Draganov 1995–97, 1997: 372 no. 7). The same type is present in the collection of the American Numismatic Society. The full descriptions of these specimens are as follows:

1. Plate 3 no. 3. AE. 18 mm, 4.68 g, 10:00.
Obv.: head of Dionysus in ivy wreath to right.
Rev.: horseman, bearded, with long hair, galloping to left, hand in greeting gesture
ANS 1944.100.36180 (E. T. Newell collection)
Find-spot: unknown

2. Plate 3 no. 4. 18 mm, 4.60 g.
Obv.: same as **1**, but different die. Above Dionysus' head, monogram **ΔI**.
Rev.: same as **1**, but different die.
Private collection of Y. Tachev, Balchik (Bulgaria)

3. Plate 3 no. 5. 18 mm, 4.94 g.
Obv.: same as **2**; cmk.: amphora,
Rev.: same as **2**; cmk: vine with bunches of grapes (?)
Museum of History, Jambol (Bulgaria), inv. no. 491.

4. Plate 3 no. 6. 18 mm, 4.91 g.
Obv.: same as **3**
Rev.: same as **3**
Private collection of Y. Tachev

Find-spots for nos. 2, 3, and 4: ruins and hinterland of Dionysopolis

The horseman on the reverses of the Dionysus/Horseman type has
typically Scythian features: long hair, Scythian costume, and a bow
case. This depiction is closely related to the image of a horseman used
by Ateas for his coins. It also has analogies with Scythian images on
Greek-Scythian toreutics of the fourth century BC (Artamonov 1969)
(cf. Plate 3 nos. 1 and 2). Probably because of the Scythian image,
the coins were originally dated to the third or early second century
BC (Draganov 1995–97: 55–56), when more Scythians moved into the
Dobrudja and established the kingdom of Scythia Minor. But the coins
of the kings of Scythia Minor borrowed the images of the autonomous
emissions and even the identical magistrate names from the Greek
poleis of the West Pontic area (Blavatskaya 1952: 144–147; Canarache
1950: 218–226; Iliescu 1975; Jouroukova 1977; Andrukh 1995: 117–147;
Tacheva 1995). The coins of the Dionysus/Horseman type are very different in style from all of the coins linked to the kings of Scythia Minor. In addition, some of the coins of the Dionysus/Horseman type
(nos. 3 and 4) bear countermarks: a vessel with two handles (amphora?
kantharos?) and a vine with bunches of grapes. The images of these
countermarks are similar to the images struck on the earliest autonomous bronze types of Dionysopolis, which are dated to the first part of
the third century BC (Canarache 1957: nos. 14, 15; Draganov 1995: 61,
1995–97: 55: nos. 10, 11). Thus, the Dionysus/Horseman coins were evidently manufactured earlier than the first autonomous bronzes of Dionysopolis. Stamped with these images and produced by Dionysopolis in
the first part of the third century BC, they circulated together with the
autonomous coins of Dionysopolis, where they were found.

The iconographic aspects of the Dionysus/Horseman type are close
to the bronze coins of Philip II (Apollo/Horseman/Horseman with
Raised Hand) (*SNG ANS 8*: 841–971). The coinage of the Macedonian
rulers occupied a specific position in the monetary economy of the
West Pontic-Thracian basin in the Early Hellenistic period (340–270
BC). Over twenty hoards (burial date in the last quarter of the fourth
century BC) and single finds show that the bronze coinage of Philip II
and Alexander III circulated in this region in great abundance (*IGCH*

732, 778–785, 787–793, 844, 845; Iordanov 1990: 51; Jurukova 1992:
91; Lazarenko 1997–99: 57). Cassander (316–298 BC), Alexander's successor in Macedonia, used Philip's type of a horseman with raised hand
on the reverse of his own issues (Ehrhardt 1973: 26). He also continued
to produce coins in Philip's and Alexander's types and supported Lysimachus' monetary needs (Thompson 1968: 164). After founding his own
mint Lysimachus, who controlled not only Thracian lands but also the
Pontic colonies, began to strike small silver and bronze coins using the
type of Philip II (*SNG ANS 8* nos. 997–1004; Thompson 1968). Lysimachus' earliest bronzes have been dated to 306/5–301/0 BC (Thompson 1968: 164). But the presence of such coins in the Drama Hoard
(*IGCH* 404, burial date c. 325–310 BC) and in the partial hoard of
royal Macedonian bronzes (burial date soon after 323 BC), recently
published by Hyla A. Troxell (2000: 195), make this chronology ques-
tionable.

The characteristic image of deities/king/galloping horseman is icono-
graphically very close to the type presented on the coinage of the
Thracian dynasts Kotys (384/3–359 BC) and Srois (second half of
fourth century BC). The Thracian rulers Seuthes III, Spartokos, Rhoi-
gos, and Skostokos, dated between 340 and 270–240 BC, also continued to strike bronze coinages bearing similar types (Peter 1997; Jurukova 1992; Dimitrov 1989). Some bronze issues of Seuthes III were re-
struck on coins of Philip II, Alexander III, and Cassander, which were
widespread in Thrace and the West Pontus at the end of the fourth
and beginning of the third century BC (Jurukova 1992: 90–97, 1976:
24). It seems that the types deities/king/horseman were a general
iconographic type for the Balkans during the Early Hellenistic age.
Thus, the coins with Dionysus/Scythian horseman with his hand raised
in greeting were influenced by Macedonian royal types and should
be seen as a transitional type between the Classical fine style of Philip II's coinage and the expressive traditions of the dawning Hellenistic
age.

Historically, the Dionysus/Scythian horseman coinage is connected
with the period of the Scythian presence in Dobrudja after the death
of Ateas and before the time of the kings of Scythia Minor. Ateas' defeat diminished Scythian power, but as historical accounts indicate
(Arrian 1.3.1–2; Just. 12.1.4), the Scythians remained a strong presence

in the region. The Dobrudjan Scyths were still powerful enough that the Greek *poleis* of the West Pontus (Callatis, Histria, and Odessus) asked for their support against Lysimachus in 313 BC (Diod. 19.73). Lysimachus forced Odessus and Istria to capitulate, drew the Thracians to his side, besieged Callatis, and drove the Scythians beyond the Danube (Blavatskaya 1952: 93–107).

This anonymous coinage with the type of the Scythian rider with greeting gesture may have been used by the Greek *poleis* in their revolt against Lysimachus. The absence of the name of a ruler on the coins is evidence that this issue was not intended for the proclamation of the king's power. It was a declaration of political alliance, wherein the Greeks adopted the image of the Scythian horseman. This imagery is a numismatic indication of the continued importance of the Scythian presence in the Dobrudja and a link between the issues of Ateas and those of the kings of Scythia Minor. The anonymous issues with the Scythian type and the coinage of king Ateas should not be consider in isolation: bringing them together and presenting their historical context helps to shed light on the ethno-political situation and extensive contact between Greek civilization and barbarian tribes in the West Pontic region.

REFERENCES

Andrukh, S. I. 1995. *Nijnedynaiskaya* Skifia *v VI- nachale I v. do n.e.* Zaporoj'e: Gosudarstvenii Universitet.

Anokhin, V. A. 1965. Moneti skifskogo tsarya Ateya. *Numismatika i Sfragistika* 2:3–15.

—. 1973. Moneti Ateya. *Skifskie drevnosti* 20–41. Kiev: Naukova Dumka.

Artamonov, M. I. 1969. *Treasures from Scythian tombs in the Hermitage Museum, Leningrad.* London: Thames & Hudson.

Blavatskaya, T. V. 1952. *Zapadnopontiiskie goroda v VII-I vv. do n.e.* Moskva: Izdatel'stvo Akademii Nauk SSSR.

Brabich, V. M. 1977. Podlinnaya li moneta Ateya is sobrania Ermitaja. In: V. M. Potin, ed., *Proshloe nashei rodini v pamyatnikah numizmatiki,* pp. 152–155. Leningrad: Izd Aurora.

Bulatovich, S. A. 1970. Klad kizikinov iz Orlovki. *Vestnik Drevnei Istorii* 2:73–86.

Canarache, V. 1950. Monetele sciților din Dobrogea. *Studii și Cercetări de Istorie Veche* 1.1:213–257.

—. 1957. Monede autonome inedite din Dionysopolis și cronologia lor relativă. *Studii și Cercetări de Numismatică* 1:61–78.

Dimitrov, K. 1989. Dynastic coinage in Thrace in the Early Hellenistic Age (340–270 B.C.): images, traditions, ideology. *Bulgarian Historical Review* 2:67–71.

Draganov, D. 1995. New coin types of Dionysopolis. *Numismatic and Sphragistic Contributions to Ancient and Medieval History of Dobroudja, International Symposium, Dobrich, 1993.* Dobroudja 12, 60-63.

—. 1995–97. Neizvesten bronzov moneten tip na Dionisopolis. *Numizmatika i Sfragistika [Sofia]* 4:54–56.

—. 1997. The bronze coinage of Dionysopolis. *Spink Numismatic Circular* 105: 371–377.

Ehrhardt, Ch. 1973. The coins of Cassander. *Journal of Numismatic Fine Arts* 2(2):25–32.

Gerasimov, T. 1967. Istinski li sa monetite s nadpis ΑΤΑΙΑΣ i ΑΤΑΙΑ. *Izvestiya na Arheologicheskiya Institut na Bolgarska Akademiya na Naukite* 30:181–186.

—. 1972. Otnobo za falshibite moneti s nadpisi ΑΤΑΙΑΣ i ΑΤΑΙΑ. *Izvestiya na Narodniya Muzei [Varna]* 8(23):3-16.

Grakov, B. N. 1954. Kamenskoe gorodishche na Dnepre. Materiali i Isledovaniya po Arkheologii SSSR 36. Moskva: Izdatel'stvo Akademii Nauk.

—. 1971. *Skifi*. Moskva: Izdatel'stvo Instituta Arkheologii.

Harmatta, J. 1970. Studies in the history and language of the Sarmatians. *Acta Antiqua et Archaeologica Univ. Attila Jozsef* 13:16–20.

Hill, G. F. 1912. Greek coins acquired by the British Museum, 1905–1910. *Numismatic Chronicle* (4th ser.) 12:134–148.

IGCH. Thompson, M., O. Mørkholm, and C. M. Kraay, eds. 1973. *An inventory of Greek coin hoards.* New York: American Numismatic Society.

Iliescu, O. 1973. Le système monétaire et ponderal à Histria, Callatis et Tomis aux Vᵉ-IIᵉ siècles av. notre ère. In: H. A. Cahn and G. Le

Rider, eds., *Proceedings of the 8th International Congress of Numismatics*, pp. 85–98. Paris and Bâle: Association Internationale des Numismates Professionels.

Iliescu, V. 1975. The Scythians in Dobrudja and their relations with the native population. In: *Relations between the autochtonous populations*, pp. 13–24. Bibliotheca Historica Romanaiae, monograph 16. Bucureşti: Editura Academiei Republicii Socialiste Romania.

Imhoof-Blumer, F. 1908. Zur griechischen und römischen Münzkunde. *Revue Suisse de Numismatique* 14:1–265.

Iordanov, I. 1990. Numizmatichnata kollektsiya na arheologicheski muzei v Balchik. Izvor na istoriyata na grada I okolnoctite mu. *Balchik: drevnost i svremue*. Dobrich. 51–52.

Jouroukova, J. 1977. Nouvelles données la sur la chronologie des rois scythes en Dobrudza. *Thracia* 4:105–121.

Jurukova, J. 1976. *Coins of the ancient Thracians*. BAR Supplementary Series 4. Oxford: British Archaeological Reports.

—. 1992. *Monetite na trakiiskite plemena i vladeteli*. Sofia: Petr Beron.

Karishkovskii, P. O. 1960. O monetakh s nadpis'iu EMINAKO. *Sovetskaya Arkheologia* 1:179–195.

—. 1961. Olvia i Rodos po numizamticheskim dannim. *Kratkie Soobtscheniya Instituta Arheologii Academii Nauk SSSR* 83:9–14.

—. 1962. Retsenziya: izvestia na varnenskogo arheologicheskdrujestva, Varna 1951–1961, Kn. 8–12, *Vestnik Drevnei Istorii* 2:146–148.

—. 1971. Skifi na Dunai. *Ukrains'kii Istorichnii Jurnal* 9:54–60.

—. 1984. Novie materiali o monetakh Eminaka. *Rannii jeleznii vek Severo-Zapadnogo Prichernomor'ya*, 78-89. Kiev.

—. 1988. *Moneti Ol'vii*. Kiev: Naukova Dumka.

Kopeikina, L. V. 1986. Zolotie blyashki iz kurgana Kul'-Oba. *Antichnaya Torevtika*, Leningrad.

Kraay, C. M. 1976. *Archaic and classical Greek coins*. London: Methuen.

Lazarenko, I. 1997–99. Nachalo i pervi etapi ot bronzovo monetosechene na Odesos. *Dobrudja (14-16), 1996-1999*. p.51-63.

Le Rider, G. 1963. *Deux trésors de monnaies grecques de la Propontide (IVe siècle avant J.-C.)*. Bibliothèque archéologique et historique de l'Institut Français d'Archéologie d'Istambul 18. Paris: Librairie Adrien Maisonneuve.

—. Sur le monnayage de Byzance au IVe siècle. *Revue Numismatique* (6th ser.) 13:143–153.

—. *Le monnayage d'argent et d'or de Philippe II.* Paris: É. Bourgey.

Mantsevich, A. P. 1987. *Kurgan Solokha.* Leningrad: Iskusstvo.

Melukova, A. I. 1979. *Scifiya i Frakiiskii mir.* Moskva: Nauka.

Peter, U. 1997. *Die Münzen der thrakischen Dynasten (5.-3. Jahrhundert v.Chr.): Hintergründe ihrer Prägung.* Berlin: Akademie Verlag.

Rogalski, A. 1956. Obrazut na Artemida vurkhu moneti ot Kalatis. *Izvestiya na Arkheologicheskoto drujestvo gr. Varna, kn.X*

—. 1961. Moneti s imeto na skitckiya tsar Atei. *Izvestiya na Varnensko Arheologichesko Drujestvo* 12:23–27.

—. 1970. Falchivi li sa monetite s nadpic **ΑΤΑΙΑΣ** i **ΑΤΑΙΑ**. *Izvestiya na narodniya Musei.* 6 (21):3–19. Varna.

—. 1974. K voprosu o monetah skifskogo tsarya Ateya. *Numismatika i Sfragistika* 5:3–13.

Segrè, A. 1928. Metrologia e circolazione monetaria degli antichi. Bologna: Nicola Zanichelli.

Shelov, D. B. 1965. Tsar Atei. *Numismatika i Sfragistika* 2:16–40.

—. 1967. Zapadnoe i Severnoe Prichernomor'e v antichnuyu epohu, *Antichnoe obshchestvo,* 219-224. Moskva.

—. 1971. Skifo-makedonskii konflikt v istorii antishnogo mira. *Problemi Skifskoiu Arkheologii* 54-63.

SNG ANS 7. 1987. *Sylloge nummorum Graecorum, the collection of the American Numismatic Society: Macedonia I: cities, Thraco-Macedonian tribes, Paeonian kings.* New York: American Numismatic Society.

SNG ANS 8. 1994. *Sylloge nummorum Graecorum, the collection of the American Numismatic Society: Macedonia II: Alexander I–Philip II.* New York: American Numismatic Society.

SNG BM. 1993. *Sylloge nummorum Graecorum, Great Britain, vol. 9: the British Museum, part 1: the Black Sea.* London: British Museum Press.

SNG Stancomb. 2000. *Sylloge nummorum Graecorum, Great Britain, vol. 11: the William Stancomb collection of coins of the Black Sea region.* London: Oxford University Press and Spink & Son.

Tacheva M. 1995. About the so-called Scythian kings and their coinage in the Greek cities of Thracia Pontica (the end of the 3rd-2nd century B.C.). *Numismatic and Sphragistic Contributions to Ancient and Medieval History of Dobroudja. International Symposium, Dobrich, 1993.* Dobroudja 12, 7-16.

Thompson, M. 1965. The coinage of Proconnesus. *Revue Numismatique* (6th ser.) 7:30–35.

—. 1968. The mints of Lysimachus. In: C. M. Kraay, ed., *Essays in Greek coinage presented to Stanley Robinson,* pp. 163–182. Oxford: Clarendon Press.

Troxell, H. A. 1997. *Studies in the Macedonian coinage of Alexander the Great.* ANS Numismatic Studies 21. New York: American Numismatic Society.

—. 2000. A partial hoard of royal Macedonian bronzes. In: S. M. Hurter and C. Arnold-Biucchi, eds., *Pour Denyse: divertissements numismatiques,* pp. 189–195. Bern.

Vinogradov, Yu. G. 1989. *Politicheskaya istoriya Ol'vijskogo polisa.* Moscow: Nauka.

Zograph, A. N. 1951. *Antichie moneti.* Akademiya Nauk SSSR. Materiali i Issledovaniya po Arheologii SSSR, #16. Moskva-Leningrad: Izdatel'stvo Akademii Nauk.

AJN Second Series 13 (2001) pp. 35–62

© 2002 The American Numismatic Society

ENGRAVED GEMS IN THE COLLECTION OF THE AMERICAN NUMISMATIC SOCIETY III: MALE DEITIES AND HEROES

(Plates 4–6)   HÉLÈNE GUIRAUD AND JAMES H. SCHWARTZ*

This article continues the series begun in 1979 (Schwartz and Schwartz 1979; Schwartz 1999) to publish the engraved gems of the Society: we catalogue 56 intaglios from the Roman period with devices that show figures at least one of which is a male deity or hero.[1] These devices occur frequently on intaglios dating from the first century BC to the beginning of the third century AD, representing almost half of the gems in published collections (Schwartz 1999: 25).

For the most part, these intaglios served as seals (Henig 1997): the image of Mercury, the god of commerce, for example, would be appropriate for merchants. They are also likely to have served as amulets or charms, each god providing specific protection: thus, Mercury for the merchant while traveling. During the Empire the various motifs became more generally familiar because of numerous representations in statues and reliefs, wall paintings, and perhaps most important, coin types. Also evident is the Roman appreciation and enthusiasm for elegant Hellenistic models.

---

* Center for Neurobiology and Behavior, Columbia University, 722 W. 168th St., New York NY 10032, USA (jhs6@columbia.edu).

[1] Excluding Eros. Intaglios with female deities will follow in another article.

Most of the gems are engraved in carnelian of varying color. Although carnelian is the stone most favored, nicolo with its clear blue surface above a dark layer, jaspers both red and brown, amethyst, sardonyx, and agate were also used. Molded glass paste imitating precious stones is also quite frequent. Most of the gems in this group are oval in shape; only nos. 15 and 47 are exceptions. With carnelian the engraved surface is slightly curved to bring out the faint transparency of the stone. With more translucent stones like no. 32, the curve (form Cc) is much greater. On the other hand, the more opaque nicolo and jasper are cut on a flat surface. Stones like nicolo and sardonyx that have many superimposed layers of different color have bevelled exterior edges (forms F2, F3, F4, and Cc).

The dimensions of the intaglios in this collection correspond to what is usually seen in other collections. Judging by size, most are likely to have been set in rings. An exception is no. 10, a carnelian showing Jupiter, Mars, and Victory, which is considerably larger than the others and may have been used in a brooch or pendant.

As usual for most antique engraved stones, the provenance of these gems is unknown, all having been obtained from dealers in the first half of the twentieth century by Duffield Osborne (1912) and Edward Newell. Osborne wrote that dealers were his source; von der Osten, who published Newell's extensive collection of oriental seals (1934), also wrote that the seals were bought from dealers (or from other collectors who had bought from dealers), and therefore had no provenance. Although there is no mention of Newell's engraved Roman gems, it seems likely that they too were purchased.

There is no completely secure way to date the gems. Choice of stone can be used as one criterion, and shape provides another. For example, nicolo and jasper were popular in the second century AD, and greatly curved stones were fashionable during the Republic. Choice of device is also significant. Representations of Mars, Mercury, Harpocrates, and Bonus Eventus were more popular during the mid-imperial period than in the late Republic and early Empire. Nevertheless, almost all of the devices originated in the Hellenistic period (Plantzos 1999).

Analysis of engraving technique has developed during the past 30 years into a way to date intaglios. Despite some differences in terminology,[2] several investigators have reached agreement on the dating of various engraving styles. The study of style is based upon an examination of the characteristic traces left by the engraver's drill. The time period for each style is quite broad, and it is likely that several techniques of engraving were in use at any one time.[3] Therefore the system of dating proposed must be standardized using the very small number of specimens that are available from proved archeological contexts.

The gems catalogued here range in date from the last half of the first century BC to the third century AD. Some of them are closely related to reverse coin types, and were placed by Newell in the Society's cabinets along with the appropriate Roman provincial issues. Several of them may be copies after the antique done in modern times (up to the nineteenth century), however. The intaglios are engraved in several styles. Two styles were used during the period of the end of the Republic and the beginning of the Empire. The pellet style[4] (second to first century BC) is characterized by small beads defining the outline of figures and their connection with objects. The modeling of bodies is usually flexible, the details of hair and clothing rendered with lines that are fine and steady. In the calligraphic style (first century BC),[5] straight lines define clothing and the outlines of bodies that are often quite squat; sometimes the engraving technique is miniaturistic.

The other styles found on the intaglios catalogued here belong specifically to the Imperial period. In the modeled classical style[6] (first century AD) the anatomy of bodies is emphasized in a realistic

---

[2] Taking into account the different terminologies used by E. Zwierlein-Diehl (1973, 1979), G. Sena Chiesa (1966), M. Maaskant-Kleibrink (1978), H. Guiraud (1988), and M. Henig (1994). See also Platz-Horster (1994: 33–40). For specific information about these styles, see Guiraud (1988:35–59).

[3] For example, see the casket buried at Pompei in 79 AD that contained thirty stones engraved in very different styles (Pannuti 1975).

[4] Italic Republican pellet style (Hague). Rundperlstil (Wien). Officine della Menade, di Ulisse, del Pegaso (Aquileia).

[5] Republican wheel style (Hague). Linearer Stil, kalligraphischer Stil (Wien). Officine del filosofo, delle offerte campestri, del citaredo (Aquileia).

[6] Imperial classicising style (Hague). Klassizistischer Stil (Wien). Officine classicistica, dei prasii (Aquileia).

manner. Figures are draped to give the impression of volume. The classical linear style[7] (first to second century AD) makes use of many fine grooves even if the bodies are drawn realistically. Grooves are used specifically to mark the outlines of faces (chin, lips, nose). In the simplified classical style (second century AD),[8] the work of the fine drill is accentuated to outline clothing, but anatomical features are neglected and gestures accentuated. The smooth style[9] (second to early third century AD) emphasizes the simplification of figures shown as cylinders without internal detail. Clothing is shown in even less detail. The figures engraved in the incoherent style[10] (second to third century AD) lack realism: the grooves forming the bodies and clothing are put together haphazardly.

CATALOGUE

For each gem we note the ANS inventory number and the type of stone (for sardonyx the color of the surface is given). Shape is described in a now almost universally accepted code (Henig 1994); since the stones are almost all oval, the outline is noted only if it is different. Next we give the dimensions in millimeters, other identifying features, and any damage, as well as prior publication and date (almost all date from the first three centuries AD). The device is described as it appears on the gem. Next we comment briefly on theme and style. Because these devices occur with great frequency on gems of the Roman period, we cite parallels only from recently published catalogues, which usually have extensive lists of similar examples. All images in the plates are reproduced at 2.5× enlargement, and all are images of the gem itself except for nos. 33 and 43, for which casts provided clearer illustrations.

---

[7] Imperial small grooves style (Hague). Klassizistisch-linearer Stil (Wien). Officine della sfinge A and B (Aquileia).

[8] Imperial round head style and cap-with-rim style (Hague). Flachperlstil (Wien). Officine della Nimfa, del Guerriero, di Iside (Aquileia).

[9] Imperial plain grooves style (Hague). Kleinteiliger Flachperlstil (Wien). Officine dei Dioscuri, delle linee grosse (Aquileia).

[10] Imperial incoherent style (Hague). Flüchtiger Stil (Wien). Officine delle linee grosse C (Aquileia).

1. 0000.999.33936. Chalcedony. Ca4. 11.1 × 8.5 × 2.5. Pierced for suspension through the head of the figure. Second century AD.

Jupiter partly draped sits on a stool (diphros), torso facing, with head in profile to the right. His raised right hand rests on a scepter. He holds a victoriola in his left hand. An eagle stands at his feet. Groundline.

This type, inspired by Phidias' cult statue at Olympia, occurs frequently on Roman imperial coins with the title Jupiter Victor and on gems, with or without an eagle. Cf. *Aquileia* nos. 2–4; *AGDS I.3* nos. 2454, 3017–3018; *AGDS IV* no. 1361; *Wien II* nos. 957, 1221–1223; *Fitzwilliam* no. 251; *Gadara* nos. 14–16.

Between the simplified classical and smooth styles. Cf. *Hague* cap-with-rim style, nos. 888, 903, 910, 912.

2. 0000.999.33835. Red jasper. F1. 12 × 11 × 3. Chip in the upper part of the stone. Second century AD.

Jupiter with a himation draped over his legs sits on a throne, torso facing and head turned right. His raised right hand leans on a scepter. He holds a thunderbolt in his left hand. One eagle stands in front of the throne, another behind. Groundline. Inscription: **RO** to the right behind the throne, **VI** under the groundline.

The motif of the Capitoline Jupiter or Jupiter Custos is familiar from imperial coinage. Single eagles or stars occur on intaglios. See *AGDS IV* nos. 1362–1364; *Wien II* nos. 958, 1230–1231; *Getty* no. 263.

Simplified classical style. Cf. *Hague* cap-with-rim style.

3. 0000.999.33879. Chalcedony. Ca2. 14 × 10.5 × 4.2. Second century AD.

Jupiter with a himation draped over his legs sits on a throne, his head turned in profile to the right. His raised right hand rests on a scepter; he extends a patera with his left hand. An eagle stands at his feet.

This motif occurs only late on imperial coinage (Severan period) but is frequent on gems. See *Aquileia* nos. 9–15; *AGDS IV* nos. 1365–1366; *Wien II* nos. 1224–1228; *Getty* nos. 262, 265–266; *Fitzwilliam* nos. 253–256.

Smooth classical style. Cf. *Hague* plain grooves style; Fitzwilliam no. 255.

4. 0000.999.33931. Carnelian. F6. 19 × 14.9 × 4. Second to third century AD.

Jupiter, a himation draped over his legs, sits on a stool with his head in profile to the left. His raised left hand leans on a scepter; he holds two ears of wheat in his right hand. Groundline.

The device represents Zeus Arotrios, who appears infrequently in coinage (Domitian and Trajan) but often on gems. See *Aquileia* no. 6; *AGDS IV* no. 1378; *Wien II* no. 1232; *Fitzwilliam* no. 236. Incoherent style. Cf. *Hague* no. 982, incoherent grooves style; *Aquileia*, Officina delle linee grosse, pl. xciii.

5. 0000.999.33801. Chalcedony. Cb1. 13.8 × 10.5 × 4.1. Second century AD.

Jupiter, a himation draped over his legs, sits on a throne, his head turned to the right. His raised right hand rests on a scepter; his extended left hand supports a bust with a mural crown personifying a city. Groundline.

Modeled classical style. Cf. *Fitzwilliam* no. 254.

6. 0000.999.33854. Carnelian. Ca5. 17 × 12 × 2.8. Chip in the lower part of the stone. Second century AD.

On the upper part of the gem a statue of Jupiter of Heliopolis is shown standing and facing; he wears a kalathos on his head and holds a whip in his raised left hand and two ears of wheat in his right. Two symmetrical humped bulls stand behind him. In the field to the left, a crescent moon; to the right, a six-pointed star. In the lower part of the gem, an eagle stands with outstretched wings.

This is the traditional image of the Syrian god, who is rarely seen with an eagle (on statues of the god, however, the eagle appears behind Jupiter). The astral signs express the cosmic power of the god (Haggar 1977), cf. *LIMC* IV s.v. Heliopolitani dei, intaglios 10–25 (our gem closely resembles no. 17 in this list). See (without an eagle) *Aquileia* no. 33; *AGDS IV* no. 1382; *Wien II* no. 1235; *Gadara* nos 23, 24.

Simplified classical style. Cf. *Hague* plain grooves style.

7. 0000.999.33939. Carnelian. Ca5. 12 × 10 × 4. Second century AD.

On the left, Jupiter with a himation draped over his legs sits on a stool. He appears in three-quarter view, his head turned toward the center. His raised right hand leans on a scepter; he extends his left hand. An eagle stands at his feet. To the right, Sol (Helios) stands facing naked, his radiating head turned toward the center, a whip and a bit of cloth against his right arm. His left hand is raised. Groundline. Inscription to the right KΛN; to the left, ARA*; below, TOC.

Other example with small variations: *AGDS I.3* no. 2461.

Simplified classical style. Cf. *Hague* no. 896, cap-with-rim style.

8. 0000.999.33791. Carnelian. P1. 11.5 × 11.1 × 3.0. Chip in the lower part of the stone. Second century AD.

Jupiter with a loose himation draped over his legs sits on a throne to the left, his head turned to the center; his elevated right hand rests on a scepter, his extended left hand supports an eagle. To the right Mercury stands naked and facing, his head in profile turned to the center, supporting a caduceus on his left arm over which a chlamys is draped. He holds a purse in his right hand. Groundline. Inscription above, between the two gods: ΛΨΔ.

Other examples with some variations in the objects: *Aquileia* nos. 37, 206; *Wien II* no. 1194.

Between the linear classical and simplified classical styles. Cf. *Hague* nos. 742, 754, 770, 773, small grooves style.

9. 0000.999.33705. Carnelian. Ca4. 14.8 × 12 × 3.2. A chip on the right side of the stone. Second to third century AD.

On the left, Jupiter seen in three-quarter view sits on a stool, his head turned toward the center, his raised right hand leaning on a scepter (that is not visible) and his left hand extended to hold two ears of wheat. On the right, Victory clothed in a chiton stands in profile to the center, extending a wreath with her left hand; a palm branch is held against her right shoulder. Groundline beneath Jupiter.

Other examples, with some variation in the objects: *Gadara* no. 17; *Wien II* no. 1195.

Between the linear classical and incoherent styles. Cf. *Hague* no. 972, rigid chin-mouth-nose style.

10. 0000.999.33880. Carnelian. F1. 22 × 16 × 5.5. Second century AD.

A divine triad. Mars Ultor stands to the left, his face turned to the center, wearing helmet, cuirass, and boots. His raised right hand leans on a scepter, his left hand balances a shield at his feet. In the center, Jupiter partly draped with a mantle sits on a stool. He is seen in three-quarter view, his head turned right; his raised right hand leans on a scepter, and he extends a thunderbolt with his left hand. An eagle stands by his feet. To the right, Victory clothed in a chiton stands in profile facing toward the center. She holds a crowning wreath in her upraised left hand. A palm branch rests against her right shoulder. Groundline under Jupiter and Mars.

Associations among the gods occur with many variations. An identical example is *LIMC* VIII s.v. Zeus-Iuppiter no. 170.

Simplified classical style. Cf. *Hague* nos. 845, 847, chin-mouth-nose style.

11. 0000.999.33932. Chalcedony. Cb7. 14 × 9.8 × 4.5. First century AD.

A male figure, possibly Sarapis, leaning on his right elbow with a himation draped over his legs, reclines on a couch turned toward the right. He wears a kalathos and holds a scepter with his right arm and two ears of wheat in his left hand. Groundline.

This device is closest to motifs representing a god of abundance (like Tellus) or river gods (like the Nile). Those representations usually show a mature male figure reclining directly on the earth, elbow resting on an urn from which water flows, but the figures do not wear kalathoi. See *Wien II* no. 977 (Tellus), 1255 (a river god). For comparison: *LIMC* VII s.v. Sarapis no. 71, Egyptian terracotta relief of Sarapis reclining on a bed holding a fan; *LIMC* VIII s.v. Zeus no. 210, relief from the fourth century BC, Zeus reclining with cornucopia and patera.

Modeled classical style. Cf. *Hague*, classicizing style, nos. 477, 626.

12. 0000.999.33881. Sardonyx (chestnut/white/chestnut). F3. 21.7 × 17.3 × 5.5. Second to third century AD.

The upper part of the gem shows the radiate head of Helios/Sarapis in profile turned to the left, wearing a kalathos. In the field before him, cornucopiae. Beneath the head, an unidentified animal (ram, lion?) stands left. Groundline.

Because of its pantheistic attributes, the head might represent several gods (Helios, Sarapis, and, with the ram's horns, Ammon). Cf. *LIMC* VII s.v. Sarapis no. 105, coins of Alexandria from the reign of Hadrian with head of Sarapis and a ram below. Intaglios: *Wien II* no. 1251 (Sarapis Pantheus); *Gadara* no. 28 for the bust of Heliosarapis; *Gadara* nos. 34–36 and *Fitzwilliam* no. 312 for Sarapis over an eagle with wings outspread and flanked by standards.

13. 0000.999.53001. Carnelian. F1. 14.3 × 10.2 × 3.1. First to second century AD.

Draped bust of (Jupiter) Sarapis. His bearded head is turned in profile to the left. A slender ribbon binds his hair, and he wears a kalathos decked with leaves as a skull cap.

The intaglio shows the traditional image of (Jupiter) Sarapis, which appears at the beginning of the Hellenistic period (*LIMC* VII s.v. Sarapis, pp. 665–692), and which frequently reappears in many different ways on gems during the Roman period. Cf. *Fitzwilliam* nos. 309–311; *Getty* no. 336 (with Isis); *Wien II* nos. 1242–1246; Hornbostel (1973).

Classical linear style.

14. 0000.999.33790. Carnelian. F1. 10 × 6.8 × 3.5. Osborne (1912: pl. XXIII, 20). First century AD.

Neptune stands naked facing, his head turned to the right. His raised right hand holds a trident; with his left hand he supports a dolphin balanced on its snout. Groundline.

Representations of Neptune on gems are rare. They usually show the god with his foot up on a prow or rock. Cf. *Aquileia* no. 48; with variation in position, *AGDS I.3* no. 2293; *Getty* no. 268. For the same pose on a coin, see *LIMC* VII s.v. Poseidon no. 97 (third century BC); on a statuette, *LIMC* VII s.v. Poseidon no. 25 (second century BC).

Modeled classical style. Cf. *Hague* no. 474, classicizing style.

15. 0000.999.33882. Carnelian. F6. Quadrangular with rounded corners. 12.5 × 10.5 × 3.5. First century BC.

Neptune stands naked, head in profile, his torso turned to the left. His right foot rests on a small rock; he rests his left arm on his elevated right knee. Part of a chlamys falls behind him. A trident is placed obliquely behind the god. Groundline. The image is surrounded by sharp, closely spaced hatching.
The figure was possibly inspired by a statue by Lysippus (but see Bartman 1992: 102–146): many intaglios show the figure of Neptune with his body not turned quite so far and his right arm positioned along his body. Cf. *AGDS I.2* no. 721; *Fitzwilliam* no. 237. Calligraphic style. Cf. *Hague* nos. 277, 335, Republican wheel style; *Fitzwilliam* no. 202. The hatching, inspired by Etruscan engraving, also appears on some pieces at the end of the first century BC: *Fitzwilliam* no. 174.

16. 0000.999.35105. Carnelian. F1. 13.8 × 11.2 × 4. Osborne (1912: pl. XXVI, 3). First century BC to first century AD.

A Triton is shown in profile to the left, a raised steering oar rests against his left arm. In his right hand he balances a dolphin by its snout.
The Triton is an uncommon image. His attributes can vary: in addition to the dolphin, they include the steering oar, keel, trophy, trident, shell, or fish. Cf. *Aquileia* no. 521; *Wien I* no. 253; *Hague* no. 355, 398; *Dalmatia* no. 132.
Between the calligraphic and classical linear styles. Cf. *Hague* nos. 342, 354, Republican wheel style and small groove style.

17. 0000.999.36774. Banded agate. C3d. 11.5 × 11.0 × 4.0. First century BC to first century AD.

Apollo with long hair stands naked in profile to the left. He holds a bow and arrow in his left hand, which is raised slightly. With his right hand he supports the forelegs of a stag that stands upright on its hind legs.
This image of Apollo originated in archaic Greek statues (*LIMC* II s.v. Apollon no. 332 for Apollo of Kanachos; Richter 1960). For more recent motifs, see *Lewis* no. 15; *LIMC* II s.v. Apollon-Apollo

nos. 159–160. The pellet style of the engraving and the nature and shape of the stone date to the end of the Republic.

18. 0000.999.35113. Carnelian. Ca4. 14.6 × 11 × 4.5. End of the first century BC to first century AD.

Apollo, turned in profile to the left, a himation draped loosely across his leg, sits on a stool. His left elbow leans on a kithara; a quiver filled with arrows is strapped to his back. In his right hand he holds a patera from which a serpent drinks. The serpent extends its head from a tripod situated to Apollo's left. Further to the left is a laurel tree. Groundline.
A complex scene in the style of Augustan landscape wall-painting. Cf. *Aquileia* no. 68; *Lewis* no. 11; *Hague* no. 478.
Modeled classical style. Cf. *Hague* nos. 477, 479, classicizing style.

19. 0000.999.33830. Carnelian. F1. 11.1 × 8 × 2. First to second century AD.

Apollo stands naked, his body facing and his head in profile to the right. His right elbow leans on a small column behind which stands a tripod. In his left hand, he holds a branch of a laurel tree with leaves. Groundline.
This traditional representation of Apollo is inspired by statues. The position of the branch, elevated or lowered, varies. Cf. *Aquileia* nos. 54, 61; *Wien I* no. 409; *Hague* no. 71; *DL* nos. 427–430; *Fitzwilliam* no. 264.
Smooth style. Cf. *Hague* no. 822, round-head style, nos. 946–947, plain grooves style; *Fitzwilliam* no. 264.

20. 0000.999.33857. Carnelian. F1. 15.5 × 10.5 × (stone broken). In a modern setting. Probably not ancient.

Male head (Apollo?) in profile to the left. The hair, encircled by a laurel fillet, is mid-length with curls.
In an ancient style. *AGDS IV* no. 1032 (Apollo?); *Wien II* no. 1336 (Genius?), 1274 (more traditional representation of Apollo).

21. 0000.999.33888. Carnelian. Ca4. 16.5 × 12 × 4. Large chip on the left part of the stone. First to second century AD.

Helios drives a quadriga to the left. There is a crescent moon above the horses. Because of damage to the stone, we see only

the charioteer's head with radiate crown and the end of an extended arm; of the chariot only a wheel is visible. Groundline.

This is the traditional representation of Helios in his astral aspect
as indicated by the crescent moon. Cf. *AGDS I.3* nos. 2650–2651;
Wien II nos. 1258–1259; *Fitzwilliam* nos. 265–266.

Linear classical style. Cf. *Hague* no. 791, small grooves style; *Fitzwilliam* no. 266.

22. 0000.999.43529. Carnelian. F7. 18.5 × 2.0 × 1.0. Second to third
century AD.

A young cavalier, his cloak flying behind him, holds a double ax
over his shoulder. The horse, in profile, strides left toward a cy-
press before which stands a flaming altar. Beyond the tree, a globe
to the far left. Groundline.

The young cavalier is a local Asiatic divinity who appears as a
reverse type on Roman provincial coins of a group of Lydian
cities: Apollonia, Blandos, Mastaura, Mostene, Thyatiera, and
Tomaris (Merlat 1960: 63). His name is Tyrimnos, and because he
is athletic and young, he was equated with Apollo. On some coins
he is also shown radiate, and therefore was equated with Helios as
well (Cook 1914: 543–601). The iconography of Tyrimnos is primarily known from local Lydian coinage: *LIMC* VIII s.v. Tyrimnos, coins of the second century (as cavalier).

23. 0000.999.33707. Carnelian. Ca4. 14.8 × 11.2 × 4.2. Osborne (1912:
pl. XXIII, 23). Second to third century AD.

Mars Ultor stands facing, his helmeted head in profile to the right.
He wears a short tunic, cuirass, and ankle boots. Behind him a
paludamentum. His raised left hand leans against a lance; his lowered right hand rests on the rim of a shield, which is shown in
profile.

This representation is particularly well established as Mars Ultor
thanks to inscriptions on many imperial coins. Augustus, who built
a new temple with a colossal cult statue, favored the title
"Avenger" for the god in recognition of his victory at Philippi in
43 BC. A similar type occurs on other gems and statues, in which
the god may appear naked or cuirassed. Cf. *Aquileia* no. 207;

AGDS III Göttingen no. 198, Kassel nos. 69–70; *DL* nos. 396–397; *Fitzwilliam* no. 271.

Incoherent style. Cf. *Hague* nos. 971, 974, rigid chin-mouth-nose style; 984, 985, incoherent grooves style.

24. 0000.999.33802. Carnelian. F1. 15 × 12.5 × 2.5. Chip on the upper right part of the gem. Osborne (1912: pl. XXIII, 22). First to second century AD.

Mars, naked and carrying a trophy over his right shoulder, marches left, his waist encircled by a loin-cloth (*subligaculum*) whose ends appear on either side of his body; he wears a helmet and ankle boots. In his left hand he holds a lance obliquely. Groundline.

Traditionally called Mars Gradivus, an old Roman god whose image is known from the end of the second century BC (*LIMC* II s.v. Ares-Mars no. 209, the god shown facing and not marching). The representation takes its present form (marching) in the second part of the first century AD on coins with several epithets: Victor, Pater. This is the usual type on gems: *Aquileia* nos. 221–225; *Wien I* no. 176 (first century BC); *Wien II* nos. 1283–1287; *Getty* nos. 357–358; *Fitzwilliam* no. 270; *Jerusalem* nos. 29–30.

Linear classical style. Cf. *Hague* nos. 667, 737, small grooves style.

25. 0000.999.33942. Chestnut-colored glass paste. F1. 14 × 10.8 × 2.2. Chip to the upper right. First to second century AD.

Same as preceding.

26. 0000.999.35114. Carnelian. Cb. 12.8 × 10 × (mounted in a modern setting). First to second century AD.

A warrior stands to the left facing, clothed in a short tunic and ankle boots. A sword and a chlamys rest against his right arm. A lance stands vertically in front of the warrior, and a trophy stands to his right. At his feet, a shield is placed vertically. Groundline.

Identification of this warrior as Mars is uncertain because the god is rarely shown facing (*LIMC* II s.v. Ares-Mars no. 245, coins of Severus). Nothing distinguishes this figure from an ordinary warrior: *Aquileia* no. 234; *Luni* no. 63; *Bonn* no. 60; *Wien II* no. 1280.

Smooth style. Cf. *Hague* nos. 950, 956, plain grooves style.

27. 0000.999.33810. Carnelian. F4. 18 × 12 × 2.8. Chip in the upper part of the stone. First to second century AD.

Mercury stands naked facing, his head in profile to the right, wearing a pileus (a brimless hat for traveling) and winged sandals. An upright caduceus rests against his right arm, on which a chlamys is draped. He holds up a purse with his left hand. Groundline.

Representations of Mercury were frequent on gems and small statues during the Roman period. The nine representations in this collection are an indication of the god's popularity. It is easy to explain Mercury's popularity since he was both the god of business and the protector of travelers. He also escorts the souls of the dead to the afterlife. Because he rarely was used as a reverse type in either imperial or provincial coinage from the first to the third centuries (with the exception of Hermanubis at the mint of Alexandria), Mercury's frequent appearance as a device on gems is likely to reflect his personal or private significance. Support for this idea is provided by the major exception—imperial coins of Marcus Aurelius for AD 172–174. Rather than reflecting the spirit of commerce, the figure of Mercury on both the silver and bronze issues is thought to honor the Egyptian god who had been invoked by the magician Arnouphis to cause the miracle of rain during Marcus' campaign in the land of the Quadi (Mattingly 1940/1968: cxxxix). His attributes vary: for example, the presence or absence of the cap and winged sandals and various animals: *Aquileia* no. 165–187; *Wien II* nos. 1296–1302; *Getty* nos. 255–256, 343; *Fitzwilliam* no. 260.

Between the modeled and simplified classical styles. Cf. *Hague* nos. 587, classicizing style (musculature), 822, round-head style (head).

28. 0000.999.33878. Carnelian. F1. 10.5 x 8.5 x 3. Second to third century AD.

Mercury stands as on the preceding gem, but without winged sandals.

Between the smooth and incoherent styles. Cf. *Hague* nos. 1010, 1029, incoherent style.

29. 0000.999.33829. Red jasper. F1. 11.1 × 9.5 × 2.8. Second to third century AD.

Mercury stands facing as in the preceding gems, without winged sandals. At his feet to the left is a ram; to the right, a rooster. Groundline.
Cf. *AGDS I.2* nos. 1198–1199; *AGDS IV* no. 1436; *Wien II* no. 1308; *Fitzwilliam* no. 259.
Between the modeled and simplified classical styles. Cf. *Hague* no. 667, small grooves style.

30. 0000.999.33877. Carnelian. Ca4. 13.5 × 10.5 × 3. Second century AD.

Mercury stands facing as on the preceding gems without winged sandals, but possibly wearing a winged cap on his head which is shown in profile toward the right. At his feet, a goat stands to the right and a rooster to the left. In front of the god's right shoulder is a turtle; a scorpion is just to the left of his right arm. Groundline.
Mercury is often accompanied by domestic animals that are symbols of abundance. He is also shown with the turtle, a reference to his exceptional intelligence and skillfulness, because he invented the lyre on the day of his birth, constructing it from the shell of a tortoise. Examples with four animals: *Aquileia* no. 191; *AGDS I.3* no. 3094; *Lewis* no. 34; *Fitzwilliam* no. 258.
Linear classical style. Cf. *Hague* nos. 742, small grooves style, 947, plain grooves style.

31. 0000.999.35112. Carnelian. Ca4. 11.8 × 8.5 × 3.5. Second century AD.

Mercury naked is seated on a rock, his head in profile to the right, his right arm extended behind him to lean on the rock. His left arm rests on his left thigh, which is slightly raised. He holds the rabdos, a magic wand, bent downward with his left hand. Groundline.
This type of Mercury seated with an arm supporting his leaning body is inspired by a statue by Lysippos of Hermes in repose (*LIMC* V s.v. Hermes no. 961 ff). Hermes is the master of technol-

ogy, trickery, mischief, and magic. The rabdos is an attribute of
Hermes already found in Homer. Cf. *AGDS I.3* no. 2294; *AGDS
III* Göttingen nos. 173–174; *AGDS IV* nos. 790–791; *Fitzwilliam*
no. 263.
Simplified classical style. Cf. *Hague* nos. 770, 773, small grooves
style, 879, chin-mouth-nose style.

32. 0000.999.33934. Amethyst. Cc. 10 × 8 × (in a modern setting). First
to second century AD.

Mercury is seated as on the preceding gem. In his left hand he
holds a caduceus horizontally. A rooster stands before him at his
feet. Groundline.
See: *AGDS III* Göttingen no. 176; *AGDS IV* no. 1444; *Hague* no. 668
(these three stones also are amethysts); *Lewis* no. 39; *Wien II* no.
1294.
Linear classical style. Cf. *Hague* nos. 668, 780–781, small grooves
style.

33. 0000.999.33839. Chalcedony. Cc4. 11.5 × 9.5 × 5.2. First century
AD.

Mercury, seated as in the preceding gems, holds a caduceus horizon-
tally in his left hand. A rooster stands in front of him. There is a
turtle behind the rock and a star beneath his right foot. Groundline.
See: *Berlin* no. 2726 (rooster and star).
Modeled classical style. Cf. *Hague* nos. 496–497, classicizing style;
Fitzwilliam no. 262.

34. 0000.999.33702. Brown jasper. F1. 12 × 10 × 2.3. Second to third
century AD.

Mercury, torso facing front, rides a ram toward the right. He
sports a winged cap on his head, which is turned in profile to the
right. His right arm, which is wrapped with a chlamys, supports a
caduceus. He holds a purse with his left hand. In front of the ram
are two ears of wheat. Groundline.
Wheat is another symbol of abundance. See *AGDS III* Göttingen
no. 187; *AGDS IV* nos. 793, 1445; *Lewis* no. 40; *Wien II* no. 1314
(with other objects).

Incoherent style. Cf. *Hague* nos. 964, rigid chin-mouth-nose style (head), 982, 998, incoherent style.

35. 0000.999.33832. Nicolo. F4a. 10.3 × 7.2 × 3. Second century AD.

Bonus Eventus stands naked in profile to the left, a chlamys draped from his shoulders. He holds a cluster of grapes in his lowered left hand and a plate of fruit with his raised right hand. Groundline.

Bonus Eventus, a Roman agricultural god personifying the bountiful outcome of the harvest and, by extension, success in all things, was similar to the Greek Agathos Daimon. He is shown in two ways, either naked facing, holding a patera and ears of wheat, or as here in profile holding a variety of objects symbolizing prosperity. The most common are plates of fruit, clusters of grapes, and ears of wheat. See *Aquileia* nos. 546–551; *AGDS IV* no. 919; *Luni* no. 77; *Wien II* nos. 1329–1330. In the East there were many deities of prosperity and good luck. There were fewer in the West, perhaps accounting for the popularity of Bonus Eventus, especially in Gaul. Another important iconographic influence may have been the Genius Populi Romani coin type.

Smooth style. Cf. *Hague* no. 935, plain grooves style.

36. 0000.999.33886. Nicolo. F4a. 12.2 × 10.5 × 3. First to second century AD.

Bonus Eventus stands in profile to the left in front of a leafy vine, a chlamys hanging from his shoulders. He holds two ears of wheat in his lowered left hand and a plate of fruit with his raised right hand. Groundline.

There are symbols of prosperity everywhere, held in his hand and shown in the background. See *Aquileia* nos. 548, 553; *Köln* no. 297; *Wien II* nos. 1322 (ears of wheat and grapes together), 1323 (leafy vine).

Modeled classical style (?).

37. 0000.999.33867. Chestnut-colored molded glass. F1. 13 × 10.2 × 2.2. Osborne (1912: pl XXIII, 5). Second half of the first century BC.

Bacchus, a youth with short hair, sits on a throne with a high back and legs that end with lion paws. His body, which appears in profile to the left, is partly draped. A beribboned thyrsus is extended obliquely in front of him. A four-legged animal lies at his feet.

The thyrsus indicates that the youth belongs to the world of Dionysus, here likely to be Bacchus. However, Bacchus is rarely shown seated. An almost identical glass paste is *AGDS I.2* no. 1064, first century BC. Related representations: *LIMC* III s.v. Dionysus-Bacchus no. 28 (wall painting at Pompeii) and no. 29 (coin of Corinth). See also *Wien II* no. 1377; *Berlin* no. 1676. Difficult to see because of the imperfect impression in the molded glass is a wine cup (*kantharos*), which the youth appears to hold out in front of him. It is also difficult to identify the animal, but it is probably the traditional panther. This type of throne, or *solium*, usually made of marble (Richter 1966), is frequently used in the representation of various important figures from the middle of the first century BC: *Gaule* no. 88; *Wien I* no. 322; *AGDS IV* no. 447. Classical linear style.

38. 0000.999.33861. Carnelian. Cb8. 13.8 × 9.6 × 4.8. Osborne (1912: pl. XV, 19). Late first century BC.

Bacchus' head, encircled with a crown of ivy, is shown in profile to the left on a herm with hair parted in rolls on the forehead and a rounded coil at the nape of the neck. Four long curls hang toward the neck.

This hairdo adorns the heads of Apollo and Bacchus, especially during the second half of the first century BC. See *AGDS I.2* nos. 1072–1073; *Wien I* no. 232; *Getty* no. 238 for Bacchus and for Apollo nos. 207 and 356. In all of these examples, the god is shown as a bust, lacking the supporting column of a herm.
Modeled classical style or modern work.

39. 0000.999.33866. Brown glass paste. F5. 13.3 × 11 × 2.8. End of the first century BC.

A satyr steps to his right, holding a pedum upright; an animal's pelt is draped over his right arm. He holds a bunch of grapes with his left hand. A panther or dog, its head raised toward the grapes, stands at his feet. Groundline.

The attitude and attributes of this figure are often seen in representations of satyrs in this period, but the presence of an animal is
unusual. See *Aquileia* no. 1082; *Wien II* nos. 1388, 1394.

Between the pellet style and the modeled classical style. Cf. *Hague*
nos. 251–252, Republican extinguishing pellet style.

40. 0000.999.35106. Carnelian. Ca5. 12.5 × 8.7 × 3.8. Second half of the
first century BC.

A satyr stands bent forward in profile to the left. A small child
rests on the satyr's right foot; he is prevented from falling by the
satyr's left hand. The satyr's right hand is raised (usually to hold
the other hand of the child which is absent here). Groundline.

A picturesque motif used in the decorative arts. The infant may be
Bacchus or a satyr. See *Aquileia* no. 405; *Hague* no. 337; *Xanten*
no. 19; *Wien II* no. 1061.

Calligraphic style. Cf. *Hague* nos. 342, 344, 346, Republican wheel
style; *Fitzwilliam* nos. 185–186.

41. 0000.999.33863. Carnelian. Ca5. 12.8 × 8.5 × 3.1. Second half of the
first century BC (?).

A satyr stands in profile to the left. In his left hand he holds a
long object to his lips (an aulos?). A small child with head turned
back climbs down his raised thigh.

The theme of a satyr with Bacchus or a child-satyr is poorly developed here: the infant usually sits straddled across the satyr's
thigh. See *AGDS I.2* no. 749; *Wien I* no. 473; *Fitzwilliam* no. 289.

Calligraphic style. Cf. *Hague* nos. 278, 335, Republican wheel
style.

42. 0000.999.33845. Carnelian. Ca5. 9.8 × 8 × 3. First century AD.

Pan prances left, his bust facing, penis erect and head turned
back. A bunch of grapes drops from his raised right hand; a goat
prepares to spring for the grapes. Pan holds a pedum with his left
hand. Groundline.

Pan is rarely seen on intaglios. His attitude, actions, and attributes are similar to those of satyrs. Typically he holds a syrinx,
his most common attribute. See *Dalmatia* no. 103; *Aquileia* no. 422;

AGDS I.3 no. 2593; *Wien II* nos. 1406 (without a goat), 1407; Jerusalem no. 75; Gadara no. 244 (without the goat, and with patera and branch).
Linear classical style. Cf. *Hague* no. 745, small grooves style.

43. 0000.999.33812. Veined jasper, with flecks of gray, black, and white. Cc4. 16.2 × 12 × 4.1. Osborne (1912: pl. xv, 17). First to second century AD.

The adolescent Harpocrates stands facing, naked. A chlamys slips from his right arm, which holds a cornucopia. His left index finger is pressed against his lips. He wears a composite crown, possibly the *pschent*. Groundline.
This is the Hellenized version of the Egyptian god, whose image spread throughout the empire mainly for private worship. See *AGDS I.3* no. 2677; *Hague* no. 501; *Xanten* no. 190; *Wien I* no. 455; *Wien II* nos. 1364–1368; *Getty* no. 277. Harpocrates' head sometimes is shown in profile, sometimes with the left elbow leaning on a small column. The iconography is illustrated in numerous representations on Roman coins of Alexandria, terracotta statuettes, and lamps, as well as bronzes: *LIMC* IV s.v. Harpocrates nos. 34 (coins), 31 (lamps), 40 (terracotta statuettes), 41 (bronze statues).
Modeled classical style. Cf. *Hague* nos. 473, 482, 501, classicizing style.

44. 0000.999.33941. Red jasper. F1. 12.5 × 9.8 × 3.8. Second century AD.

A standing figure is shown naked, his mature body facing, his head in profile to the left and wearing a *hemhem* crown. His raised left hand leans against a tall stick. His lowered right hand holds a vase. Groundline.
The identification of this figure is uncertain. The *hemhem* crown is worn by Harpocrates (*LIMC* IV s.v. Harpokrates nos. 134, 148b, 188a); as a child the god is often shown in terracottas statuettes holding a vase (*LIMC* no. 134) but not a staff. The adolescent Harpocrates appears with a spherical object (a pomegranate?) and a small branch on tetradrachms of Gallienus to Diocletian from Alexandria (*LIMC* no. 357) and on intaglios (*Lewis* no.

126). Alternatively the figure might represent Dionysus-Osiris (see *LIMC* VII s.v. Osiris, p. 116). In *AGDS III* no. 57, the god holds a kantharos in one hand and a staff with the other. He also wears a tripartite headgear that might be meant to be a *hemhem* crown. Smooth style.

45. 1944.100.83573. Red jasper. F2. 10.7 × 7.7 × 2.3. Second to third century AD.

Mithras wearing a Phrygian cap rides a prancing horse in profile to the left. An altar with a pointed flame stands in front of the horse, and a tree stands behind. Groundline.

Representations of Mithras on engraved gems are rare: he is shown either as a bust of a young man wearing a Phrygian cap or, less frequently, slaying the bull. The device of Mithras as cavalier, close to the image of the Thracian horseman, appears on Roman provincial coins of Trebizond during the first part of the third century. See *LIMC* VI s.v. Mithras nos. 308–313 (various coins), no. 311 (cavalier with altar and tree, dating from the middle of the third century); intaglios: *Berlin* no. 2935; *AGDS III* Braunschweig no. 80, Kassel no. 209.

46. 1944.100.83572. Red jasper. F4a. 14.2 × 10.9 × 2.5. Third to fourth century AD.

Mithras. Similar to the preceding gem. The horseman is wearing a pileus, not a Phrygian cap, and raises his left arm in a gesture characteristic of imperial cavaliers. There is a six-pointed star above the altar. See *LIMC* IV s.v. Mithras no. 313, cavalier with tree, altar, and star on a coin of Gordian III.

47. 0000.999.33864. Red jasper. Octagonal. F2. 15.5 × 13 × 5.2. Second century AD.

A draped bust with a bearded head wearing a Phrygian cap is shown in profile to the left. Inscription **ME** to the right behind the head; **APH** in front of the head to the left; and **C** below the bust.

Identification is uncertain. The god Men would have a crescent moon placed with points upward behind his shoulders. As a rule,

Men is shown as a youth without a beard (*LIMC* VI s.v. Men nos. 8, 19), as are Mithras, Attis, and Perseus. The beard may indicate Priam or Aeneas, but they are rarely depicted alone (*LIMC* VII s.v. Priamos no. 1; *LIMC* I s.v. Aineias no. 5). An unidentified parallel image is *AGDS I.2* no. 1057.

48. 0000.999.33892. Carnelian. Ca5. 18.2 × 15 × 4. Second century AD.

The Dioscuri. Two naked youths; a chlamys passes behind them, rolled over their arms. They stand on a groundline, facing symmetrically, heads turned toward each other. Each twin leans on a lance placed toward the center of the device. Above each head is a six-pointed star.
The twin heroes are easily recognized by the stars and lances. Cf. *Aquileia* nos. 491–493; *AGDS IV* no. 1550; *Xanten* no. 193.
Smooth style. Cf. *Hague* nos. 882, 888 (head) cap-with-rim style.

49. 0000.999.35107. Sardonyx, orange, white, and brown. Cc3. 14.5 × 12 × 5.8. First to second century AD.

A Genius is shown as a partially dressed youth standing and facing. He carries a cornucopia against his right arm under which a chlamys is draped. He holds a patera in his left hand. Beneath the patera is an altar with burning incense. Groundline.
A Genius is represented in the same way, whether for personal or public use. It is only possible to determine his significance by inscription, provenance, or place. On intaglios and other personal objects, the Genius can have the appearance of a public image, for example as the Genius Populi Romani. Variations occurs with and without the altar: *AGDS I.3* nos. 2311, 2691–2692; *Wien II* nos. 1334–1335.

50. 0000.999.33889. Carnelian. F1. 18.5 × 15 × 4. Small chips in the lower part of the stone. Second to third century AD.

On the left, Aesculapius stands facing, wearing a loose himation around his legs, his head turned toward the center. His left hand rests against a short rod around which a serpent winds. On the right Hygieia stands facing, dressed in chiton and himation, her head turned toward the center. She holds a patera in her right hand. A serpent winds around her lowered left hand, its head appearing below the patera. The two gods are placed upon a tall quadrilateral base, suggesting that the figures are meant to be statues.

Aesculapius is commonly associated with Hygieia. The presence of the imposing base is unusual. See (without a base) *Aquileia* nos. 509–510; *AGDS I.3* no. 2596; *Hague* nos. 664, 848; *Wien I* no. 205 signed by the engraver Heius; *Wien II* no. 1200.

Simplified classical style. Cf. *Hague* no. 815, round-head style, 952, plain grooves style.

51. 0000.999.33846. Carnelian. Cb4. 14 × 12.5 × 4.4. Osborne (1912: pl. XXIV, 19). Second to third century AD.

Aesculapius and Hygieia as on the preceding gem, but the deities stand on a simple groundline.

Classical linear style. Cf. *Hague* no. 664, small grooves style.

52. 0000.999.36781. Carnelian. C4a. 14.5 × 7.0 × 2.0. Second to third century AD.

Ganymede and the eagle. A naked youth shown seated on a rock in profile to the left, a pedum behind him. He offers a phiale for the eagle to drink. The eagle faces Ganymede, his wings spread upward; he stands on one foot, the other is upraised to grasp Ganymede's thigh.

Ganymede, a Trojan prince and a shepherd (hence the pedum), was carried off by an eagle sent by Jupiter who was charmed by the boy's beauty. In the Roman period, the motif of the prince providing the bird with drink, an action that anticipates Ganymede's ultimate office on Mount Olympus as cupbearer of the gods, is often shown in two ways. In one, Ganymede stands (*LIMC* IV s.v. Ganymedes nos. 108–114 [mosaics, gems], 115–137 [small statues]). The eagle is placed on a column, a tree, or the ground. In the other, Ganymede is seated (*LIMC* IV s.v. Ganymedes nos. 138ff, 144–164); also see *Aquileia* no. 44; *Gaule* no. 451. See Sichtermann (1953).

Incoherent style. Cf. *Hague* nos. 1053–1054, incoherent grooves style.

53. 0000.999.33828. Nicolo. F4. 11.8 × 10 ×3.4. Second to third century AD.

Ganymede stands partly to the left wearing a Phrygian cap, a chlamys draped down his back. In his right hand he holds a vase. Groundline.

The Phrygian cap and the pedum would indicate Paris, but the presence of a vase (*skyphos*) indicates Ganymede. An identical figure occurs with the drinking eagle (*Getty* no. 427). Since the eagle is absent, however, perhaps the Ganymede shown here is already on Olympus ministering to the gods (a motif that occurs on Attic vases of the fifth century B.C: *LIMC* IV s.v. Ganymedes nos. 59–68). For the motif of Ganymede alone, see *LIMC* s.v. Ganymedes nos. 3, 4 (*Aquileia* no. 45); *Gaule* no. 452.

Modeled classical style. Cf. *Hague* nos. 536, 555, 600, classicizing style.

54. 0000.999.36800. Banded agate. C4c. 13.0 × 12 × 6. First to second century AD.

The crowned head of Hercules in profile to the left. His hair is short, his brow furrowed, and his neck thick-set.

On intaglios as on coins, Hercules appears either as a young man without a beard and with curly hair or as a mature man, bearded and with hair cropped. Often the pelt of a lion is tied around his neck or worn on his head. Following Alexander the Great certain emperors, particularly Commodus, favored Hercules as a device on coins (Speidel 1993). For the young head: *LIMC* IV s.v. Herakles nos. 126–164, coins of the fifth century BC to second century AD; *Wien II* no. 661. For the mature head: *LIMC* nos. 191–206, from the third century BC to the third century AD; *Wien II* no. 664 (with club behind the head); *AGDS IV* no. 190; *Fitzwilliam* no. 199–200. Classical linear style.

55. 0000.999.36636. Carnelian. F1. 22.0 × 9 × 1.5. Second century AD.

Hercules stands facing, head turned to the left. He carries a club at an oblique angle over his left arm, which is separated from his chest. A lion's pelt hangs from his right arm. He holds something (apples?) in his right hand. Groundline.

This representation of Hercules, which occurs during the Imperial period in many artistic forms, was inspired by fourth-century BC statuary (*LIMC* IV s.v. Herakles pp. 745–747, diverse variants, for example, Hercules with bow and arrow or apples in his left hand; on coins, no. 285 at the beginning of the third century; terra sigillata, no. 314). On gems, *AGDS IV* no. 1545; *Fitzwilliam* no. 335.

Smooth style. Cf. *Aquileia*, Officina dei Dioscuri, pl. XCII (round the head style), nos. 943, 950, 956 (plain grooves style).

56. 0000.999.35204. Carnelian. F5. 13.5 × 11.5 × 3. Chipped in the lower left part of the stone. First century BC.

Hercules mingens. The hero stands in profile to the left, leaning forward with legs spread apart, urinating. A lion's pelt hangs down his back, the club rests on his right shoulder. Groundline.

The image of the drunk Hercules is known from the second century BC; it appears on gems, small statues in bronze or marble, in the decorative arts, and even in fountains. Intaglios: *AGDS IV* nos. 306–308; *Getty* no. 349.

Imitation of the pellet style. Cf. *Hague* nos. 165, 171, Italic-republican blob style, 225, Italic-republican pellet style; *Fitzwilliam* nos. 147–149.

ABBREVIATIONS FOR THE CATALOGUE

AGDS I = Brandt, E., A. Krug, and E. Schmidt. 1968–1972. *Antike Gemmen in deutschen Sammlungen I: staatliche Münzesammlung, München*. München: Franz Steiner Verlag.

AGDS III = Scherf, V., P. Gercke, and P. Zazoff. 1970. *Antike Gemmen in deutschen Sammlungen III: Braunschweig, Göttingen, Kassel*. Wiesbaden: Franz Steiner Verlag.

AGDS IV = Schlüter, M., G. Platz-Horster, and P. Zazoff. 1975. *Antike Gemmen in deutschen Sammlungen IV: Hannover, Kestner-Museum; Hamburg, Museum für Kunst und Gewerbe*. Wiesbaden: Franz Steiner Verlag.

Aquileia = Sena Chiesa 1966.

Berlin = Furtwängler, A. 1896. *Beschreibung der geschnittenen Steine im Antiquarium*. Berlin: W. Spem Enn.

Bonn = Platz-Horster, G. 1984. *Die antiken Gemmen im Rheinischen Landesmuseum Bonn.* Köln: Rheinland-Verlag.

Dalmatia = Middleton, S. H. 1991. *Engraved gems from Dalmatia.* Oxford: Oxford University Committee for Archaeology.

DL = Vollenweider, M.-L. 1984. *Deliciae leonis: antike geschnittene Steine und Ringe aus einer Privatsammlung.* Mainz: Philipp von Zabern.

Fitzwilliam = Henig 1994.

Gadara = Henig, M. and M. Whiting. 1987. *Engraved gems from Gadara in Jordan: the Sa'd collection of intaglios and cameos.* Oxford: Oxford University Committee for Archaeology.

Gaule = Guiraud 1988.

Getty = Spier, J. 1992. *Ancient gems and finger rings: catalogue of the collections.* Malibu: J. Paul Getty Museum.

Hague = Maaskant-Kleibrink 1978.

Jerusalem = Amorai-Stark, S. 1993. *Engraved gems and seals from two collections in Jerusalem.* Jerusalem: Franciscan Printing Press.

Köln = Krug, A. 1980. *Antike Gemmen im römisch-germanischen Museum Köln.* Sonderdruck aus Bericht der Römisch-Germanischen Kommission 61. Frankfurt: Römisch-Germanische Kommission des Deutschen Archäologischen Instituts.

Lewis = Henig, M. 1975. *The Lewis collection of engraved gemstones in Corpus Christi College, Cambridge.* BAR Supplementary Series 1. Oxford: British Archaeological Reports.

LIMC = *LIMC* 1981–1997. *Lexicon iconographicum mythologiae classicae.* Zürich: Artemis Verlag.

Luni = Sena Chiesa, G. 1978. *Gemme di Luni.* Roma: Giorgio Bretschneider.

Wien II = Zwierlein-Diehl 1979.

REFERENCES

Bartman, E. 1992. *Ancient sculptural copies in miniature.* Leiden: E. J. Brill.

Cook, A. B. 1914. *Zeus, a study in ancient religion, vol. II: Zeus, god of the dark sky (thunder and lightning).* Cambridge: Cambridge University Press.

Guiraud, H. 1988. *Intailles et camées de l'époque romaine en Gaule (territoire français).* Gallia supplément 48. Paris: Éditions du CNRS.

Hajjar, J. N. 1977. *La triade d'Héliopolis-Baalbek*. Leiden: E. J. Brill.

Henig, M. 1994. *Classical gems: ancient and modern intaglios and cameos in the Fitzwilliam Museum, Cambridge*. Cambridge: Cambridge University Press.

—. 1997. Roman sealstones. In: D. Collon, ed., *7000 years of seals*, pp. 88–106. London: British Museum Press.

Hornbostel, W. 1973. *Sarapis: Studien zur Überlieferungsgeschichte, der Ercheinungsformen und Wandlungen der Gestalt eines Gottes*. Leiden: E. J. Brill.

Maaskant-Kleibrink, M. 1978. *Catalogue of the engraved gems in the royal coin cabinet, the Hague: the Greek, Etruscan, and Roman collection*. The Hague: Government Publishing Office.

Mattingly, H. 1968 [1940]. *Coins of the Roman empire in the British Museum, vol. IV: Antoninus Pius to Commodus*. London: British Museum.

Merlat, P. 1960. *Jupiter Dolichenus*. Paris: Presses Universitaires de France.

Osborne, D. 1912. *Engraved gems: signets, talismans, and ornamental intaglios, ancient and modern*. New York: Henry Holt.

Pannuti, U. 1975. Pinarius Ceralis, gemmarius pompeianus. Bollettino d'Arte 60:178–190.

Plantzos, D. 1999. *Hellenistic engraved gems*. Oxford: Clarendon Press.

Platz-Horster, G. 1987. *Die antiken Gemmen aus Xanten I*. Köln: Rheinland-Verlag.

—. 1994. *Die antiken Gemmen aus Xanten II*. Köln: Rheinland-Verlag.

Richter, G. M. A. 1960. *Kouroi, archaic Greek youths*. London: Phaidon Press.

—. 1966. *The furniture of the Greeks, Etruscans and Romans*. London: Phaidon Press.

Schwartz, F. M. and J. H. Schwartz. 1979. Engraved gems in the collection of the American Numismatic Society I: ancient magical amulets. *ANS Museum Notes* 24:149–197.

Schwartz, J. H. 1999. Engraved gems in the collection of the American Numismatic Society II: intaglios with Eros. *American Journal of Numismatics* 11:13–45.

Sena Chiesa, G. 1966. *Gemme del Museo Nazionale di Aquileia*. Padova: Associazione Nazionale per Aquileia.

Sichtermann, H. 1953. *Ganymed: Mythos und Gestalt in der antiken Kunst*. Berlin: Gebr. Mann.

Speidel, M. P. 1993. Commodus the god. *Journal of Roman Studies* 83:109–114.

von der Osten, H. H. 1934. Ancient oriental seals in the collection of Mr. Edward T. Newell. Chicago: University of Chicago Press.

Zwierlein-Diehl, E. 1973. *Die antiken Gemmen des kunsthistorischen Museums in Wien, Band I: die Gemmen von der minoischen Zeit bis zur frühen römischen Kaiserzeit*. München: Prestel Verlag.

—. 1979. *Die antiken Gemmen des kunsthistorischen Museums in Wien, Band II: die Gemmen der späteren römischen Kaiserzeit*. München: Prestel Verlag.

AJN Second Series 13 (2001) pp. 63–80

A SIXTH-CENTURY TREMISSIS FROM PSALMODI
(GARD, FRANCE)

(PLATE 6)   SEBASTIAN HEATH* AND DAVID YOON*

The Benedictine monastery at Psalmodi in Gard, France, is most prominently marked by the standing south wall of the twelfth-century triple-aisle church. Now the site of a farm whose main product is flowers for the European market, the first indications of permanent occupation revealed by the Williams College excavations conducted between 1970 and 1989 date to the middle of the fifth century; only a few residual sherds of the Bronze Age, Iron Age, and early to mid Roman periods indicate earlier use of the site. No certain architectural features survive from the late antique settlement but there is abundant, though poorly stratified, ceramic evidence indicating that the inhabitants of Psalmodi had ready access to products from the main exporting regions of the Mediterranean during the late fifth and sixth centuries AD.

Psalmodi is located between Saint-Laurent-d'Aigouze and Aigues-Mortes, on the edge of the Petite Camargue, the western side of the Rhône delta. Although now several kilometers from the shore, in the Middle Ages and before it would have been on a small island within a coastal lagoon, subsequently filled by alluvial silts, at the mouth of the

* The American Numismatic Society, Broadway at 155th Street, New York, NY 10032, USA (heath@amnumsoc.org; yoon@amnumsoc.org).

Vistre river. In this location, the site was well placed for access both to the interior and along the coast, and profited from control of coastal resources (salt pans, in particular) as well as land-based production in its hinterland. During the sixth century, moreover, this location was at the margin between Visigothic Septimania to the west and Ostrogothic/ Frankish Provence to the east.

The excavations at Psalmodi, originally directed at the twelfth-century abbey church whose remains dominate the site, revealed the foundations of an earlier church underneath, probably representing multiple phases of Carolingian and Romanesque date (Dodds 1977; Dodds et al. 1989). Around the northeast end of this early church, still earlier deposits were found, containing mostly artifacts of the fifth and sixth centuries AD.

THE COIN

In 1988, during cleaning of an excavation face from an earlier year in the area of the north aisle of the twelfth-century church (northeast of the earlier Carolingian or Romanesque church), a pseudo-imperial tremissis was found (catalogue number PS88.102.11).

AV Tremissis, 19 mm, 1.49 g, 6:00 (Plate 6 no. 1).
Obv.: Bust diademed and draped r. See below for discussion of legend.
Rev.: Victory advancing r. holding palm branch and wreath. See below for discussion of legend.
The coin is well struck and centered on a thin flan. There is some wear on high points and a few scratches are present near the edge. Some original luster and flow lines are preserved.

The lettering is not entirely competent, allowing for some ambiguity of reading. The obverse legend is readable but blundered enough to allow different interpretations. It is possible to interpret the legend as DN IVSTINI PP AVG, DN IVSTINS PP AVG, or DN IVSTINIS P AVG, referring to Justin I (518–527). The legend is continuous over the top of the head of the imperial bust, however, which is normal on coins of Anastasius (491–518) but not Justin. The same legend could just as well be interpreted as DN ANASTINI PP AUG, DN ANISTIVS PP AVG, DN

ANSAIIVS PP AVG, or the like. Other possible readings have been published based on two other coins struck from the same die (see below). The AVGVSTORVM of the reverse legend is thoroughly blundered, with the third to fifth letters being the most illegible: an approximate reading of the legend would be VICTORIA IC*CACCA*. The legend in the exergue on the reverse is CONOB.

The imperial bust on the obverse is relatively naturalistic for this series, with a tall face, an exaggerated chin, loosely drawn drapery that forms a distinctive hook shape on the chest, and an exaggerated round fibula. On the other hand, the Victory on the reverse shows some tendency toward deterioration into a bird-like or dragon-like creature: the skirt has turned into two streamers on the right side, almost becoming a new pair of legs, and a tail-like appendage on the left, and the wreath with the arm holding it resembles a small head with a long, thick neck.

At least two other published coins were struck from the same obverse and reverse dies: a coin in the Cabinet des Médailles of the Bibliothèque Nationale de France (Plate 6 no. 2; BN 236), published as Lenormant (1853) pl. VII no. 8, Belfort (1894) no. 5113, and Tomasini (1964) no. 122, and another in Nîmes (Plate 6 no. 3; Nîmes 228), published as Amandry et al. (1989) no. 45. All three are well struck and have good preservation of detail; the Psalmodi coin is perhaps somewhat less worn than the other two. The ambiguity of the lettering can be seen in the diverse readings found in the publications of the other two examples: MNANASINIZAIVC I VICTORIAICANACCV I CONOZ (Lenormant 1853: 311; Belfort 1894: 37), DNANASTAIVSPAVC I VICTORIAIC////// I CONOB (Tomasini 1964: 199), DN ANASTASIS PAVC I VICTORIA [ ]ACCA I CONOB (Lafaurie in Amandry et al. 1989: 35).

NUMISMATIC CONTEXT

Pseudo-imperial tremisses, produced by many mints in several kingdoms over a period of about a century and a half, have been resistant to classification due to their diversity and lack of explicit statement of mint or issuing authority. In the absence of more explicit criteria, study has been based primarily on stylistic resemblances and relationships, supplemented where possible by the evidence that hoards provide for date and provenance. Some fairly clear general categories can be defined on the basis of reverse type: for example, the Cross in Wreath reverse is early and associated with the Visigoths and Suevians, whereas the Victory with Globe and Cross reverse is associated with the Ostrogoths and northern Frankish regions (Tomasini 1964; Grierson and Blackburn 1986). The Victory with Palm and Wreath (VPW) type, to which the subject of this article belongs, presents the most difficulties. It appears to have been issued under Ostrogothic, Visigothic, Burgundian, and Frankish auspices at the least, in Italy, France, and the Iberian peninsula, for much of the duration of the sixth century. It occurs in a confusing welter of stylistic variants for which the most detailed arrangement is that of Tomasini (1964); the types found in the Iberian peninsula have also been classified by Reinhart (1940–41).

The VPW series is thought to have begun perhaps around 509 with a group of tremisses attributed by Wroth (1911) to the Rome mint under Theoderic (Tomasini 1964; Grierson and Blackburn 1986: 35). The engraving on this issue is close to (or better than) the standard of imperial issues, with minor differences such as some stylization of the drapery on the obverse bust, resulting in a somewhat more two-dimensional appearance. As coins from this tradition came to be copied in the mints of Gaul and Spain, various innovations appeared.

The rapid stylistic evolution of this series suggests that dies were generally cut using recent examples as models, rather than being based on older or more stable exemplars. As a result, stylistic change tends to take the form of accumulation of successive "mutations" over time. Therefore, the affinities of coin types in this series can be estimated according to the innovations that they share.[1]

The coin from Psalmodi has several derived features relative to the presumed ancestral type: apart from idiosyncratic features (such as the

---

[1] This simple picture could be complicated, of course, if a die-cutter used two different coins as models for the same die, as may often have occurred. It is even conceivable that the obverse legend on the coin presented here could have resulted from attempting to copy two models, one in the name of Anastasius and one in the name of Justin.

hook-shaped line in the drapery on the obverse bust), the most notable is the Victory on the reverse, whose flaring skirt has turned into streamers on the right and a thick tail-like appendage on the left. The blundered lettering may also be considered a derived feature. On the other hand, various other innovations that occur on pseudo-imperial tremisses of the early sixth century are absent, such as an elongated neck, simplified delineation of the face, or a pectoral cross on the obverse and a monogram or a "stick-figure" rendering of the Victory on the reverse.

Tomasini attributes his no. 122 to his group A6, which he considers to be probably Burgundian, on the basis of stylistic resemblance to group A5, which contains coins generally accepted as Burgundian issues (1964: 96). However, as Lafaurie (1966) has pointed out, it does not fit Tomasini's definition of the type. Although the obverse type is fairly close to the ancestral type, like many Burgundian issues (as well as other early VPW tremisses that are not considered to be Burgundian), the derived features of the reverse type are associated primarily with what is considered to be Visigothic coinage rather than what is thought to be Burgundian coinage (typically characterized by a simplified but clearly drawn long skirt on the Victory, for example).

This does not mean, however, that the coin was necessarily minted under Visigothic auspices. In fact, coins of this general appearance, with a conservative obverse and a moderately distorted Victory on the reverse, have been attributed to the Franks by Lafaurie (1968, 1983: e.g., nos. 56–60).[2] However, considering the frequently changing political boundaries and weak administrative control typical of this period, attribution to kingdoms may not be the most useful approach to classifying this series. Broad regional groupings, as suggested by Grierson and Blackburn (1986: 110), may provide a more useful starting point for future progress. Regardless of who authorized them, the coins with conservative obverse and moderately stylized Victory are clearly associated with what is today southern France: for example, a majority of such specimens in Belfort (1894) are referenced to Robert

---

[2] Including the one in Nîmes struck from the same dies as the Psalmodi coin (Amandry et al. 1989: no. 45).

(1879), a work devoted to coins that Robert believed to have been found in (or otherwise associated with) Languedoc.

Not only attribution but also detailed study of the function and chronology of these coins is hampered by the lack of any known archaeological context for most examples and by the paucity of well-documented hoards. The hoards that are most relevant by date and location to the context of the coin described here are those of Roujan (c. 520, Hérault: Dhénin and Landes 1994, 1995–96), Gourdon (c. 530, Saône-et-Loire: partially reconstructed in Lafaurie 1958) and Alise-Sainte-Reine (c. 550, Côte-d'Or: partially reconstructed in Lafaurie 1983), and Viviers (c. 570–80, Ardèche: Lafaurie and Morrisson 1987) and Var (c. 570–80, Var: Lafaurie and Morrisson 1987), both dated by Lafaurie to c. 570–80 but containing mostly earlier coins.

The Roujan hoard, found between Béziers and Montpellier and dating to the reign of Justin I, contained twenty-four tremisses as well as four solidi. One of the tremisses is of distinctively Ostrogothic type (not VPW); of the remaining twenty-three, Dhénin attributes one in the name of Anastasius to the Visigoths, and of the others, all in the name of Justin, one to the Burgundians, nine to the Visigoths, and twelve to the Franks (Dhénin and Landes 1995–96). Although some of the specific attributions may be controversial, it is noteworthy that this hoard found in the heart of Visigothic Septimania included not only a Byzantine solidus and an Ostrogothic tremissis, but also a large number of tremisses that do not have the derived characteristics (pectoral cross, in particular) shared by most Visigothic tremisses minted in the name of Justin. In fact, several of the pieces are more conservative in design than the Psalmodi specimen, even though they were minted in the name of Justin. It is also noteworthy that this hoard, though probably formed early in Justin's short reign, is composed mostly of coins in the name of Justin rather than Anastasius, suggesting (if, as the diverse attributions suggest, the hoard was formed from circulating coinage) that the turnover of types in circulation was quite rapid.

The Gourdon and Alise-Sainte-Reine hoards, both found in Burgundy in the nineteenth century, dispersed without having been adequately recorded, and subsequently studied by Lafaurie (1958, 1983), present somewhat different patterns. The Gourdon hoard appears to have consisted mostly of coins from Burgundian sources, with a few others, such as two fifth-century East Roman solidi and a Frankish tremissis in the name of Justinian that was probably associated with this hoard (Lafaurie 1958: 64, 73–75). This suggests a circulation pattern with a greater emphasis on political boundaries. The Alise-Sainte-Reine hoard, on the other hand, is very diverse; the reconstructed portion includes significant numbers of coins attributed to the Visigoths and Burgundians and smaller numbers of Ostrogothic and Imperial coins, in addition to the majority attributed to the Franks. Both the Gourdon hoard and the Alise-Sainte-Reine hoard contained a significant proportion of pseudo-imperial tremisses in the name of Anastasius, even though they were later than the Roujan hoard.

The Viviers hoard from the middle Rhône valley, composed mostly of solidi rather than tremisses, follows the same pattern as that of Alise-Sainte-Reine, with a mixture of imperial, Ostrogothic, Frankish, and Visigothic types, including many in the name of Anastasius and Justin I (as well as earlier imperial issues) in a hoard dating to the reign of Justin II (Lafaurie and Morrisson 1987: 77–80). A smaller hoard found somewhere in the Var is very similar in composition (Lafaurie and Morrisson 1987: 75–76).

It appears from the hoard evidence that tremisses circulated fairly freely, without much regard to political boundaries (too little is known about the Gourdon hoard for one to be certain that it contradicted this pattern). The preponderance of the evidence suggests that tremisses could remain in circulation for several decades during this time; the Roujan hoard appears to be exceptional, perhaps having been formed in a different manner. These conclusions add little to our knowledge about the tremissis from Psalmodi as an individual object: if coins of different origins circulated freely, there is little basis for attributing the Psalmodi piece to a particular kingdom, and if tremisses circulated for several decades, the relatively unworn condition of the coin is the only evidence suggesting deposition early in the sixth century. Nevertheless, by indicating the general patterns of circulation, the hoard evidence provides a valuable context for understanding what the functional significance of this artifact may have been.

ARCHAEOLOGICAL CONTEXT

As mentioned, the coin was found while cleaning off the face of an earlier excavation. It came from a layer (Context 88.102.26) that contained mostly sixth-century artifacts, but the stratigraphic position of the layer is directly between a mid-sixth-century pit and the floor preparation for the twelfth-century church, so it could have been deposited there anytime between those dates. It is very unusual to find gold coins as stray site finds; their value makes casual loss or discard highly unlikely. Most sixth-century tremisses are found in hoards or in graves; of the few other finds with documented proveniences, most either lack stratigraphic associations (Bonifay et al. 1998: 106) or are thought to be from disturbed graves (Lafaurie 1970).

The area in which the Psalmodi coin was found was used for burials from late antiquity to the twelfth century and then was heavily disturbed by the construction of the church in the late twelfth century. Therefore it is possible that this coin was originally deposited in a grave but was subsequently redeposited by the digging of a later grave or by construction activity. The possibility that it was found in an intact sixth-century deposit should not be excluded, though; Goury (1997) has reported finding a tremissis in the name of Anastasius in a pit fill associated with refuse from craft production and sixth-century pottery.

ECONOMIC SIGNIFICANCE

The discovery of this coin at Psalmodi may hold considerable importance for the economic status of the site and deserves further commentary. The interpretive weight which this piece can bear is, of course, limited by the relative lack of both material and textual evidence, but, as will be seen, the two can be usefully combined at Psalmodi.

Among the uncertainties is the purchasing power of the coin under consideration. Durliat has pointed out that an estate of 50 solidi is the generally accepted lowest limit for a person to be considered of means in the late Roman and early medieval world (1990: 297). Using predominantly eastern evidence he has also established broad price ranges for certain commodities (Durliat 1987:345). For example, by Durliat's calculations one solidus (i.e., three tremisses) could purchase between 12 and 68 liters of olive oil depending on quality. For the same amount one could acquire 87 liters of wine suitable to serve to soldiers or lesser bureaucrats. The laws found in the Visigothic *Forum Iudicum*, issued in the seventh century, also help to establish the purchasing power of gold (e.g., Barral i Altet 1976: 72–74). The theft of a cow is punishable by payment of two tremisses, that of a calf only by one.

The narrative history of Gregory of Tours also makes occasional reference to the use of gold coins in the late sixth century (Stamm 1982/84). The Gallo-Roman aristocrat Mummolus extracted "multa nummismati auri milia" from Saxon raiders (*HF* 4.42). In a more specific reference, the Syrian merchant Eufronius offered 200 "aureos" to the same Mummolus so that the aristocrat would not press his demands to see a relic in the foreigner's possession (*HF* 7.31). At the low end, Gregory relates that during the famine of 585 merchants sold "modium annonae aut semodium vini uno triante." (*HF* 7.45) These numbers are not cited as direct evidence of the purchasing power of the Psalmodi tremissis but rather as a rough indicator. Any gold coin had considerable value, but a tremissis by itself is in no way an indicator of great wealth.

The total supply of gold in the region has also been roughly assessed. The calculations of Depeyrot (1996: 29, 33–35) show a decrease in total gold supply following a peak in the late fourth century as well as decreasing relative share of that supply in the western Mediterranean. His calculations for the sixth and seventh centuries in France (1994: 96–102) show relative stability in total supply but at a dramatically reduced level. These conclusions are complemented by Banaji's study of sixth-century hoards (1996). While it is true that determining the purchasing power and supply of gold remains a largely qualitative exercise, even the limited extent to which the problems can be approached indicates that the Psalmodi piece can indicate the presence of some individuals of relative wealth at the settlement.

Expressing the purchasing power of this tremissis in terms of oil and wine is useful because the ceramic record at Psalmodi makes clear that

the sixth century inhabitants had ready access to both. The archaeological deposits contemporaneous with the coin are distinguished by the
presence of imported amphora sherds that would have carried oil and
wine from North Africa and the Eastern Mediterranean, and for the
presence of imported coarse wares and table wares that are further
evidence of the site's relative prosperity and access to long-distance
exchange networks.

The pottery from the deposit in which the tremissis was found
(PS88.102.026) numbered only 37 sherds and includes substantially
later material. A single partially preserved rim of a Keay 62a North
African amphora datable to the sixth century AD is nonetheless notable.
A sixth-century pit filled with domestic refuse only a few meters east of
the findspot of the tremissis did, however, produce a ceramic assemblage
large enough to help elucidate the economic circumstances of Psalmodi
in the sixth century. Contexts PS88.102.024 and PS88.102.028
form the recorded portions of a pit that produced a total of 262 sherds
weighing just under 4 kilograms. This pit is remarkable for the diversity of imported ceramics that it produced. Discounting the 16 residual
and unidentified sherds, imports make up 52% of the deposit by sherd
count and fully 74.8% by weight. The imbalance is caused by the relatively large size of the individual North African amphora sherds.

This is not the venue in which to present the ceramics from this
deposit in detail, but the highlights are relevant. North African products are the most common ceramic imports in this pit and among
sixth-century deposits at the site generally. African Red-Slip, the most
common category of fine ware in the Western Mediterranean at this
time, is represented by fourteen sherds, including three rims whose
chronological ranges overlap in the second half of the sixth century: a
Hayes 91d flanged bowl, a Hayes 104a plate, and a Hayes 87c plate.
(Hayes 1972, Py 1993) North African amphoras are present only as
body sherds, but the substantial number and weight—64 sherds and
2.1 kilograms respectively—indicate the continued importation of food-
stuffs from that region during the sixth century. Elsewhere at the site,
diagnostic fragments of Keay 55, Keay 62, and Keay 61 amphoras
show that this was a regular feature of the economy of the site from
the late fifth century through the sixth and possibly into the seventh
(Keay 1998).

In addition to the North African products, which are common at many sites in the region, the pit also produced imports from the Eastern Mediterranean. While these are well known in southern France, they are not nearly so common as the African products, particularly on smaller sites. The main exporting regions represented in Pit 88.102.24/28 are the Aegean, the Cilician coast of Asia Minor, and ancient Palestine. From the Aegean come two categories of vessel, the globular amphora with grooved upper body known as Late Roman Amphora 2 and the cooking pot known in France as Com-Medit 5. Late Roman Amphora 1, probably a product of the Cilician coast and the only import from eastern Asia Minor in this pit, is represented by one rim and eleven body sherds.

Like the Aegean material, the imported ceramics from ancient Palestine include both amphora and coarse ware forms. Late Roman Amphora 4 carried the wine for which Gaza was famous in Late Antiquity. It is widely exported to the west from the fourth through seventh centuries and is represented in Pit PS88.102.24/28 by one base and seven body sherds. Less common on Western Mediterranean sites is the coarse ware form known in France as Com-Medit 4. Pit PS88.102.24/28 produced a rim/handle as well as a body sherd of this form.

Taken by themselves imported ceramics are an uncertain indicator of wealth. There should be no *a priori* assumption that ARS and the imported wine and oil carried by the amphoras found on the site are luxury items, though scholars have certainly argued that this is the case (Lebecq 1997: 73). For the imported wine at least there is written evidence that matches quite well with the ceramic record. Gregory of Tours in his *History of the Franks* and his *Glory of the Confessors* relates two episodes that do suggest that Gaza wine was held in high esteem. He describes the murder of an out-of-favor royal official after he had sent his servants away to fetch wines, among them Gaza, which he thought would seal his friendship with the king's emissary (*HF* 7.29). Gregory also writes of a sixth-century woman of senatorial family who makes a regular donation of Gaza wine to the Church of St. Mary in Lyon in memory of her dead husband (*GC* 64–65). After one visit a subdeacon replaces the wine with vinegar, but the switch is exposed when the pious widow is miraculously visited by the dead man's ghost.

These and other anecdotes suggest that imported wine did have a special status in the society of southern France; it could mark toasts of friendship and was the object of theft. It is important to note, however, that the widow of Lyon came to church "semper sextarium Gazeti vini praebens". This indicates that she did not have trouble acquiring it, or at least that it seemed reasonable to Gregory as narrator of the story that a pious widow would have ready access to one of the finest wines of the time. While this small observation of Gregory's opens the door for assessing the relative value of imports in southern France, it is the archaeological evidence that makes the point.

Archaeological investigation at urban sites and at smaller rural settlements has shown that imported ceramics such as those found at Psalmodi are common in southern France but are not universal. Marseille was the largest city in southern France at this time and as such had access to an even wider range of imports than found at Psalmodi. Throughout the sixth century North African amphoras, table wares, and coarse wares continued to enter its port and are found in deposits throughout the city. In contrast to the abundance at Marseille, the sixth century is not well represented at Nîmes (Monteil 1999: 437–438), the city closest to Psalmodi. Excavations on the Rue de Sauve and near the Palais de Justice revealed deposits tentatively dated to the sixth century that contained a small number of North African amphoras and finewares (Leenhardt et al. 1993).

Many rural sites have also produced substantial numbers of sixth-century ceramic imports. The hilltop site of Saint-Blaise, near the coast of the Mediterranean and approximately 20 km west of Marseille, ranked as a major settlement in the pre-Roman period but saw only limited use under the empire (Démians d'Archimbaud 1994). In the fifth and sixth centuries the site saw multiple periods of intense construction and occupation. These were accompanied by ready access to imported products from North Africa, Italy, and the main exporting regions of the Eastern Mediterranean. Indeed, in the sixth century African Red-Slip makes up a greater share of the fineware assemblage than at Marseille. At Saint-Propice, another hill-top site, a brief occupation in the late fifth or early sixth century is typified by a large number of African Red-Slip vessels—over 20% of the total fine ware assemblage—and a small number of eastern Mediterranean products

(Boixadera 1987). Closer to Psalmodi, excavations of the late Roman and early medieval levels of the small farm site at Dassargues have revealed a relatively impoverished site in comparison to Psalmodi but one which in the fifth and sixth centuries had access to African Red-Slip as well as to African and Eastern Mediterranean amphoras (Garnier et al. 1995).

In addition to these three secular sites, Maguelone provides an important comparison for Psalmodi. It is also an insular site with late antique origins that developed into a substantial religious establishment, which saw its greatest period of prosperity in the eleventh and twelfth centuries. A bishop is first recorded there in the late sixth century, and recent excavations in a mortuary church to the east of the standing Romanesque structure have revealed the prosperity of the site in the early Middle Ages (Martin 1976; Paya 1996; Raynaud 2001: 259). The limited ceramic information available from earlier work shows that the site, like Psalmodi, had at least some access to imported ceramics in the sixth century. These four sites, then, firmly show that imports are not unusual on rural sites in southern France. Indeed, this assessment is confirmed in the growing number of regional surveys which now regularly emphasize the economic dynamism of the post-Roman countryside (e.g., Raynaud 1996, 2001; Trement 2001). The imported ceramic record is a clear indicator of this continued economic activity but one that diminished towards the end of the century. The distribution of regional wares, which is beyond the scope of this article, suggest that this activity persisted, even if at a reduced level, into the seventh century (Leenhardt et al. 1993).

This very brief overview of a few of the well-published urban and rural sites in southern France contemporaneous with the Psalmodi tremissis is intended to place that site in its regional context. Balance is the key here. Psalmodi's preferential access to imports in comparison to rural sites such as Dassargues suggests relative wealth, even though the presence of imports on other sites indicates that they are by no means unattainable luxuries. Psalmodi is also marked out by the presence of the tremissis. At the risk of making a circular argument, the exceptional combination of the coin and its contemporary ceramics in a rural context suggest a site of elevated wealth.

Because this is one of the few tremisses found during excavation, the Psalmodi piece cannot by itself contribute much to our understanding of the circulation of these coins. This is particularly true given that it is likely that the coin was originally deposited in a burial and is not evidence of purely economic use. That said, the discovery of this coin on a small rural site certainly expands the range of this denomination, as does the roughly contemporary piece from the Camp de César (Goury 1997).

The nature of the early settlement at Psalmodi is currently uncertain, but the tremissis may provide a link to its later history. The later documentary sources indicate that Psalmodi was a monastic establishment by the late seventh century and there was a Carolingian church on the island by the ninth century (Dodds 1977; Dodds et al. 1989). It is uncertain, however, at what point the site became home to an explicitly Christian community. Young and Carter-Young (1988) have previously suggested that the material evidence points to early monasticism. This coin, together with the ceramic evidence, suggests a relatively wealthy site. Lérins, the more famous insular monastery in eastern Provence, was the recipient of substantial aristocratic patronage (Klingshirn 1994: 23), and the general tendency of southern Gallic aristocrats to replicate their luxurious lifestyle in monastic settings has been discussed by Van Dam (1993: Ch. 1). The combined evidence of coin and ceramics, then, could be taken either as evidence of an early start for Psalmodi's religious life or as an indicator of a social and economic context that later contributed to monastic use.

ACKNOWLEDGMENTS

We thank Jean-Louis Foncelle, the current owner of the site, and Brooks Stoddard, director of the Williams College excavations at Psalmodi, for the opportunity to publish this coin. We also thank Bailey Young for clarifying the circumstances and location in which it was found, the Musée Archéologique Henri-Prades in Lattes for photographing it, and Michel Amandry for confirming the die-identity with the Bibliothèque Nationale specimens and for giving permission to reproduce images of the BN and Nîmes specimens.

REFERENCES

Amandry, M., Cl. Brenot, M. Dhénin, J. Lafaurie, and C. Morrisson. 1989. *Monnaies d'or des Musées de Nîmes II: catalogue des monnaies d'or grecques, gauloises, romaines du Ve siècle, ostrogothique, franques, mérovingiennes, lombardes et byzantines.* Cahiers des Musées et Monuments de Nîmes 7. Nîmes: Musées d'Art et d'Histoire de Nîmes.

Banaji, J. 1996. The circulation of gold as an index of prosperity in the central and eastern Mediterranean in late antiquity. In: C. King and D. Wigg, eds., *Coin finds and coin use in the Roman world: the thirteenth Oxford symposium on coinage and monetary history, 25.-27.3.93*, pp. 41–53. Studien zu Fundmünzen der Antike 10. Berlin: G. Mann.

Barral i Altet, Xavier. 1976. *La circulation des monnaies suèves et visigotiques: contribution à la histoire économique du royaume visigot.* Beihefte der Francia 4. Munich: Artemis Verlag.

Belfort, A. de. 1894. *Description générale des monnaies mérovingiennes, par ordre alphabétique des ateliers,* tome IV: *monnaies indéterminées, supplément.* Paris: Société Française de Numismatique.

Boixadera, M. et al. 1987. L'habitat de hauteur de Sainte-Propice (Velaux, B.-du-Rh.), l'occupation de l'Antiquité tardive. *Documents d'Archéologie Méridionale* 10:91–113.

Bonifay, M., M.-B. Carré, and Y. Rigoir, eds. 1998. *Fouilles à Marseille: les mobiliers (Ier -VIIe siècles ap. J.-C.).* Études Massaliètes 5. Paris: Errance.

Démians d'Archimbaud, G., ed. 1994. *L'oppidum de Saint-Blaise du Ve au VIIe s.* Documents d'Archéologie Française 45. Paris: Éditions de la Maison des Sciences de l'Homme.

Depeyrot, G. 1994. *Richesse et société chez les Mérovingiens et Carolingiens.* Paris: Éditions Errance.

—. 1996. *Les monnaies d'or de Constantin II à Zenon (337–491).* Wetteren: Éditions Moneta.

Dhénin, M. and C. Landes. 1994. Vingt-cinq monnaies d'or de l'antiquité tardive au Musée Archéologique H. Prades de Lattes (Hérault). *Revue du Louvre* 5/6:7–8.

—. 1995–96. Le trésor «de Roujan» (VIe siècle). *Études Héraultaises* 26–27:11–14.

Dodds, Jerrilyn. 1977. Carolingian architecture in southern France: some observations in light of the excavations of Psalmodi. *Gesta* 16(1):23–28.

Dodds, Jerrilynn, Brooks W. Stoddard, Whitney S. Stoddard, Bailey K. Young, and Kitch Carter-Young. 1989. L'ancienne abbaye de Psalmodi (Saint-Laurent-d'Aigouze, Gard): premier bilan des fouilles (1970–1988). *Archéologie Médiévale* 19:7–55.

Durliat, Jean. 1987. Philologie et numismatique: à propos de quelques prix protobyzantins. In: G. Depeyrot et al., eds., *Rythmes de la production monétaire de l'antiquité à nos jours,* pp. 343–357. Louvain-la-Neuve: Séminaire de Numismatique Marcel Hoc.

—. 1990. *Les finances publiques de Dioclétien aux Carolingiens (284–889)*. Sigmaringen: J. Thorbecke.

Garnier, B., A. Garnotel, C. Mercier, and C. Raynaud. 1995. De la ferme au village: Dassargues du Ve au XIIe siècle. *Archéologie du Midi Medieval* 13:1–71.

Goury, D. 1997. L'oppidum du Camp de César à Laudun (Gard): premières acquisitions de la recherche 1990–1994. *Revue Archéologique de Narbonnaise* 30:125–172.

Grierson, Philip and Mark Blackburn. 1986. *Medieval European coinage,* vol. 1. Cambridge: Cambridge University Press.

Hayes, John. 1972. *Late Roman Pottery*. London: British School at Rome.

Keay, Simon. 1998. African amphorae. In: L. Saguì, ed., *Ceramica in Italia: VI–VII secolo,* pp. 141–155. Firenze: Edizioni all'Insegna del Giglio.

Klingshirn, William. 1994. *Caesarius of Arles: the making of a Christian community in late antique Gaul.* Cambridge: Cambridge University Press.

Lafaurie, J. 1958. Le trésor de Gourdon. *Bulletin de la Société Nationale des Antiquaires de France* [1958]: 61–76.

—. 1966. Compte rendu: W. J. Tomasini, *The barbaric tremissis in Spain and southern France. Revue Numismatique* 8:336–338.

—. 1968. Monnaies d'or attribuables à Thierry Ier, fils de Clovis. *Bulletin de la Société Nationale des Antiquaires de France* [1968]:30–39.

—. 1970. Trouvailles de monnaies des VIe–VIIIe siècles à Tourouzelle (Aude). *Bulletin de la Société Française de Numismatique* 25:479.

—. 1983. Trésor de monnaies du VIe siècle découvert à Alise-Sainte-Reine en 1804. *Revue Numismatique* 25:101–138.

Lafaurie, J. and C. Morrisson. 1987. La pénétration des monnaies byzantines en Gaule mérovingienne et visigothique du VIe au VIIIe siècle. *Revue Numismatique* 29:38–98.

Lebecq, Stéphane. 1997. Routes of change: production and distribution in the West (5th–8th century). In: L. Webster and M. Brown, eds., *The transformation of the Roman world, AD 400–900*, pp. 67–78. Berkeley and Los Angeles: University of California Press.

Leenhardt, M., Cl. Raynaud, L. Schneider, et al. (1993). Ceramiques languedociennes du haut Moyen Age (VIIe–XIe s.): études micro-régionales et essai de synthèse. *Archéologie du Midi Medieval* 11:111–228.

Lenormant, Ch. 1853. Lettres à M. de Saulcy sur les plus anciens monuments numismatiques de la série mérovingienne, VIII et IX. *Revue Numismatique* 1853:277–316.

Martin, Th. 1976. Céramiques romaines tardives de Maguelone (Hérault). *Archivo de Prehistoria Levantina* 15:231–251.

Monteil, M. 1999. *Nîmes antique et sa proche campagne: étude de topographie urbaine et périurbaine.* Monographies d'Archéologie Méditerranéenne 3. Lattes: UMR 154 de CNRS.

Paya, D. 1996. Autour des recherches de Frédéric Fabrège, des découvertes archéologiques restées inédites à Maguelone, Villeneuve-les-Maguelone (Hérault). *Archéologie du Midi Médiéval* 14:69–95.

Py, Michel, ed. 1993. *Dicocer: dictionnaire des céramiques antiques (VIIe s. av. n. è. - VIIe s. de n. è.) en Méditerranée nord-occidentale (Provence, Languedoc, Ampurdan).* Lattara 6. Lattes: Association pour la Recherche Archéologique en Languedoc Orientale.

Raynaud, Claude. 1996. Les campagnes rhodaniennes: quelle crise? In J.-L. Fiches, ed., *Le IIIe siècle en Gaule narbonnaise: données régionales sur la crise de l'Empire*, pp. 189–212. Sophia-Antipolis: Editions APDCA.

—. 2001. Les campagnes languedociennes aux IVe et Ve siècles. In: P. Ouzoulias et al., eds., *Les campagnes de la Gaule à la fin de l'Antiquité*, pp. 247–274. Antibes: Éditions APDCA.

Reinhart, W. 1940–41. Die Münzen der westgotischen Reiches von To-
ledo. *Deutsches Jahrbuch für Numismatik* 3/4:69–101.

Robert, P. Ch. 1879. *Numismatique de la province de Languedoc, vol. 2:
période wisigothe et franque.* Toulouse: Édouard Privat.

Stamm, V. 1982/84. Geld und Schatz bei Gregor von Tours. *Hamburger
Beiträge zur Numismatik* 36/38:113–118.

Tomasini, W. J. 1964. The barbaric tremissis in Spain and southern
France. ANS Numismatic Notes and Monographs 152. New York:
American Numismatic Society.

Trement, F. 2001. Habitat et peuplement en Provence à la fin de
l'Antiquité. In P. Ouzoulias et al., eds., *Les campagnes de la Gaule
à la fin de l'Antiquité,* pp. 275–302. Antibes: Éditions APDCA.

Van Dam, Raymond. 1993. *Saints and their miracles in late antique
Gaul.* Princeton: Princeton University Press.

Wroth, Warwick. 1911. *Catalogue of the coins of the Vandals, Ostrogoths
and Lombards and of the empires of Thessalonica, Nicaea and Trebizond in the British Museum.* London: British Museum.

Young, Bailey K. and Kitch Carter-Young. 1988. Psalmodi: un site pa-
léochrétien sur le littoral de Septimanie. In: Ch. Landes, ed., *Les
derniers Romains en Septimanie, IVe–VIIIe siècles,* pp. 151–156.
Lattes: Imago, Musée Archéologique de Lattes.

AJN Second Series 13 (2001) pp. 81–88

NEW DATA ON THE MONETARY CIRCULATION OF MEDIEVAL UZGEND: COINS FROM THE KASHKA-TEREK HILLFORT

MICHAEL FEDOROV*

Eight kilometers northwest of the medieval city of Uzgend (Ūzkand) is the Kashka-Terek hillfort, a medieval settlement that belonged to the suburbs of Uzgend, the capital of East Farghana under the Qara-khanids (Goriacheva 1983, Addenda, fig. 15), and hence of the same area of monetary circulation (Figure 1). I had a brief opportunity to examine a small but interesting collection of coins (GIK 512 Fn. 155 nos. 1–19) in the Osh History Museum (Kirghiz Republic) that had been found at Kashka-Terek by a shepherd, who was prompted to donate them to the museum by the late E. V. Druzhinina, then archae-ologist on the museum's staff. Unfortunately it was not possible for me to photograph the coins at the time, and the Osh History Museum is regrettably no longer in existence.

This collection provides information about monetary circulation around Uzgend between the late tenth and early thirteenth centuries AD. It was possible to identify seventeen coins (two others being completely unreadable). Though small in number, the collection includes some rare and interesting coins. The coins of the tenth to elev-

* Humboldtstrasse 20, D-98693 Ilmenau, Germany.

enth centuries are copper *fulūs*; the coins of the twelfth to early thirteenth centuries are silvered copper dirhams. Note that the last letter
of *ḍuriba* and the first letter of *hādhā* are often connected on these coins.

CATALOGUE

1. **Saghaniyan. 365/975–76. 27 mm.** This coin, minted in the half-in-
dependent principality of Saghaniyan about 600 km southwest of
Uzgend, is of such interest that it has been made the subject of a
special article (Fedorov 1989: 73).

2. **Bukhara. [3.]6 AH. 26.5 mm.** The coin is badly effaced. Judging
by its appearance, it is likely to have been minted around the
end of the tenth century.

3. **Ferghana-Akhsiket. 400/1010–11. 27 mm.**

Obverse. In the field a figure made of mutually intersecting semi-
circles, forming a kind of triangle in the center of the figure. Within
the triangle:باد شاه. Mint/date legend forms a triangle on the sides of
the central figure: الفلس بفر غانه / سنة احد اربعمئة / ---
Reverse. Within a circle:(sic) لله محمد / رسول / الله / بخسيكت .
Circular legend: مما أمر به الامير نصر بن على ----المومنين .

Similar coins with the mintname "Farghana" in the circular legend
of the obverse and "Khsiket" (i.e., Akhsiket) written in small letters under the main legend of the reverse field, minted in 390, 391
and ..1 AH, have been published previously (Kochnev 1984: 62).
This coin, however, provides a new type and date: 401 AH. The
fals was minted by Ilek Nasr b. 'Alī, who after conquering the Sa-
manid capital Bukhara in 999 created a new Qarakhanid dominion
in Mawarannahr.

4. **Ilaq. 403/1012–13. 27 mm.**

Obverse. Within a beaded circle:
سنا / لا اله الا / الله وحده / لاشريك له / الدولة .
Circular legend:
بسم الله ضر بهذا [sic] الفلس بايلاق سنة ثلث و اربع مائة

Reverse. Within a beaded circle:

.لله / محمد رسول الله / الـ ــ ـ دل/ خان

Circular legend: مما امر به الامير السيد اــ ـ المظفر ارسلان تكين

Ilaq was a medieval province in the valley of the Angren River, now in the modern Tashkent Oblast' in the Uzbek Republic. The only *fals* of AH 403 from Ilaq known hitherto was of a different type (Kochnev 1995: 225 no. 310).

5. Uzgend. 420/1029. 25 mm.

Obverse. Within a circle:قادر خان . Above and under this title within two parallel crescents, turned with their backsides to one another, the words:ملك / المشرق. Circular legend:

.بسم الله ضربهذا الفلس باوزكند سنة عشرين و اربع ـ ـ ـ

Reverse in the field: .ـ ـ ـ / ـ ـ ـ محـ ـ ـ ـ / ســ ـ ـ بن هارون / الدولة
Circular legend:

.مما امر به الامير ـ ـ ـ قلر خان بن بغ[را]خان ـ ـ ـ المومنين

So in the circular legend of the reverse Qadir-khan b. Boghra-khan is mentioned once again. In the reverse field his vassal S... b. Harun ... al-Daula is mentioned. A coin of Uzgend dated 421/1030, found in the village of Ivanovka (about 33 km east of Bishkek), gives the full name of this Qarakhanid. Therefore, I give a description of that coin here as well.

5a. Uzgend. [4]21/1030. 24 mm.

Obverse. In the field: لا اله الا / الله وحده / لاشريك له. Circular legend: .بسم الله ضر بهذا الفلس بلوزكند سنة احدى و عشرين [!] Reverse. In the field: لله / محمد / رسول الله / ملك المشرق. Circular legend: .مما امربه الامير سليمن بن هارون مولى امير المومنين

In the reverse field "Malik al-Mashriq" (i.e., Qadir-khan, the suzerain) is mentioned, and in the circular legend his brother and vassal Suleiman b. Harun is mentioned as an immediate owner of the town, by whose order (مما امر به) the coin in question was minted.

6. Uzgend. [42]3/1031–32. 29 mm.

Obverse. Within a beaded circle an equilateral triangle is inscribed. Within the triangle the title خان is placed. Circular legend: .بسم الله ضر بهذا الفلس بلوزكند سنة ثلث [!]

Reverse. Within a double circle (inner solid, outer made of radial notches): كوج تكين / عضد الدولة . Circular legend:

. ‫ ‬--- امر به الامير الاجل --- مولى امير ---

The name of the ruler in the reverse circular legend is effaced, but on an AH 423 Uzgend *fals* of the same type Yusuf b. Harun (Kochnev 1995: 254 no. 752)—i.e., Qadir-khan—was mentioned.

On all the coins of AH 420–423 from Uzgend (Kochnev 1995: 252 nr. 715) the title "Kuch-tegin" was placed on the reverse—the more "prestigious" place, where caliph and suzerain were mentioned—and the *laqab* "'Adud al-Daula" was on the obverse, where a vassal or subvassal was usually mentioned. Such disposition of title and *laqab* could be interpreted two ways: 1) they both belong to one and the same person; 2) they belong to two different persons and Kuch-tegin, since he is mentioned on the reverse, was higher in rank than 'Adud al-Daula. On the fals of AH 423 from Uzgend published here, the title and *laqab* were placed on the same side of the coin (reverse field) and the *laqab* "'Adud al-Daula" was placed *above* the title "Kuch-tegin". If these were two different persons, it would mean that 'Adud al-Daula was higher in rank than Kuch-tegin. However, since on all the other coins of Uzgend the disposition of title and *laqab* in question implies the opposite, this can only mean that the *laqab* and the title belonged to one and the same person.

7. Uzgend. 4.. AH (not earlier than 416, when Qadir-khan conquered Uzgend, and not later than 424, when Qadir-khan died). 25 mm.

Obverse. Within a circle:

. عضد / لا اله الا / الله وحده / لاشريك له / الدولة
Circular legend: بسم الله --- الفلس باوزكند سنة --- اربع [!]
Reverse. Within a beaded circle:

. لله / محمد / رسول الله / قادر خاقان / كوج تكين
Circular legend: --- . به الامير قد --- خان مولى امير المومنين

8. Uzgend. 430/1038–39. 25 mm.

Obverse. Within a double circle (inner solid, outer beaded):

طنغا / خان . Circular legend:

. بسم الله ضرب بهذا الفلس باوزكند سنة ثلثين اربع مائة

Reverse. Within a border as on the obverse: محمد / رسول / الله .
Circular legend: مما امر به ___ الخان [الحسن؟] ___ مير المومنين .
This coin is the first *fals* known to have been minted by Tongha-khan.

9. [Fargh]ana. 431/1039–40. 25 mm.

Obverse. Within a beaded circle: لا اله الا / الله وحده / لاشريك له .
Circular legend:

بسم الله ضر بهذا الفلس ___ نة سنة احد و ثلثين و ار ___ .

Reverse. Within a beaded circle:

لله / محمد / رسول الله / الخاقان ___ / [طنغا؟] ___ .

Circular legend: [!] مما امر به الامير ___ وؤيد ال ___ مولى امير .

The title of the ruler is effaced. If it was Tongha, the coin published here is the first one of this ruler known to have been minted with the mintname Farghana. This hypothesis is implied by the date and the fact that in 430–433/1038–1042 coins of Uzgend (then the capital of Farghana) cited Tongha-khan (Kochnev 1995: 259 no. 830).

10. Farghana. 421/1030. 31 mm.

Obverse. Within a circle: لا اله الا / الله وحده / لاشريك له . Inner circular legend: ناصر الحق مولى امير المومنين ___ . Outer circular legend: بسم الله ضر بهذا الفلس بفرغانه سنة أحد عشرين و أربع ___ .
Reverse. Within a circle:

لله / محمد / رسول الله / الملك المشرق / قلر خان .

Circular legend: ___ . الأجل ___ [؟] الحق ___ امير ___ .

This is a new, hitherto unknown *fals* of AH 421 from Farghana, minted by Qadir-khan.

The coins of Uzgend minted in the twelfth to early thirteenth centuries from the Kashka-Terek hillfort are silvered copper dirhams. They appeared as a result of the so-called "silver crisis" and were fiduciary coins, a kind of metallic bill with forced face value. Many examples have already been published. Therefore, I do not give here a full description of the dirhams found at Kashka-Terek, presenting instead a simple enumeration with reference to previous publications. All the coins are in a poor state of preservation. Many of them could be identified only by type.

11–12. Uzjend (as the name of the town was spelled in the twelfth and thirteenth centuries). Two dirhams minted by the Qarakhanid ruler Arslan-khan Ibrahim b. Husayn around 559–568/1163–75 (Davidovich 1979: 195–197, 429 fig. 1 no. 1).

13. Uzjend. Dirham minted by Arslan-khan Ibrahim around 570–574/1174–79 (Davidovich 1979: 203-204, 429 fig. 1 no. 2).

14–15. Uzjend. Two dirhams minted by the Qarakhanid ruler Qadir-khan in 579/1183–84 (Davidovich 1979: 208, 429 fig. 1 no. 39).

16. Uzjend. Dirham minted by Qadir-khan in 58. AH. Coins of this type are known with the dates 584/1188–89 (Davidovich 1979: 214, 430 fig. 2 no. 1) and 587/1191 (found by the archaeologist A. K. Abetekov in Seidy Kum village, Bazar korgon raîon, Osh Oblast', Kirghiz Republic).

17. Uzjend. Dirham minted by Qadir-khan in 596/1199 (Davidovich 1979: 216, 430 fig. 2 no. 4).

DISCUSSION

Judging by to the finds from the Kaska-Terek hillfort, the monetary circulation around Uzgend/Uzdjend was based mainly on the production of the local mint. This group includes not only the coins specifically naming Uzgend, but also the coins with the mintname "Farghana" (without any additional mintname, as there was in the case of Akhsiket). Uzgend, or in the twelfth and thirteenth centuries Uzjend, was under the Qarakhanids the capital of Farghana, and coins minted in Uzgend could well have had the mintname "Farghana", just as coins with the mintname "Shash" were even more numerous in Shash than coins with the mintname "Binket", which was the capital of Shash province.

But of course the production of other Qarakhanid mints also played some role in the monetary circulation of Uzgend in the eleventh century. According to the finds at Kashka-Terek, coins minted in

Saghaniyan, Bukhara, Ilaq, and Akhsiket were present. It was not the same, though, in the twelfth and early thirteenth centuries, when fiduciary silvered copper dirhams appeared: they had only local circulation. Only gold coins would be accepted everywhere, not fiduciary dirhams, because their circulation was confined to the province (or principality) where they were minted.

Of course, a hoard, being a snapshot of the money in circulation taken at the moment when the hoard was deposited, would give a more precise picture. The collection of coins found at the Kashka-Terek hillfort gives a less precise but much broader picture, which as a whole corresponds to the picture given by another collection of 100 coins of about the same period, found in the Farghana valley (Fedorov 1991: 3–15). Another collection of coins of that period found in Farghana, kept by the Bishkek antiquary V. Koshevar (the publication of which I am preparing) also corresponds to that picture.

REFERENCES

Davidovich, E. A. 1979. *Klady drevnikh i srednevekovykh monet Tadzhikistana*. Moskva: Izd Nauka.

Fedorov, M. N. 1989. Redkii saganianskii fel's iz okrestnostei Uzgenda. *Izvestia Akademii Nauk Kirgizskoĭ SSR* 4:73–77.

—. 1991. Materialy k izucheniiu ekonomicheskikh sviazei i denezhnogo obrashcheniia Iuga Kirgizii v X nachale XIII vv. In: *Nekotorye voprosy arkheologii i etnografii Kyrgyzstana*, pp. 3–15. Bishkek.

Goriacheva, V. D. 1983. Srednevekovye gorodskie tsentry i arkhitekturnye ansambli Kirgizii. Frunze: Izd-vo "Ilim".

Kochnev, B. D. 1984. Novye dannye o karakhanidskom monetnom dvore Fergany (= New data on the Qarakhanid mint in Fergana). *Soobshcheniia Gosudarstvennogo Ermitazha* 49:62–63.

—. 1995. Svod nadpisei na Karakhanidskikh monetakh: antroponimy i titulatura. *Vostochnoe istoricheskoe istochnikovedenie i spetsial'nye istoricheskie distsipliny* 4:201–279.

Figure 1. Map showing Uzgend and Kashka-Terek.

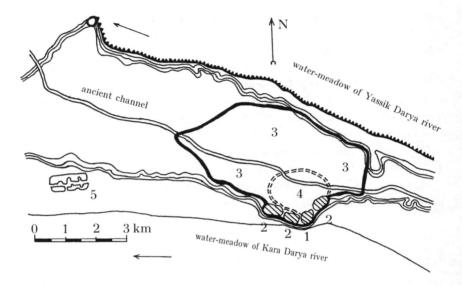

1 citadel. 2 ancient Uzgend. 3 Uzgend in XIII c. 4 Uzgend in XVI c. 5 Kashka-Terek.

AJN Second Series 13 (2001) pp. 89–108

JOSEPH J. MICKLEY'S DIARY FOR 1852:
AN ANNOTATED TRANSCRIPTION

JOEL J. OROSZ*

In 1980, at the Antiquarian Booksellers Association of America Book Fair, held that year in New York City, numismatic bookseller George Frederick Kolbe made an exciting discovery: a daily diary kept for nearly three years by the "father of American coin collecting", Joseph J. Mickley. A Philadelphia manufacturer and repairer of pianos and other musical instruments, Mickley was one of the earlier systematic coin collectors in the United States. Over a collecting career that spanned nearly 50 years, Mickley amassed numismatic holdings that were unprecedented in America for their scope: US and foreign, ancient and modern, business strike and proof. He was for decades an intimate of officials at the United States Mint, and they actively helped him build his collection. When an 1867 robbery carried off part of his coins and most of his collecting spirit, Mickley sold his numismatic holdings to Boston dealer W. Elliot Woodward, whose auction catalog of Mickley's great coin cabinet, held 28 October 1867 (and following days) became an instant numismatic classic.

Given Mickley's iconic status, the diary Kolbe discovered proved to be of great historical interest to numismatists and bibliophiles alike. With a beginning date of August 1866, and an ending date of June

* 4300 Old Field Trail, Kalamazoo, MI 49008, USA (joelorosz@aol.com).

1869, its timeframe included the robbery on 13 April 1867, the sale of the collection to Woodward on 1 May 1867, and Mickley's surprised reaction to the high prices realized at the auction. Quite apart from its historical significance, many numismatists simply looked upon the diary itself, replete with Mickley's holographic entries and signatures, with a sort of veneration.

The chain of ownership for the 1866–69 diary adds to this aura of awe. Robert Batchelder, the noted autograph merchant and one-time coin dealer, had brought the diary to the ABAA sale in 1980. Kolbe purchased it from Batchelder and subsequently sold the volume to the late Armand Champa, the first "marquee name" numismatic bibliophile in the United States. The Mickley diary did a star turn at the 100th anniversary convention of the American Numismatic Association held in Chicago in 1991, when it was item 42 in Champa's landmark "Numismatica Americana" exhibition. After Champa's death, the diary became lot 414 of the Bowers and Merena sale of the Armand Champa library, part one. The purchaser, for $3,960, was the Dallas numismatist Harry Bass. Recognizing the historical and educational value of the volume, Bass presented it to the library of the American Numismatic Society, where it resides today (see the *American Numismatic Society Annual Report for 1995*, pp. 44-45).

Given that Mickley was such a faithful diarist for nearly three years in 1866–1869, the obvious question was whether he had created other diaries, and if so, what had become of them? The first question can be answered by referring to the testimony of Mickley's friend William E. Du Bois (1810–1881), the curator of the Mint Cabinet of Coins. Writing in the *American Journal of Numismatics*, Du Bois (1871) asserted that Mickley had kept a journal "nearly all his life". The second question has proved more vexing, for numismatic bibliophiles diligently but fruitlessly searched for another volume of Mickley's diary for two decades after Kolbe's find. This sustained period of failure did not prevent collectors from continuing to search for the missing volumes, referred to by this author (Orosz 2000) as "missing masterpieces" of American numismatic literature, nor from appreciating the one that had been found.

One of these "missing masterpieces" has now come to light. During the 109th anniversary convention of the American Numismatic Association, held during the year 2000 in Philadelphia, the author of this article searched the manuscript repository of the Historical Society of Pennsylvania, seeking items of numismatic significance. Residing there, with catalog number AM 1039, was another Mickley diary, covering most of the year 1852. It had been donated to the Historical Society on 18 November 1958 by one Paul Jones, who was then a columnist for the Philadelphia *Evening Bulletin*. This 1852 diary is quarto in size (its cover is taller than 25 centimeters), bound in brown half-Morocco leather with marbled boards. Physically, it is quite similar to the 1866–69 volume.

Before examining the contents of this 1852 diary, however, it seems appropriate to consider the content of its creator's life. Joseph J. Mickley was born on 24 March 1799 in Whitehall Township (then known as Northampton County), Pennsylvania. According to family lore, his ancestors, surnamed Michelet, were among the persecuted French Protestants called the Huguenots. It is known that the first Mickley to emigrate to the United States embarked in Amsterdam; John Jacob Mickley, the great-grandfather of Joseph J., arrived in Philadelphia in 1733. Two of John Jacob's children were killed by Native Americans, an event that his great-grandson chronicled in a book (Mickley 1875) more than a century later. The Mickley clan settled near present-day Allentown, Pennsylvania and so prospered there that for a time in the 19th century there was a village named "Mickleys", which has since been absorbed by Allentown.

Joseph J. Mickley received an elementary education, and showing considerable mechanical aptitude and a great fondness for music, he was apprenticed to a pianoforte maker in Philadelphia. On 25 August 1822 he established a business in Philadelphia specializing in the building and repair of pianofortes; due to success in his trade (and the receipt of a large bequest), he was able, after a few years, to scale back his activities, although he continued to tune pianos virtually all of his life.

Mickley was an avid hobbyist, noted as a bibliophile, an autograph collector, and particularly as a numismatist. Accounts vary as to when he began collecting coins, from as early as 1816 to as late as the 1830s, but by his own account it was around 1820. This information comes from an obscure article written by Mickley's friend, Jacob Bunting (1885); thanks are due to Karl Moulton (2001) for bringing this article to the attention of scholars. Bunting quotes a memorandum written by Mickley in the latter part of 1872, in which the elderly collector lamented:

> I have become rather indifferent about numismatics, or, at least, about collecting coins. It was a great source of amusement for a period of over 50 years. But having been so unfortunate at different times with my coins, it is, as it were, a warning to desist from collecting any more. In the year 1827, the United States dollars from 1794 to 1803, all good specimens, together with some foreign coins, were stolen. In 1848 about 20 half dollars were taken. In 1854, after showing my collection to three Southern gentlemen (as they called themselves), I missed three very scarce half-eagles. The great robbery was in 1867.

Although repeated thefts eventually dulled Mickley's numismatic enthusiasm, for more than 50 years he had been the consummate coin hound, seeking out new specimens with both ardent spirit and careful discrimination. Jacob Bunting recalled that "although guileless as a child and the easy victim of numerous thefts throughout his life, he was scarcely ever deceived in the value of a coin, token or medal". Without question, the contents of the great Mickley collection, even after the robbery of 1867, corroborated Bunting's assessment.

The story of Mickley's collection, the notorious robbery on 13 April 1867 that sharply curtailed his interest in numismatics, and the auction sale of his remaining holdings, has been told elsewhere (Orosz 1995). In brief, fearing another robbery—indeed fearing for his life—the venerable numismatist quickly moved the balance of his collection to the Philadelphia Mint for safekeeping, then sold it to W. Elliot Woodward less than a month after the break-in. Woodward sold the United States gold coins in the collection to William Sumner Appleton, a notable Boston numismatist, but offered the balance in New York City on 28 October 1867 and the following days (Woodward 1867). The 3,349 lots brought $13,285, then a record realization for a coin collection in the United States at public auction. The catalogue of the sale remains the *magnum opus* of Woodward's career.

Joseph Mickley was granted eleven years of life after the conclusion of this sale, which years he used to travel widely overseas, to work extensively on a history of New Sweden, and even to begin once more to collect coins. He died in Philadelphia on 15 February 1878.

Although the great collector was gone, a portion of his life in numismatics lived on in the diaries he left behind. The discovery of the 1852 diary doubles the number of volumes known, although it obviously covers less ground than the 1866–69 discovery piece. Both of the known volumes of Mickley's diaries are currently in institutional collections, at the American Numismatic Society and the Historical Society of Pennsylvania. One other volume of the diary is definitely known to have existed, although its whereabouts cannot be determined today. Jacob Bunting (1885) quotes from Mickley's 1871 diary, in which the aged collector, on a trip to Stockholm, encountered to his astonishment an example of the very rare US 1815 half-eagle at the National Museum.

We know for certain, therefore, that Mickley created diaries in the years 1852, 1866, 1867, 1868, 1869, and 1871. William Du Bois's observation that Mickley had kept a journal "nearly all of his life" suggests that there was once an unbroken string of such volumes, stretching backward from his death in 1878 to the 1830s or even the 1820s. Because our knowledge of numismatic history in the United States prior to the widespread popularization of the coin hobby in the late 1850s is sketchy at best, the Mickley diaries from the early years would comprise the numismatic analogue of the Dead Sea scrolls. The first-hand testimony to be found within could settle many arguments and illuminate dark corners. The only problem is that, even with the discovery of the 1852 diary, the vast majority of Mickley's volumes are still "missing masterpieces".

It seems probable that other volumes of the Mickley diaries may still exist, if for no other reason than that a systematic search has never been mounted for them. The 1852 journal, for example, had been lying undisturbed at the Historical Society of Pennsylvania for 42 years before the author simply looked it up in that institution's old card catalogue. Additional Mickley volumes may be like Poe's purloined letter, hiding in plain sight, needing only a minimal effort to discover. Others may require strenuous efforts to uncover. The facts recorded in them, however, would undoubtedly be significant enough to justify even the most difficult search.

JOSEPH J. MICKLEY'S DIARY FOR 1852

During the year 1852, Joseph J. Mickley kept a daily diary, written in brown ink in a neat cursive hand. The diary actually began on 1 January 1852 as a family affair, for each date initially contained entries by Joseph, by Hannah C. Mickley (Joseph's daughter, b. 1835), Josephine C. A. Mickley (daughter, 1830–1887), and Joseph P. Mickley (son, b. 1842). Gradually, however, the other entries ended, and only those of the father of the house, invariably signed "Jos. J. Mickley", continued. Finally, Mickley's entries also ceased in the autumn of 1852, with the last numismatic one dated Sunday, 26 September.

Mickley was a keen observer of the weather, so virtually every entry contained a reference to the temperature and meteorological phenomena of the day. Another of Mickley's interests was music, and several passages made reference to duos, trios, and quartets in which he had played with friends. Numismatics was Mickley's other great passion, and the excerpts quoted hereafter comprise verbatim transcriptions of all of the 1852 diary entries pertaining to numismatics, plus a few that are non-numismatic, but important to the context. Mickley's original spelling, punctuation, syntax, and capitalization have been retained. Footnotes are annotations by the author of this article to explain important passages in Mickley's text more fully.

> Philadelphia, January 1, 1852 Got myself weighed found myself weighing to 165. My height is 5f. 5 and 4/10
>
> Philadelphia, January 12, 1852 Rec^d a lot of English Coins consisting of 20 English Coins in a very good state of preservation & one medal of Washington.
>
> Philadelphia, January 13, 1852 Went to the Mint & brought $30 worth of 3 cent pieces...[1] Mr. Jacob Morris[2] a Coin Collector called

---

[1] This purchase, and the subsequent purchase of three-cent pieces mentioned in the entry for 25 February 1852, seem to have been for commercial purposes, for no three-cent pieces appear in the W. Elliot Woodward sale of the Mickley collection (Woodward 1867).

[2] Jacob Giles Morris (1800–1854) was one of the leading early coin collectors of Philadelphia. He was a noted philanthropist, and a first cousin once removed of the scientist Caspar Wistar, after whom the flowering shrub wisteria was named.

to see me to show me a Coin which he pronounced "unique" it was a specimen of One Cent of 1792 of the United States Mint, a little larger than a Common Half Cent with a small piece of Silver inserted in the centre, on the principle of the pattern Coins which had been struck a few years past at the English & French Mints.[3] It is however not "unique" for my friend James Hall of Allentown has one in his collection.[4]

Morris was one of the US Mint's "pet collectors" as early as 1839 (Newman and Bressett 1962:118), and was named as one of the four major coin collectors in Philadelphia in 1842 by William Du Bois (1872). Another early coin collector and author, Samuel Breck (1771–1862), in his eulogy of Morris after the latter drowned in the wreck of the S.S. *Arctic* in the North Atlantic on 27 September 1854, said that Morris made many trips to Europe to add to his coin collection, which was one of the finest in the nation (Breck 1854). After Morris's death, his collection went to his sister, then to his niece, who later bequeathed part of it to the University of Pennsylvania, and sold the balance in two Lyman Low sales on 18 September and 29 October 1901. The coins of the University of Pennsylvania collection were deaccessioned in the early 1950s and sold privately to dealers Philip Ward, Jr., and B. Max Mehl. For more background on Morris, see Orosz (2002).

[3] P. Scott Rubin (1985) does not list either Morris or Hall as owners of silver center cents. Walter Breen (1988) ascribes a University of Pennsylvania provenance for his silver center no. 1369-2 but says that it came earlier from the Brock collection, not the Morris collection. Breen asserts that "Morris" was the first owner of Silver Center 1369-4, but the next owner given is James G. Sloss, a twentieth-century numismatist. Unlike Rubin, Breen did not consistently supply citations to buttress his opinions. With regard to the pattern coins struck at the British and French mints to which Mickley referred, the British pieces may have been the 1844 model half-penny and the 1844 model penny (both of which were struck at the private mint of Allen & Moore in Birmingham) and the 1848 gilt crown. The first two had a brass or white metal center surrounded by copper. The 1848 crowns had the same composition, but as the name implied, they were gilded. The coin from the French mint was probably an 1848 one-centime piece, which had a copper core washed on one side with silver and on the other with gold.

[4] James Hall (1773–1861) made his living as the Register of Wills in Lehigh County and commenced coin collecting in 1788. According to his obituary (Mickley 1865–66), Hall lost his sight in 1853 and sold his collection of coins and books for $850, no mention of to whom. It may have been Mickley; his diary entry for 13 January 1852 suggests that on that date both Morris and Hall had a silver center cent but Mickley did not. However, lot 2135 of Woodward's Mickley sale was a 1792 silver center, in "remarkably fine" condition. It was purchased by Baltimore numismatist Mendes I. Cohen (see n. 33).

Philadelphia, February 3, 1852 A young man called with some coins, and I made an exchange with him.[5]

Philadelphia, February 7, 1852 Saw a notice of the death of my venerable friend Mr. Adam Eckfeldt, he died yesterday in the 83rd year of his age, he held a situation in the United States Mint ever since its establishment, to which place he was appointed by President Washington [he] was for many years Chief Coiner, which situation he resigned several years ago. He was a man of unblemished character, beloved by every one of his acquaintances for his integrity, his mild & amiable disposition, his death is universally regretted.[6] Mr. Jacob Morris called to see me in the afternoon & got some Coins of me, 2 Half Dollars 1794, 1795, 1 Ten Cent Piece 1796 & One Cent 1793.[7]

Philadelphia, February 8, 1852 In the afternoon went to Camden with Joseph to Mr. Mason, tuned his Piano & spent the afternoon there, Mr. Mason gave me a Medal of Lafayette & a Six Pence of George the Third.[8]

[5] This brief mention underlines an important means of building early collections that is largely forgotten today. While attention has been paid to buying coins at public auction, or at private sale, early collectors also made many exchanges with each other, usually trading duplicates to augment each other's holdings.

[6] Adam Eckfeldt (1769–1852) was the first in a long line of Eckfeldts to work for the United States Mint (the last, Jacob Bausch Eckfeldt, did not leave the Mint's employ until 1929, 137 years after Adam began his service). As Chief Coiner from 1814 to 1839, Adam Eckfeldt was instrumental in striking and restriking pieces for collectors, including Robert Gilmor, Jr. (Orosz 1990). It is highly likely that Eckfeldt performed the same service for Mickley.

[7] Examples of all of these pieces appeared in the 1867 Mickley sale by Woodward, so it is highly probable that all of the coins traded to Morris were duplicates. Of these coins, however, only the dime was included in Lyman Low's sales of the residue of the Morris collection, on 18 September 1901, and that was only in "fair" condition (see lot 75). It is interesting to note the very matter-of-fact manner in which Mickley recorded parting with such major rarities.

[8] This passage suggests that Mickley also built his collection by taking numismatic items in trade for his piano tuning services. "Joseph" was his son Joseph P. Mickley; it is possible that "Mason" was Ebenezer Locke Mason, Jr. (d. 1902), who later became a coin dealer. We know that Mason worked in Philadelphia as early as 1855 (Mason 1882:25); it is conceivable that he lived in Camden prior to moving to Philadelphia.

Philadelphia, February 9, 1852 Mrs. Wood called with her two children to look at my Coins.[9]

Philadelphia, February 16, 1852 Received Two Coins from Mr. McMullen, one Swiss & one Danish.[10]

Philadelphia, February 19, 1852 Wrote a letter to Mr. Barnum requesting him to engage Mr. Schmitz's children at his museum.[11]

Philadelphia, February 20, 1852 Called on Mr. Hockling to see about a Coin Case he is making for me, he told me it would be finished by Thursday next.[12] Called on Mr. F. Peale about the American Medals.[13]

---

[9] This entry confirms the reminiscences of Jacob Bunting, William Du Bois, and others that Mickley was a genial host who delighted in showing his collection to many people of all ages.

[10] Mr. McMullen is not known to have been a coin collector. It is possible that he was a source from whom Mickley bought coins, such as a broker, an exchange agent, or a jeweler.

[11] It was not previously known that Mickley had had any contact with Phineas Taylor Barnum (1810–1891), the famed showman. It does make sense, however, for prior to his career as a circus impresario, Barnum was the proprietor of the American Museum in New York City from 1841 to 1867. Over the years, Barnum bought out the museums established by the painter Charles Willson Peale (1741–1827) and his family, starting with the branches in New York City and Baltimore, and eventually the original Peale Museum in Philadelphia, which Barnum purchased in 1849. It would have been natural for Mickley to be interested in Peale's (and later Barnum's) Philadelphia museum, for Dr. James Mease (1771–1846) noted that it contained a collection of medals as early as 1811 (Mease 1811:313), and Augustus B. Sage (1867) also was complimentary about Barnum's American Museum collection. Sage said that it "contained a very fair cabinet, a miscellaneous collection it is true, but scattered here and there in the cases were some very rare specimens of our earlier coinage."

[12] Like most nineteenth-century collectors, Mickley stored his coins in a wooden cabinet with lined drawers. In the 1867 Mickley sale by Woodward, the final lot (lot 3349) consisted of "two nice little cabinets of black walnut". The lot description is hand-corrected to read "one" in some copies of the catalogue. This was probably not the case made by Mr. Hockling, for Woodward noted that the cabinets had been completed only recently.

[13] Franklin Peale (1795–1870), the son of painter and museologist Charles Wilson Peale (see n. 11), had a turbulent tenure as Chief Coiner of the United States Mint from 1839 to 1854. Although all conceded that he made valuable improvements in

Philadelphia, February 21, 1852 Went to Mr. Bacon to order paper trays for my Coins.[14]

Philadelphia, February 25, 1852 Went to the Mint & got $ 30 worth of 3 Cent pieces, also the Medals of the Presidents.[15] Saw a Gold Medal at the Mint worth in gold $ 350, it was struck in France, given to Gen. McIntosh, the Head of Charles X is on the obverse, it was sent from the City of Washington to the Mint, was got at the Gambling table, but it is not known who lost it there.[16]

the Mint's coining technology, he was also accused of using the Mint's facilities and employees for his private gain and was ultimately removed from his position. It seems clear from this entry and from subsequent entries on 18 March and 28 May that Peale conducted some of this illicit business with Mickley, although there is no evidence to suggest that Mickley was aware that Peale was profiting personally. Adam Eckfeldt struck pieces for collectors too, but Eckfeldt did so to enrich the Mint Cabinet of Coins, not himself. The term "American Medals" is ambiguous; it could refer to the series of US Mint medals struck to honor the heroes of the Revolutionary War and the War of 1812, or it could refer to Indian Peace Medals.

[14] The words "paper trays" are also ambiguous. Mickley could have meant "envelopes" when he wrote "trays". Alternatively, "paper trays" may have referred to pasteboard dividers in his coin cabinet. Nothing further is known about "Mr. Bacon".

[15] Again, the three-cent pieces were probably for spending, not hoarding. The "Medals of the Presidents" is yet another ambiguous reference; it may refer to the series today known as Indian Peace Medals, which feature a portrait of the sitting President at the time that the medal was struck, or it could refer to other medallic likenesses of the thirteen Chief Executives from George Washington to Millard Fillmore.

[16] A search of Eckfeldt and Du Bois's *New Varieties of Gold and Silver Coins* (Eckfeldt and Du Bois 1852), which contained the second edition of Du Bois's *Pledges of History*, which described the collection of the Mint Cabinet of Coins, does not reveal any information about this piece. Snowden (1860:170) does mention a 1592 gold crown of the pretender called Charles X. Comparette (1913) lists an *écu d'or* of 1592 depicting Charles X of the League. Those mentioned, however, are coins, not medals, and are too small to be the enormous medal struck in honor of the pretender to the French throne described by Mickley. Eckfeldt and Du Bois (1852:20) peg the 1852 value of gold at $20.67 per ounce. In order to have an intrinsic value of $350, then, the medal would have had to contain slightly less than 17 ounces of gold. The "Gen. McIntosh" mentioned may have been General Lachlan McIntosh (1725–1806), a Revolutionary War soldier remembered more today for his exploits on the field of honor than on the field of battle. In April of 1777, McIntosh killed Button Gwinnett,

Philadelphia, February 28, 1852 Received a letter from Mr. Barnum declining to make an engagement with Mr. Schmitz's children for the present.[17]

Philadelphia, March 1, 1852 My Coin Case was sent to me.

Philadelphia, March 2, 1852 Called on Mr. Bacon, but found he had not made my paper trays for my Coin Case yet, but promised to have them done in a few days.

Philadelphia, March 9, 1852 Wrote a letter to Alexis I. duPont near Wilmington.[18]

Philadelphia, March 11, 1852 Received my Paper Trays for the Coins, began to arrange the American Coins in the evening.

Philadelphia, March 12, 1852...Staid [sic] at home & arranged some of my Coins.[19]

a signer of the Declaration of Independence, in a duel. Alternatively, if the medal depicted the real Charles X of France (reigned 1824–1830), the "Gen. McIntosh" mentioned by Mickley could have been John McIntosh (1755–1826), nephew of Lachlan and major general of militia in the War of 1812, or William McIntosh (1775–1825), a Creek Indian chief and brigadier general.

[17] While the great numismatist may have been acquainted with the great showman, apparently Mickley had little influence with Barnum. Nothing further has been learned about the identity of Mr. Schmitz.

[18] According to Marc Duke (1976), Alexis Irenée du Pont (1816–1857) was the son of Eleuthère Irénée du Pont, the founder of the E.I. du Pont de Nemours Company of Wilmington, Delaware. At the time of Mickley's correspondence with him, du Pont was the superintendent of the DuPont powderworks (where he lost his life in an 1857 explosion). Alexis is not known to have been a numismatist, but the grandson of his older brother Alfred Victor du Pont, one Lammot du Pont, would later become a notable numismatist, owning, among other rarities, two 1804 silver dollars.

[19] Mickley was obviously a careful collector, as opposed to a mere hoarder, for he spent the evening of 11 March and all day 12 March arranging his American coins in the new paper trays and coin cabinet. This squares with the recollections of his contemporaries, who had high regard for his knowledge about coins.

March 18, 1852...Went to the Mint & got some medals of Mr. Peale.[20]

Saturday, March 20, 1852 Received a letter from Mr. Chaffers, Coin dealer in London, informing [me] among other things, that a Silver Crown of Henry the Eighth had been sold at public sale for the enormous sum of £130!!! he says that there are only three known to exist.[21]

Wednesday, March 24, 1852 This is my birthday. I am now 53 years of age...Went to the Mint by invitation of Mr. Dubois, who gave me great numbers of American Silver & Copper Coins, also a Washington Cent.[22]

---

[20] This entry provides more evidence that Mickley availed himself of Peale's "entrepreneurial" restriking operation, albeit innocently.

[21] A search of the Historical Manuscripts Commission at the United Kingdom Register of Archives reveals only one Chaffers in business in London during the nineteenth century, a William Chaffers, who is identified as a "woolen draper", with records on file from 1813 to 1841. Manville and Robinson (1986) record two auction sales in which William Chaffers was the consigner. These are Sotheby's 9–14 and 16 February 1857 sale (no. 1857-6) and Sotheby's 17–20 February 1857 sale (no. 1857-8). The most likely candidate for the "public sale" in which the Henry VIII crown sold for £130 is Sotheby's 4–6 and 8–10 March 1852 sale of the George Marshall collection Part I (no. 1852-4). Marshall, the author of a work entitled *View of the Silver Coinage of Great Britain, 1662-1837*, amassed a collection rich in Anglo-Saxon, English, Scottish, and Irish coinage, patterns and proofs, tokens, medals, and numismatic books. Sotheby's described part of his collection in an auction catalogue of 820 lots and 64 pages. Recent advances in steam technology had rendered it possible to relay news from Britain to the United States in less than two weeks. Alexander Crosby Brown (1961) noted that on 19 April 1851, the Collins Line steamer *Pacific* became the first ship to make the westbound crossing in less than ten days: to be precise, 9 days, 20 hours and 15 minutes. It was thus possible for Mickley to have learned the results of the Marshall Sale by March 20.

[22] Du Bois was Chief Assayer of the Philadelphia Mint, curator of its Cabinet of Coins, and a numismatic author (see note 16). Writing in 1872, he remembered that there were four coin collectors in Philadelphia in 1842, Mickley, Jacob Giles Morris, Dr. Lewis Roper (d. 1850), and Du Bois himself, all of whom helped each other to build their collections (Du Bois 1872). This passage demonstrates just how helpful Du Bois could be to Mickley, for his birthday present of a 1791 Washington cent and several American silver and copper coins besides was very generous. Although the entry clearly states that they were a gift, it is possible that they were given in

Friday, April 30, 1852 Received a lot of English Coins.[23]

Friday, May 21, 1852 Went to the Mint to see Mr. Peale, was told he had not been there today on account of indisposition.

Saturday, May 22, 1852 Called on Mr. Peale this morning, the girl informed me that he had been confined to his bedroom all day yesterday & today with [a] severe cold.

Friday, May 28, 1852 Went to see Mr. Peale at the Mint who gave me two Proof Half Dollars of the year 1838, on the obverse is a beautiful Head by the late C. Gobrecht (then Dyesinker [sic] of the Mint) on [the] Reverse on [sic] has a Flying Eagle & the other an eagle without the Shield.[24]

trade for coins that Mickley had previously presented to the Mint Cabinet. In any case, Mickley's connections to Adam Eckfeldt, Franklin Peale, and William E. Du Bois made for unrivaled access to the Mint's resources in his collection-building. It should be noted that when Du Bois (1872) said that there were only four coin collectors in Philadelphia in 1842, he was referring only to major coin collectors. He was aware that there were others, as proved by a list he made in 1843 that was reprinted by Newman and Bressett (1962:72).

[23] This enigmatic entry begs the question of Mickley's source, not to mention the exact contents of the lot.

[24] Again, the passage implies that Mickley received these two pattern half dollars as an outright gift, which is perhaps even more surprising in that the source of the gift was noted more for selling Mint products than for making presents of them. Certainly, however, these coins made for handsome gifts. The first of the two mentioned by Mickley (the Flying Eagle Reverse) is no. 77 in Pollock (1994), while the second is no. 75. Pollock estimates that originals of each are R-7 (4 to 12 known), while restrikes are R-5 (31 to 75 known). Whether Peale handed Mickley originals or restrikes cannot be proved, but Peale's known proclivity to restrike makes the latter possibility seem probable. In Woodward's Mickley sale, lot 2159 is a Flying Eagle Reverse, while lot 2160 is a Spread Eagle Reverse. If these were the identical coins given to Mickley by Peale, W.E. Woodward's note on lot 2159 might add some credence to the notion that they were restrikes. Woodward described it as "one of the earliest impressions, being from the die before it was injured by breaking, brilliant proof". This sounds more like a piece specially struck for a collector than a piece that had been lying about the Mint for 14 years. In any case, Mickley's statement that "on the obverse is a beautiful head by the late C. Gobrecht" contradicts the assertion by James Ross Snowden (1860:118) that it "has a bust of Liberty by Mr. Kneass". The question is therefore open as to whether Christian Gobrecht or James Kneass deserves credit for designing the obverse.

Monday, May 31, 1852 This day makes it 26 years since I moved to Market St. No. 285 from 3rd [above] arch.[25]

Saturday, June 5, 1852 Went to the Mint in the morning to get the Treasurer of the Blind Institution (Mr. Edelman) to sign an order for me to draw the amount of my Bill (due by the Institution) at the Bank.[26]

Saturday, June 12, 1852 Paid James Swaim a visit who showed me some of his curiosities he brought with him from Europe. It consists in old carved & inlaid furniture, Books, medals & coins, and a part of the Books but [I] did not see one fourth part of them.[27]

Thursday, June 17, 1852 Mr. J. Morris the Coin Collector called in the evening & gave me some Coins.[28]

[25] This entry pinpoints the exact dates Mickley lived and worked at his residences/workshops in Philadelphia. As it happens, the 3rd and Arch address was but a single block from the former location of the American Museum of Pierre Eugène Du Simitière, which displayed its proprietor's coin collection, and was the site on 19 March 1785 of the earliest known public auction of a coin collection in the United States (Orosz 1988).

[26] The Pennsylvania Institution for the Instruction of the Blind was a favorite charity of Jacob Giles Morris, who served for four months (from December 1844 to March 1845) as its interim chief executive officer. Mint director Robert M. Patterson, like Morris, served on the Institution's Board of Governors (trustees). Mickley apparently was able to use the good offices of the Philadelphia Mint to aid in his financial transactions.

[27] James Swaim may have been related to William Swaim, the inventor of Swaim's Panacea, one of the most widely used patent medicines in antebellum America. According to James Harvey Young (1961), William Swaim started manufacturing his celebrated Panacea, which consisted of sarsaparilla, wintergreen, and mercury, in Philadelphia around 1820. Its high price of $3 per bottle made Swaim a wealthy man by mid-century and allowed him to spend considerable time abroad (Young 1961: 74). If James was a relative of William, it would explain his ability to go coin-hunting in Europe.

[28] This was Morris's third visit to Mickley in 1852, and apparently he used it to pay Mickley back for the coins he had received from Mickley on 7 February. Interestingly, Mickley seems to have made no effort to return these visits by going to see Morris.

Monday, June 21, 1852 Went to Mrs. Bowie, who showed me a quantity of English Gold & Silver Coins, which were imported by her father Mr. Ashhurst, they gave me a great [deal] of pleasure.[29]

Saturday, July 3, 1852...Stopped at Pennington's [*sic*] Bookstore who told me he would have some Coins for me in a few days.[30]

Wednesday, August 25, 1852 [Mickley wrote this entry on a visit to New York City] After breakfast I went to try to get some Cotton velvet to line the drawers of my Coin case, I succeeded in find [*sic*] it yesterday I went in a great many stores without being able to find it.[31]

Monday, September 6, 1852...In the evening had a visit from Mr. Vail, the Poet, who is also a Collector of Coins, made some exchanges with him.[32]

Saturday, September 18, 1852 Had a visit from L.W. Washington & Dr. Cohen, the latter a resident of Baltimore, who is a Collector of Autographs & c. he told me he had all the Signers of the Decla-

---

[29] In S.H. Chapman's *Catalogue of the Fine Collection of Foreign Silver Coins and Gold, Silver and Copper Coins of the United States of Richard L. Ashhurst, Esquire of Philadelphia* the following note appears: "The collection contained in this catalogue was commenced by the father of the present Mr. Ashhurst, about 1830, whilst traveling in Europe" (Chapman 1908). The Chapman sale took place on 27 May 1908. Presumably Mrs. Bowie was the sister of Richard L. Ashhurst, and the daughter of the man who commenced the collection about 1830.

[30] In *McElroy's Philadelphia Directory* for 1850 (McElroy 1850), John Penington, Sr., (not "Pennington" as Mickley spelled it) was a bookseller at 10 S. Fifth Street, with his residence located at 13th below Locust. Penington (1799–1867) was apparently a coin dealer on the side at least four years before Ed Cogan (1803–1884) took up the trade.

[31] This suggests that Mickley, in his entry for February 21, meant "paper envelopes" when he wrote "paper trays", for the coin cabinet drawers were to be lined with cotton velvet.

[32] John Cooper Vail, a poet, was one of the more colorful of America's early numismatists. Augustus P. Sage (1867) remembered Vail: "It was about this time [1857] that I first met John Cooper Vail, the poet. Poor Vail, many a time have I seen him since, a martyr to that curse of Americans, rheumatism. Vail I believe was the first man in this country to advertise for rare coins, and he obtained by that means a number of the rarer specimens of our earlier coinage." Vail's first collection of verse, entitled simply *Poems*, had been published only the year before (1851).

ration of Independence, the Presidents & c. his object now is to get specimens of the Continental Money. I gave him some of which I had duplicates.[33]

Monday, September 20, 1852 Went to No. 106 South Wharves to look at a lot of Coins, a person has for sale, his price is $400, intrinsically worth about $60. There are only 3 or 4 pieces among them that I have not got in my Collection, of course I did not buy any of him.[34]

Thursday, September 22, 1852 Had a visit from Mr. Vail the Poet, we exchanged some Coins.[35]

Friday, September 24, 1852 Called on James Swaim who showed me a great many Prints & other Curiosities, which he collected while in Europe, among [them] were different views of Gräfenburg, the Establishment of the "Water Cure" of the celebrated Priessnitz, Mr. Swaim & his Lady spent a considerable time at it.[36]

---

[33] "Lawrence" was a family given name in George Washington's clan, borne by both his elder brother (from whom he inherited Mount Vernon), and his great-great grandnephew, who was born at Mount Vernon in 1854. Since the older Lawrence was long since dead, and the younger not yet born, it is probably the case that Mickley's visitor was Lewis W. Washington of Jefferson County, Virginia (now West Virginia), a great-grandnephew of the first President. Mendes I. Cohen (1796–1879), the second (after Robert Gilmor, Jr.) in a long line of great Baltimore numismatists, was also a serious collector of autographs. Among his numismatic exploits, Cohen owned one of the eight class I examples of the 1804 silver dollar. His collection was ultimately sold at auction by Ed Cogan on 25–29 October 1875. Interestingly, Woodward's sale of the Mickley collection does not contain any examples of Continental bills. It is known that, besides selling the US gold in Mickley's collection separately, Woodward also detached Mickley's British Conder tokens for separate sale. Perhaps he did the same for Mickley's Continental notes.

[34] This entry demonstrates that Mickley bought from individuals, if the coins were desirable and priced right, which these were not. In the rudimentary state of the 1852 numismatic market, intrinsic value was a major consideration. Either Mickley was disinclined to "cherry pick", or the person would sell only as a lot.

[35] Vail's visit to Philadelphia apparently extended over several days.

[36] Vincent Preissenitz of Silesia advocated a "water cure" in place of the largely ineffective medical treatments of the mid-nineteenth century. His regimen involved perspiration, ice-cold showers, lying under wet sheets, and the consumption of

Saturday, September 25, 1852 Went to the Post office & to Pennington's [sic] whom I requested to send an order for some Coins to London.[37]

Sunday, September 26, 1852 In the afternoon I put the lining in the drawers of the Coincase & arranged of the Coins...[38]

Thus end the diary's numismatic entries for the year 1852. Although sometimes cryptic, Mickley's words tell us much of historical value. First, they confirm his status as a "pet collector" at the United States Mint, for Adam Eckfeldt, William Du Bois, and Franklin Peale helped him build his numismatic holdings. Second, it sheds considerable light on the restriking activities carried on by the Mint during 1852, and presumably earlier, since Mickley does not record any of them as something novel. Third, the entries chronicle Mickley's active interaction with fellow collectors Jacob Giles Morris, Mendes I. Cohen, James Swaim, and John Cooper Vail. This demonstrates that there was a community of collectors in Philadelphia long before the Civil War, and that these collectors mingled with brother collectors from New York City and Baltimore. Fourth, the diary demonstrates that Mickley, besides making use of the Mint and other collectors to augment his holdings, also turned to part-time coin dealers like William Chaffers in London and John Penington, Sr., in Philadelphia. Fifth and finally, it paints a picture of Mickley as a disciplined and systematic collector, one who avoided overpayment for coins, and who spent hours rearranging his cabinet and studying the coins within.

twenty to thirty glasses of water daily. If James Swaim was indeed a relative of William Swaim, it is interesting to note that the celebrated Panacea was apparently not sufficient to keep him in good health!

[37] This entry, and the one immediately previous, demonstrate two different methods for participating in the trans-Atlantic coin trade in 1852, namely, purchasing coins during a visit or importing them through an intermediary. This entry indicates that Penington was not merely a coin dealer in the sense of saving unusual pieces that came over the counter in trade but rather a full-fledged coin dealer, with sources in London from whom he could order coins.

[38] This confirms that Mickley housed his collection in a cabinet with drawers lined with cotton velvet. Still unsettled is the question of whether Mickley placed individual coins in paper envelopes.

Joseph J. Mickley's diary is, ultimately, a window affording those living in the twenty-first century a glimpse into the lost world of numismatics in the nineteenth century. Mickley built his collection at a time when Revolutionary War veterans still walked the streets, a time before the great ordeal of union purged the land of slavery, a time when numismatics was not an industry, nor even yet a hobby, but rather the pastime of a handful of aficionados. It is a time we can never completely recapture, nor even fully understand, but which we can begin to appreciate through the 1852 diary of the "father of American coin collecting", Joseph J. Mickley.

REFERENCES

Bowers and Merena, Inc. 1994. *The Armand Champa library, part one.* Auction by Bowers and Merena Galleries, Baltimore, November 17, 1994.

Breck, Samuel. 1854. *Sketch of the benevolent services of Jacob G. Morris: in the Pennsylvania Institution for the Instruction of the Blind, and in other charitable institutions in the city of Philadelphia.* Philadelphia: John C. Clark.

Breen, Walter. 1988. *Walter Breen's complete encyclopedia of U.S. and colonial coins.* New York: Doubleday.

Brown, Alexander Crosby. 1961. *Women and children last: the loss of the steamship* Arctic. New York: Putnam.

Bunting, Jacob. 1885. Joseph J. Mickley: a biographical sketch. *Lippincott's Magazine,* July 1885. Reprinted in Mickley, Minnie F. 1893. *The genealogy of the Mickley family of America.* Mickleys, Pa: published by the author.

Chapman, S. H. 1908. *Catalog of the fine collection of foreign silver coins and gold, silver and copper coins of the United States of Richard L. Ashhurst, Esq. of Philadelphia.* Auction by Davis & Harvey, Philadelphia, 27–28 May 1908.

Comparette, T. L. 1913. *Catalogue of coins, tokens, and medals in the numismatic collection of the Mint of the United States at Philadelphia, Pa.,* 2nd ed. Washington: Government Printing Office.

Du Bois, William E. 1846. *Pledges of history: a brief account of the collection of coins belonging to the Mint of the United States, more particularly of the antique specimens.* Philadelphia: C. Sherman.

—. 1871. [Letter]. *American Journal of Numismatics* 1st series 5:84–85.

—. 1872. [Letter]. *American Journal of Numismatics* 1st series 7:18–19.

Duke, Marc. 1976. *The du Ponts: portrait of a dynasty.* New York: Saturday Review Press.

Eckfeldt, Jacob Reese and William E. Du Bois. 1852. *New varieties of gold and silver coins, counterfeit coins, and bullion; with mint values,* 3rd ed. New York: G. P. Putnam.

Kolbe, George Frederick. 1991. *Catalogue of an exhibition of "Numismatica Americana" comprising books, periodicals, sale catalogues and memorabilia from the library and collections of Armand Champa, held during the one hundredth anniversary convention of the American Numismatic Association in Chicago, Illinois, at the Rosemont-O'Hare Conference & Exhibition Center, August 13th to August 18th, 1991.* Crestline, Calif: George Frederick Kolbe.

Manville, Harrington E. and Terence J. Robinson. 1986. *British numismatic auction catalogues, 1710–1984.* Encyclopedia of British numismatics, vol. 1. London: A. H. Baldwin.

Mason, E. 1882. Personal numismatic reminiscences, no. 2: the numismatic chums. *Mason's Coin Collectors' Magazine* 4:25–27.

McElroy, A. 1850. *McElroy's Philadelphia directory for 1850.* Philadelphia: A. McElroy.

Mease, James. 1811. *The picture of Philadelphia, giving an account of its origin, increase and improvement in the arts, sciences, manufactures, commerce and revenue.* Philadelphia: B. & T. Kite.

Mickley, Joseph J. 1865–66. Hall [obituary]. *Proceedings of the Numismatic and Antiquarian Society of Philadelphia* 1865–66:62.

—. 1875. *Brief account of murders by the Indians, and the cause thereof, in Northampton County, Penn'a., October 8th, 1763.* Philadelphia: Thomas William Stuckey.

Moulton, Karl. 2001. Notes on Joseph J. Mickley: pioneer American numismatist. *Bowers & Merena Rare Coin Review* 142:19–24.

Newman, Eric and Kenneth E. Bressett. 1962. *The fantastic 1804 dollar.* Racine: Whitman.

Orosz, Joel J. 1988. *The eagle that is forgotten: Pierre Eugène du Simitière, founding father of American numismatics.* Wolfeboro, NH: Bowers and Merena Galleries.

—. 1990. Robert Gilmor Jr. and the cradle age of American numismatics. *The Numismatist* 103:704–712, 819–822, 829–830.

—. 1995. The Mickley countermark mystery. *The Numismatist* 108:973–978, 1041–1043, 1049.

—. 2000. Missing masterpieces: the twilight zone of American numismatic literature. *The Asylum* 18:73–79.

—. 2002. Jacob Giles Morris: patrician pioneer of coin collecting. *The Numismatist* 115:504–519, 552–557.

Pollock, Andrew W. 1994. *United States patterns and related issues.* Wolfeboro, NH: Bowers and Merena Galleries.

Rubin, P. Scott. 1985. Auction appearances and pedigrees of the 1792 silver center cent. In: *America's copper coinage, 1783–1857,* pp. 131–148. COAC Proceedings 1. New York: American Numismatic Society.

Sage, Augustus B. 1867. Recollections of a coin collector, no. 3 [letter]. *American Journal of Numismatics* 1st series 2:8–9.

Snowden, James Ross. 1860. *A description of ancient and modern coins in the cabinet collection at the Mint of the United States.* Philadelphia: J. B. Lippincott & Co.

Woodward, W. Eliot. 1867. *Catalogue of the numismatic collection formed by Joseph J. Mickley, Esq., of Philadelphia.* Roxbury, Mass: Leavitt & Strebeigh.

Young, James Harvey. 1961. *The toadstool millionaires: a social history of patent medicines in America before federal regulation.* Princeton: Princeton University Press.

AJN Second Series 13 (2001) pp. 109–132
© 2002 The American Numismatic Society

YUGOSLAV COUNTERMARKS ON
AUSTRO-HUNGARIAN GOLD COINS

Aleksandar N. Brzić*

For my mother, Radmila Miljković-Brzić, in memoriam

With all the progress of modern numismatic research in Europe, one is rather surprised to discover here and there another "terra incognita", still waiting to be explored. Yugoslav[1] countermarks on Austro-Hungarian gold coin issues are one of them. Although not a wholly unknown phenomenon, even the most specialized literature is rather cursory when it comes to them. Only the most encyclopedic of works, like Viennese *Repertorium* (Prokisch et al. 1999: 147–150) list the very few references available. What could be the reason for this?

First of all, the material itself is quite scarce, recently becoming increasingly rare. Although definitely not of the highest rarity, these coins are quite difficult to come by. Austrian numismatists and collectors tend to see them as a "Balkan" phenomenon and mostly don't collect or research them. On the other hand, Yugoslav numismatists usually lack the means to collect gold coins at all, and the scarce

* Zeezigt 388, NL-1111 TT Diemen, The Netherlands (aleks@brzic.com).

[1] In view of the political turmoil of recent years, I wish to state that my references to "Yugoslavia", "Bosnia", and "Serbia" are all to the Kingdom of Yugoslavia which ceased to exist in 1945 and its respective parts as they were known then and subsequently before the partition of the Socialist Federative Republic of Yugoslavia (SFRJ) in 1991 and nothing else. No other implication is wanted or intended.

numismatic institutions in the country, if not devoted to Greek and
Roman coinage, are typically interested in Serbian medieval coinage
and nothing else. Finally, the very few serious collectors in Europe
who might be tempted to collect them face the problem of not having
a definitive publication about these issues and therefore not really
knowing what to collect. Most importantly though, auction houses
don't really have the time nor will to deal with this (surprisingly!)
rather inexpensive material which nobody really wants or knows much
about.[2] Quite an intolerable situation!

Although several local authors have indeed cursorily addressed this
issue—the best source is the standard catalogue of Yugoslav coins by
R. Mandić (1995)—it is quite surprising that the English-language numismatic literature has totally neglected this series (e.g., nothing at all
about it in Krause and Mishler 2000). German publications do address
this series, but only up to a point: if anything is to be found at all,
only two dates are mentioned for the 1- and 4-ducat issues: 1914 and
1915 (for example, Schlumberger 1997: 823–824). The widely read Ger-
man-language coin monthly *Money Trend*[3] also has this listing and values it accordingly. One of the most interesting references for both variety and values is the Swiss Bank Corporation (UBS) auction catalogue
No. 43/1997, where a small number of very unusual host coins are
listed. Spink-Taisei, Zürich, auction catalogues were also an infrequent
but most interesting source for this material. Most frequently, though,
these coins are found in the H. D. Rauch auctions and in the lists of
E. Mozelt, both in Vienna.

We hope that this publication will help to make the series better
known in English-speaking countries. The research for this article has
been based on the author's extensive (for this series) collection of
countermarked coins and on the analysis of relevant auction catalogues
and sales lists for the last thirty years. Only catalogues in author's possession or in the library of the Institute of Numismatics of the Univer-

---

[2] Many dealers and auction houses will flatly refuse to deal with this material and
some would even call its authenticity in question. Many times we have heard the
reasoning that a "serious auction house does not deal in fantasies" and so on.

[3] Available online at http://www.moneytrend.at

sity of Vienna were considered. We feel that this sample is comprehensive: out of several hundreds of catalogues, only a couple were missing.

SOME DUCAT TYPES USED IN THE BALKANS

There is abundant historical evidence (e.g., Ugričić 1967: 51–52; Vinaver 1970: 187–212) that ducats have been used for centuries in the Balkans as *de facto* trade currency. Although different coin types predominated in different geographical regions (zecchini mostly in the South, ducats mostly in the North), the principle remained the same during several centuries of Turkish rule: local Ottoman minor currency with gold from one of the large neighboring countries. Particularly towards the end of the eighteenth century and beginning of the nineteenth century, economic growth caused an even greater need for gold coins. This coincided with power struggles within the Ottoman Empire, and the use of coins of other countries often had political overtones beyond purely economic needs. Figure 1 depicts some of the more common Austro-Hungarian types encountered.

FIGURE 1.
Some common ducat types.

Although the 1-ducat coin type had been established for a very long time, multiples were relatively rare and accordingly not much used. But again with increasing wealth, the multiples became more and more an everyday necessity, and from approximately the reign of Emperor Franz II (1792–1835) the 4-ducat coin type became a regular issue and started to be used accordingly.[4] These coins became very important in the Transdanubian trade, which was to become an economic backbone of the young Serbian state and, to a somewhat lesser extent, the Bulgarian state. The use of these coins would become such an integral part of the monetary system of these countries that their own gold coin issues had to wait quite a long time to appear. When they finally did, they remained largely an urban phenomenon because the farming population stuck with the ducats they already knew and trusted. (After all, ducats were .986 fine gold rather than the .900 fine gold of the first gold dinar or lev issues towards the end of the nineteenth century.) This situation continued until World War I, when the supply of ducats from Austria-Hungary suddenly and nearly totally stopped. After the war, the impoverished rump state of Austria was for a while wholly unable to satisfy the demand for gold ducats,[5] and eventually both Bulgaria and later the Kingdom of Yugoslavia issued their own trade coinage.

Bulgarian issues,[6] a wholly private enterprise, can be seen as having followed two lines: the more "official" one, with the bust of Czar Fer-

---

[4] Of particular importance are the 4-ducat coins issued during the reign of Franz Joseph I (1848–1916). An exceptionally useful and well-illustrated overview of these and other gold coins of this reign can be found in the auction catalog Spink Taisei 45 (Zurich, 1993).

[5] Hahn was recently able for the first time to explore and publish the total statistics of the Austrian ducat restrikes from World War I onwards. This has now given a sound basis to many conjectures by several authors (Wieser, Mandić, Schlumberger, among others) of recent decades.

[6] Fuchs (1983) states that these issues were made much later than the dates on the coins suggest and in Belgrade, not Sofia, but fails to mention his source or to substantiate this conjecture any further. We disagree and think that Schlumberger and Mandić are right and that these coins were not made in Belgrade but in Sofia. Given the political alignments at that time it would have been impossible to do any minting in a country which remained a virtual enemy until the rapprochement in the early 1930s. Belgrade did indeed mint some coins for Bulgaria in 1933–1934, but the crown countermark used on Bulgarian coins had been used much earlier in Bulgaria and therefore cannot have been used in Belgrade at any time.

dinand and later Czar Boris on them, and the more "unofficial" one, with busts resembling either Franz Joseph I of Austria or Alexander II of Russia.[7] While the first issue adhered more or less to preset weight and fineness standards, the second one showed signs of hastily conceived commercial enterprise: deteriorating design, fantasy dates and legends, and very significant variation in fineness and weight (invariably lower than expected for this type). Finally, brass and even cardboard issues were offered for the less well off. Nevertheless, in all cases the real gold issues were properly and consistently countermarked with the Bulgarian crown mark: to our knowledge, not a single example of an unmarked coin has surfaced so far.

The latest ducat series to appear was that of the Kingdom of Yugoslavia from 1931 to 1934. Administrative order No. 311, which regulated this, was signed by the Minister of Finances, Dr Šverljuga, on 17 June 1931 and published in the *Službene Novine*, as usual. The circumstances of this issue are very interesting and deserve some discussion. King Aleksandar I Karadjordjević had already had a gold coin of 20 dinara issued in 1925 (Figure 2). His wish to have a gold coinage like his predecessors[8] was well known and after the big political changes of the turbulent period of 1929–1931, the Kingdom was about to embark on an overall restructuring of finances and coinage. The crisis that the whole world was in at that time only served to increase the impetus for this restructuring.

FIGURE 2.
The 1925 20-dinara coin of the Kingdom of the Serbs, Croats, and Slovenes.

[7] For a number of very rare examples of this issue with no holes or traces of mounting, see the auction catalogue Ira & Larry Goldberg, Dr. John Kardatzke Collection, part 3, June 7, 2000, Beverly Hills, lots 4223–4225. The coins are here, as is usual nowadays, erroneously attributed to Russia.

[8] Although some of them didn't quite succeed: for example, the archive of the French Mint in Paris is full of letters of intent from the reign of Aleksandar I Obrenović, which all came to nothing.

Not only were several new coin types introduced in 1931–1932, a series of bond issues (Omerović et al. 2001) on the world market (1931–1933) also marked this new beginning. The ducat issue could be seen as both the "crowning" of the coinage series and a propaganda device (Figure 3).[9] A large, imposing double eagle covers nearly the whole available area of the reverse, while the conjugate busts of the King and the Queen are given most of the space on the obverse of the 4-ducat piece.[10]

FIGURE 3.
Design of the Yugoslav 1- and 4-ducat types.

Yugoslav ducat issues therefore had a long prehistory (see Prokisch et al. 1999: nos. 23.12.2-1.2/1 and 23.12.2.5.1/6) and turned out to be quite a sophisticated product in the end. The Viennese engravers Placht and Prinz made a series of very high-quality designs; trial pieces were first made in Paris and trial strikes in small quantities subsequently in Vienna. These were, possibly unexpectedly, recalled on

[9] The king was extremely eager to establish a "Yugoslav" identity in a country used to centuries of ethnic hatred and warfare.

[10] It is interesting to note that first design trials with much smaller double eagle and busts were rejected and the radical redesign was adopted some time later.

short notice (see note 10) and the well-known issue ensued later in Vienna and Belgrade.[11] These recalled trial strikes are of the highest rarity, and in some cases only a single example is known.[12] The countermarking of these ducats was done with very high consistency and professionalism: according to the law on which this ducat issue was based, no ducat could be issued without the authorized countermark. Of the regular issue, it is thought that only one unmarked piece exists.[13] Although several more examples without countermarks have surfaced since, all but that one seem to be Italian forgeries published by Mandić (1995). Of the trial strikes, several genuine pieces are known without countermarks. As discussed, the countermarks used on the coins were specified by the respective laws and cannot be disputed. For this article we did not perform any particular study of the countermarks found on the regular issue as these are totally uniform, very numerous, and very well documented in both collectors' and research literature.

Like many other things at that time, this issue continued in diminishing quantity for a short period (1 ducat until 1934 and 4 ducats only until 1933, *not* 1934 as stated by Krause and Mishler 2000) and then fizzled out. In particular, the uncertainty about the future of the kingdom after the assassination of Aleksandar I in Marseilles in October 1934 made many plans impossible, if not entirely obsolete. Although short-lived, this issue was far superior to others at the time and therefore remains a valuable witness of the numismatic history of this period. Nowadays this series is accepted as an integral part of the coinage of the Kingdom of Yugoslavia; in fact, the biggest rarities of the whole Yugoslav series come from this group.

---

[11] The law clearly states that the ducats had to be made in Belgrade but many authors think that Vienna nevertheless did the bulk of the work. This widely accepted conjecture has not been firmly established as yet.

[12] Schlumberger (1997) has much better photographs and is more systematic than Krause and Mishler (2000) in this case.

[13] A 4-ducat coin dated 1931 from Auction 257, Hess, Lucerne, November 1986, lot 904.

USE OF AUSTRIAN GOLD COINS IN THE BALKANS

The largely farming population of the eastern Balkans (the area now shared between Serbia and Bulgaria) was under Ottoman rule for several centuries. The coinage of the Ottoman Empire had its frequent ups and downs and, arguably, never quite projected the confidence the issuer intended. Vinaver (1970) explains how, in the sixteenth to eighteenth centuries, Venetian and Austrian gold coins circulated normally alongside Ottoman issues and were very often preferred because of their stable gold content and weight.

The downfall of the Austro-Hungarian and Ottoman Empires early in the last century inevitably triggered many social and industrial changes. The monetary situation, always a mirror of the times, followed suit. The young and upcoming nation states found themselves in a new situation: acceptable and stable coinage had to be introduced and produced, including gold coinage, whose use had been customary in the Balkans for centuries. After World War I, the Vienna Mint, traditionally the largest supplier of gold ducats, was not able to supply them in the required quantities anymore: the First Austrian Republic, with its industrial and political troubles, simply did not have the means to satisfy the requirements of the whole region anymore, well into late 1920s. Although it actually continued to strike 1- and 4-ducat pieces with the date 1915 on them through most of those years (and still does today!), the quantities actually minted in some years were quite small compared with the usual pre-war output (cf. Hahn 2001). The newer Balkan countries responded to this by striking look-alikes (Bulgaria) or their own ducat issues of variable success (Yugoslavia).

But there was another factor: even well into this century, on Sunday afternoons people would go to the village center to talk, promenade, and very often dance the local dances. Every eligible girl's family wanted to show off their wealth, so the large and imposing Austrian 4-ducat pieces were holed, strung up, and worn around the neck or as a headdress (Figure 4).[14] Some of these "necklaces" were very large

---

[14] This practice sometimes had such detrimental effects on the strained economy of the country that the authorities reacted. Ugričić (1967: 48) cites a law from the first half of the nineteenth century whereby every family head who wanted his

and contained several kilograms of gold (looking at the jewelry of the Byzantine empress Theodora, we sometimes ask ourselves whether anything changed at all over the centuries). Figure 4 is from a contemporary article by Zegga (1925), but this practice continued well into 1970s.

FIGURE 4.
Two bridal outfits from different regions in Serbia.

Zegga's article is also important for another reason: it is the only proper numismatic analysis of the jewelry pieces (*djerdani*) we have been able to trace so far. By and large, Zegga paints a picture consistent with our conclusions: from the humble beginnings with Turkish aspers earlier on, the nineteenth century saw the increasing economic potential of the farming population mirrored in increasing use of large silver coins and eventually small gold coins like zecchini and single ducats from Austria-Hungary. Finally, the large 4-ducat multiples became the coin of choice for people who could afford them: thin enough not to be too heavy in large groups but large enough to show off.

"female folk" to wear gold visibly had to buy this right by giving the same amount of gold to the Treasury!

It is therefore very interesting to note that despite the local gold coinage becoming available in Serbia after about 1880 and even after the arrival of Yugoslav 4-ducat pieces in 1931, people still kept demanding and using the Austrian 4-ducat pieces, mostly ones with Franz-Joseph on the obverse.[15] This extended use of foreign-made gold objects (ducats in this case) certainly increased the need for proper hallmarking and, in case of coins, countermarking. This was finally done toward the end of the 1920s. As the Austro-Hungarian Empire already had a very well established hallmarking system, and many parts of Yugoslavia used to be in the empire, the goldsmiths and financial officials knew about it and were accustomed to it. It is therefore logical that when the time came, a similar system was chosen to replace the now defunct one of the Austro-Hungarian Empire.

Nowadays the picture has changed: ducats are used nearly exclusively for jewelry; other currencies like the US dollar and the German mark have taken over the trade function of a trusted external currency that gold had fulfilled in earlier centuries.

COUNTERMARKS IN YUGOSLAVIA BEFORE WORLD WAR II

In the coin catalogues two countermarks are usually mentioned for Yugoslavia: "sword for Bosnia" and "ear of corn for Serbia". Unfortunately, neither the description of the stamps nor the localization are really accurate. It is not clear why this "for Bosnia" and "for Serbia" taxonomy was introduced in the numismatic literature; at the time the ducats were issued, these two entities were not even known under those names!

---

[15] When I last saw my mother's family's bridal gift that had been used for generations, I noticed that it contained about 400 single ducats and 75 4-ducat pieces. This all amounted to about 2 kilograms of gold. Although there were Austro-Hungarian ducats as old as 1821, the majority were the 1915 restrikes. Not a single one was from the Yugoslav 1931–1934 series! The aunt who was in charge of keeping them properly strung, to be used by several brides in the family, assured me that indeed no other sorts of ducats or other gold coins were considered "appropriate" for jewelry.

Let us start with obvious facts: there are altogether three counter-marks decreed by law (or hallmarks, the law does not make any distinction) relating to the Kingdom of Yugoslavia which appear on coins, Yugoslav or otherwise.[16] Two were intended for use on small gold objects of local origin and one on small gold objects of any other (foreign) origin. The law decreeing them, passed by the Ministry of Trade and Industry of the Kingdom of the Serbs, Croats, and Slovenes (the name "Kingdom of Yugoslavia" was not used before 1931), was no. 1253/922, signed by the minister, Dr. Marković, on 27 February 1922. This law is important in several ways: not only did it introduce a system by which everybody was able to buy and sell gold products of certain fineness and quality, it also reintroduced a hallmarking system quite similar to that of Austria-Hungary.[17]

For locally made objects with the minimal gold content of .750, the countermark was a pair of birds with a tree branch between them and a small sign of "I" for first quality or fineness (Figure 5). For all small gold objects of foreign origin with the minimal gold content of .750, the countermark was to be a sword between two laurel twigs and again the small sign of "I" for first quality or fineness (Figure 6).

[16] Our most recent research (Brzić and Hahn 2002) has brought to light an extremely rare trial or transitory countermark type, the Double Eagle countermark. This has been found on only thirteen coins in all so far. None of them are Austro-Hungarian "1915" restrikes: all are on host ducats dated 1914 or earlier. Heraldic analysis and other methods (Brzić and Hahn 2002) enabled us to attribute this countermark to the early period of the Kingdom of the Serbs, Croats, and Slovenes (as the Kingdom of Yugoslavia was known at that time), quite precisely between 1919 and 1922. Not even the most painstaking research in *Službene Novine* for this period has yielded any law or decree pertaining to it, though.

[17] The gold market in Yugoslavia before World War II was at first totally free (Ugričić 1967: 195). Importation and exportation had to be registered with the National Bank and there were certainly duties and excise imposed, but in essence there was a free market. Only after 1936 did the authorities see a need for tighter control, for example introducing a measure by which all refined gold had to be sold to and/or via the National Bank.

.750

Figure 5.
Birds countermark.

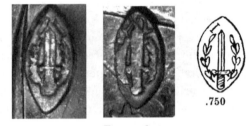

.750

FIGURE 6.
Sword countermark.

Recently, a most interesting example of a countermarked *hayrıye al-tin* of Mahmud II (year 21 = AD 1828/29, gold .873, KM 638) has been brought to our attention.[18] Next to the name mark of the goldsmith, it appears to have a (forged?) Birds stamp with a 4-I combination on it (Figure 7). The somewhat crude appearance, and the fact that this countermark should not have been on a foreign coin in the first place, both point towards an improper countermarking with forged stamp in order to legitimize a coin which otherwise possibly would have had some problems. Interestingly, the coin itself does *not* appear to be a forgery. Apart from the fact only two other occurrences of Yugoslav countermarks are known on coins of countries other than Austria-Hun-

---

[18] We are most grateful to Prof. Hahn for letting us examine this coin.

gary, this would also be one of only two known examples of a coupling of this countermark with another.[19]

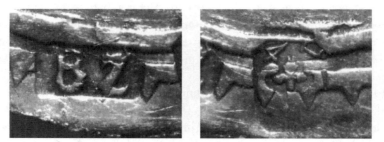

FIGURE 7.
Goldsmith's mark and (forged?) Birds countermark on Turkish coin.

According to the law mentioned above, the Arabic numerals serve to designate the city where the hallmarking was done: the law explicitly lists them all. The numbers encountered on specimens in our collection do indeed show a certain logic in distribution. For example, the above-mentioned *hayrıye altın* coin, of Turkish origin, was marked with "4", which meant Sarajevo. Given that Sarajevo's bazaar was one of the centers of Ottoman trade in the Balkans, this does not appear strange in the least. Other numbers encountered include 1, 2, and 7: these were Belgrade, Zagreb, and Subotica, respectively. This is also to be expected: aside from the previous Serbian capital, Belgrade, the city of Zagreb had been the largest economic center in the Slavic part of the Austro-Hungarian Empire; Subotica, a city north of the Danube and nowadays just south of the Yugoslav-Hungarian border, is not that far from it and also had been in the Austro-Hungarian Empire prior to World War I. These numbers therefore fit very well into the expected economic geography of this countermarking. Although many more locale numbers[20] were provided by the law, most others are seldom encountered and some of them are very improbable indeed.

---

[19] The other one is coupled with the Kingdom of Serbia "eagle" mark on an Austrian 4-ducat piece and is in a private collection we were able to examine. It is illustrated in Brzić and Hahn (2002).

[20] The 1922 law provided for twelve locales. The subsequent law no. 4389 of August 1929, signed by Dr. Drinković, which prolongs the use of these marks, provides even more numbers for locales: 21 in all!

Apart from the numeral combinations 1-I and I-2 illustrated above, we have found several others: I-4, I-7, and 2-I. Most countermarks we have seen so far bear the I-2 variant, though, which possibly might suggest that the bulk of the countermarking was done in Zagreb, now the capital of Croatia. All of them are of consistent size, and allowing for wear on the coin and the stamp itself, the overall appearance is remarkably consistent.

Finally, two unique cases are known of coins from other countries that were countermarked: Great Britain and Russia. The rarity of these occurrences points to a probable mistake in countermarking, although formally their fineness justifies the deed. No host coins of other countries (apart from the somewhat special Turkish specimen described above) have been found so far, and it is our feeling that, if found at all, these would remain mere exceptions to the rule.[21]

Later on, in 1931–1933, the Ministry introduced a different countermark for the locally made small gold objects. This is how the third countermark, the Ear-of-Wheat countermark, came into being (Figure 8). It again has a small "I" in the corner. It is interesting to note that although many coins dated 1931 and 1932 are known with this mark, the mark itself was decreed only in May 1933. This could support a conclusion that the coins were marked not at minting but when released and/or sold. Figure 8 demonstrates two interesting phenomena relating to the countermarks:

- the Arabic numerals used on stamps can differ from coin to coin on Austro-Hungarian issues; on regular Yugoslav ducats there is only "1" for Belgrade.
- the Roman numeral does not vary but can (though not often) be placed in different corners of the countermark.

---

[21] The final law concerning us in this paper even stipulates that only the trade coinage, i.e., ducats, can and should be marked. It explicitly says that normal gold currency should be left unmarked. This law also ended the validity of the sword countermark for foreign coins in the form encountered on coins known to us. It prescribes a new sword countermark, which we have not encountered on any coins. This law was no. 3022/933, of 30 May 1933, signed by Dr. Šumenković.

.950

FIGURE 8.
Ear-of-Wheat countermark.

These observations are true for all three countermarks. On the 1-ducat piece, both Austrian and Yugoslav, the countermark is always placed (more or less) under the king's bust; on the Yugoslav 4 ducats it is always to the right of the conjugate busts. On Austrian 4-ducat coins, however, the sword countermark is normally to the left of the bust of Franz Joseph I. We have seen very few exceptions to this, even in case of forgeries! The directions in which they were stamped vary considerably, but this is to be expected, given the small size of the countermark: it would have been impractical to align it always in the same direction.

All official Yugoslav ducat issues with both countermarks have always a Roman I and an Arabic 1 on them. The Roman I is for the fineness and the Arabic 1 simply points to the fact that all were made and countermarked in Belgrade.[22] Some of the early Viennese trial strikes were also countermarked in Belgrade! We have now seen several hundreds of these coins and have never found any exception to this number "1". If indeed there were one, it would be quite rare. We do not expect this, however, as the probability that somebody other than the central authority in Belgrade countermarked these ducats is most likely zero. This is a very important distinction: while the Austri-

---

[22] Some authors think that many of these ducats were produced in Vienna but bear the Belgrade moniker **KOVNICA A.D.** on the obverse. Vienna does remain a possibility (after all, the engraving was done there), but by that time this private Mint in Belgrade was already capable of producing substantial amounts of coinage, for example a part of the common 10-dinara 1931 (London issue) silver coin. It also speaks for Belgrade that the law on the issuing of ducats explicitly states that the minting is to be done by unspecified institutions in Yugoslavia and not abroad. We know, however, from earlier times that even when the law stipulated this, there could be significant exceptions.

an ducats were countermarked in various places, the Yugoslav issues were marked exclusively in Belgrade.

So how did these marks come to be known as the "sword for Bosnia" and "ear of corn for Serbia"? The "sword for Bosnia" clearly refers to the branch between the two birds, which indeed looks rather like a sword. Why this (according to the standard coin catalogues) is thought to be for Bosnia only, we do not know. The original law very definitely intended to make the countermarking traceable by using the number for the city, but nothing was intended to refer to a geographic area. By inference we would conclude that the later Ear-of-Wheat (the word "corn" should be understood in the British sense) countermark was also meant to be for the whole of the Kingdom of Yugoslavia (as it was known by then), and not only for Serbia. It is therefore our strong suggestion that cataloguers and writers in the future refrain from using this Bosnia/Serbia distinction and refer to the countermarks as means of verifying the fineness/purity of the gold.

OCCURRENCES OF COUNTERMARKED AUSTRO-HUNGARIAN DUCATS

It is impossible to know the exact range of dates of the coins that were countermarked, as there were absolutely no records about this. What we have been able to find seems to paint a consistent picture, though: with some notable exceptions, the later the host ducat's date gets toward 1915, the more probability there is that an example will exist with a countermark.

Table 1

	Denomination	Date	C/M	Relative Rarity
Austria-Hungary	*1 sovrano*	*1786M*	*Sword*	*Unique*
	1 ducat	1833A	Sword	Very rare
	1 ducat	1838KB	Sword	Very rare
	1 ducat	1848A	Sword	Very rare
	1 ducat	1855A	Sword	Very rare
	1 ducat	1859A	Sword	Very rare
	1 ducat	1863A	Sword	Rare
	1 ducat	1873	Sword	Rare
	1 ducat	1882	Sword	Common
	1 ducat	1884	Sword	Rare
	1 ducat	1886	Sword	Rare
	1 ducat	1895	Sword	Rare
	1 ducat	1897	Sword	Rare
	1 ducat	1910	Sword	Rare
	1 ducat	1912	Sword	Rare
	1 ducat	1913	Sword	Common
	1 ducat	1914	Sword	Common
	1 ducat	1915	Sword	Very common
	10 crowns	*1909*	*Sword*	*Unique*
	10 crowns	*1911KB*	*Sword*	*Unique*
	20 crowns	1894	Sword	Very rare
	20 crowns	*1902KB*	*Sword*	*Unique*
	4 ducats	1900	Sword	Common
	4 ducats	1907	Sword	Rare
	4 ducats	1910	Sword	Rare
	4 ducats	1911	Sword	Common
	4 ducats	1912	Sword	Rare
	4 ducats	1914	Sword	Common
	4 ducats	1915	Sword	Very common
Great Britain	*1 sovereign*	*1890*	*Sword*	*Unique*
Russia	*10 roubles*	*1902*	*Sword*	*Unique*

Unique coins are given in italics. The relative rarity takes into account every single appearance of the type, even if it is possibly the same coin appearing in a sale again, as well as the subjective likelihood that more coins of that date could emerge; in this sense we would rather think of this relative rarity as a prognosis for future appearances rather than exact rarity at this point in time. (The photographs in auction catalogues analyzed were usually of such quality that double appearances could not be excluded with total certainty.)

For this survey we consulted private collectors and the relevant catalogues and sales lists (UBS, Spink-Taisei Zürich, Rauch, Mozelt, and Schenk-Behrens). We were quite surprised by how few coins this actually yielded: altogether not more than about 70 coins were sold in auctions and another 50 or so are in private collections. Allowing for some doubling, this yields roughly a mere 100 coins! Records of auctions support the hypothesis that these coins are all indeed from earlier times and not modern fantasies: countermarked ducats appeared in auctions before the downfall of Communism in Eastern Europe with similar frequency as afterwards. Against the hypothesis of private fantasy manufacture speaks also the professional and consistent design of the punches and the lack of any repeat pattern in auctions and firms auctioning them. In other words, we are quite satisfied that these countermarks are a genuine phenomenon from the epoch between the two World Wars.

The coins known to us are listed in Table 1. The regular, non-countermarked pre-1915 issues were never made in real proof quality; some later years will very occasionally be found in proof-like condition. Wholly uncirculated specimens can sometimes be seen in the 1915 date but nearly always in the 1-ducat denomination. The 4-ducat coin is just too large and has too much empty space in the fields not to receive at least some hairlines. Mounted or pierced and plugged specimens are common, since these coins were usually seen as jewelry rather than numismatic material. It is however important to note that they can be found without holes/mounting/plugging much more often than the Bulgarian series.

CONCLUSION

Having stated all of the above, the question is, who did it, why, and when precisely? Let us be very frank at this point: the scarcity of sources and general lack of information make final conclusions quite difficult. Right now we can only present our hypotheses. On the other hand, we felt that at this point in time, discovery of any major and relevant new source is very unlikely, and time has come to put together what is currently known.[23] While obviously not trying to second-guess the future, we would be more than surprised if this question will ever be resolved at the level usually expected in modern numismatics.

The first hypothesis starts from the observation that after World War I, Yugoslavia (in the form of the Kingdom of the Serbs, Croats, and Slovenes) received a part of the Austro-Hungarian State Bank assets, mostly in gold. This process took some time and it is possible that countermarking was used to count or control the gold received.[24] The relative rarity of the series could not be explained unless one took into account that nearly all of this gold (approximately 5800 kg) was used for the minting of the 20-dinara 1925 coin in Paris. The records of the Paris mint (Darnis 1996: 103, though there erroneously attributed to Serbia instead of Yugoslavia) show that the gold was indeed received from Yugoslavia and not bought on the market; they unfortunately do not specify in what form the gold was received. How probable it is, we simply don't know. (A crucial problem with this hypothesis would be the sheer physical and logistics demands of countermarking tons and tons of coins. Did they really do this? If they did, the process ought to have been of such large proportions that records would have survived. We have found none.)

A second hypothesis is that it could have been a simple fiscal measure: whoever dealt in or possessed these coins had to "legalize" them fiscally by having them counted and stamped; for this a tax was to be paid. In that case, one would have expected many more surviving specimens. The reason for the relative rarity may have been explained recently when one of our older relatives told us that, when paying taxes on gold, only every hundredth ducat piece was actually counter-

---

[23] Perusing the *Službene Novine* has been quite a tedious task because of the general lack of indices for some periods. We have been greatly helped by the books written by Frantlović (1923) and Djordjević (1937), which provide consistent indexing by subject for the period of interest to us. We feel, therefore, that the survey has indeed been comprehensive.

[24] In all, about 30 million gold crowns (Austro-Hungarian currency) was received, most of it in gold, a small part in silver and other currencies.

marked! If correct,[25] this indeed could make sense: marking every coin would have taken a lot of time and wouldn't have been efficient; the possession of one or more countermarked coins could have been enough proof that the taxes had indeed been paid.

However, the third scenario is most probable. During the period of 1920–1934, the important events were as follows:

- the 1922 law regulating the countermarking of precious-metal objects of domestic and foreign origin,
- the issue of the Yugoslav 20-dinara gold coin in late 1925–1926,
- the renewed activity of Vienna Mint which again started making 1915 ducat restrikes in substantial quantities in the mid 1920s,
- the 1929 law regulating the countermarking of precious metal objects of domestic and foreign origin,
- the 1930 decisions of the Council of Ministers and Royal Chancellery about new coinage, including new trade coinage, i.e., ducats,
- the 1931 law defining the production and circulation of ducats, and finally,
- the change of the Birds countermark used originally on Yugoslav ducats into the Ear-of-Wheat countermark in 1933.

After World War I, the Yugoslav gold bullion market was left largely without any fresh supply of ducats from the Vienna mint. The last regular issue, of 1915, was made in very small quantities and, because of the war, did not circulate widely at all. For a number of years there was not much gold to buy on the free market, and the Ministry of Finance was forced to try to increase the supply by issuing the 20-dinara 1925 gold coin late in 1926. This coin, however, failed completely as an issue; its acceptance was very low and most of the issue remained in the vaults. Roughly at the same time, the activity of the Vienna mint again reached the levels of before World War I and these

---

[25] In spite of an extensive search, we have been unable to find any relevant law in the official *Službene Novine*. This is not definitive, however: financial laws and measures were sometimes published by the Ministry of Finances or the Ministry of Trade in the daily press only.

ducats, invariably bearing (somewhat surprisingly[26]) the date 1915, started coming into Yugoslavia in larger quantities. The increasing appearance of "1915" ducats around, say, 1926–1928 must have aroused suspicion, and the authorities felt they had to do something. The hallmarking law of 1922 and its prolongation in 1929 offered a seemingly simple solution: a Sword countermark was already available for all objects of foreign origin, and although this law does not mention coins anywhere in the text, the step of using the mark on qualifying foreign gold trade coins must have been very easy to make. This step was taken possibly at the same time, i.e., around the beginning of 1931, as the issue of the Yugoslav ducats.

The 1931 law ordering the issue of Yugoslav ducats speaks about "old" and "new" ducats. As there were no previous ducat issues of Serbia or Yugoslavia, it must have been referring to Austro-Hungarian ducats as "old" ones and the Yugoslav issue as "new" ones. The law further clearly states that no ducats could be issued or sold without proper examination and countermarking by local authorities. Most probably the "old" ducats in the possession of the authorities were therefore made legal by countermarking them together with "new" ones. Finally, after seeing that the Birds countermark looked too similar to the Sword countermark, which would have started appearing very frequently in circulation, they soon decided, again in 1931, to change the Birds countermark into the Ear-of-Wheat countermark. This was then retained until the end of the issue in 1934. This means that Austro-Hungarian ducats were most probably countermarked in Yugoslavia between 1931 and 1934, but possibly starting as early as 1922. Sporadic countermarking after this period cannot totally be excluded; however, the general economic circumstances and stringent tightening of the gold market regulations after this period make it highly improbable.

Finally, let us point out the fact that this Yugoslav countermarking is one of the very few ways (for another, see Hahn 2001 and Höflich 1971) to tell the contemporary restrikes of the 1915 ducat issues from

---

[26] The Austrian State Mint in Vienna has never actually explained why it continued to issue the ducats with the year 1915 on them. The only logical reason, stated by Hahn (2001), is that this was the year of the last really regular issue.

more modern ones. These countermarks are a sure sign that the coin indeed comes from that date range.

ACKNOWLEDGMENTS

I would like to express my deep gratitude to Prof. Dr. W. Hahn of the Institute of Numismatics of the University of Vienna, Austria, for extremely interesting and helpful discussions concerning this area. His insights and constant encouragement have helped shape this article much beyond the level of mere interest. Many, many sincere thanks to Dr. Hubert Emmerig, also of the Institute of Numismatics of the University of Vienna, Austria, for years of friendly advice and particularly the help in preparation of this text: his finding of the article by Zegga in a rather difficult-to-obtain Austrian ethnological journal has been of great importance to this work. Prof. Dr. Djura Paunić of the University of Novi Sad, Yugoslavia, has been most kind to verify obscure contemporary Yugoslav legal sources. Finally, thanks to Mr. J. Richter of UBS Basel/Zürich, for letting me use some of his company's photographic material in this article, besides my own.

REFERENCES

Brzić, Aleksandar and Wolfgang Hahn. 2002. Eine bisher unbestimmte Punze auf Dukaten der österreichisch-ungarischen Monarchie. *Money Trend* 2/2002:126–128.

Darnis, Jean-Marie. 1996. *Catalogue des fonds d'archives de la Monnaie de Paris, tome I.* Paris: Direction des Monnaies et Médailles.

Djordjević, N. 1937. *Zakoni uredbe i ostali propisi kraljevine Jugoslavije izdani od 1. decembra 1918. do 31. decembra 1936.* Beograd: Izdavačko i knjižarsko preduzeće Geca Kon A.D.

Frantlović, B. J. 1923. *Registar-indeks* Službenih Novina *za 1919–1922 god.* Beograd: Izdavačka knjižarnica Gece Kona.

Fuchs, W. 1983. Die 4-Dukatenprägungen von 1875 und 1905 der Belgrader Münzprägeanstalt Kovnica A.D. *Geldgeschichtliche Nachrichten* 96:181–183.

Hahn, Wolfgang. 2001. Die österreichischen Dukaten als Handelsgold-münzen—Alt- und Neuprägungen ("1915"). *Money Trend* 9/2001: 56–59.

Höflich, Peter. 1971. Der kleine Unterschied. *Helvetische Münzen-Zeitung* 4/71, Nr. 4: 123.

Krause, C. L. and C. Mishler. 2001. *2001 standard catalog of world coins*, 28th ed. Iola, Wis: Krause Publications.

Mandić, Ranko. 1995. *Katalog metalnog novca 1700–1994, III izdanje*. Beograd: Ranko Mandić.

Omerović, N., N. Mitrović, D. Pavlović, and Z. Ilić. 2001. *Katalog Akcija*. Beograd: Srpsko Numizmatičko Društvo.

Prokisch, B. et al. 1999. *Repertorium zur neuzeitlichen Münzprägung Europas, Band XVIII: Südosteuropa*. Veröffentlichungen des Institutes für Numismatik Wien, Band 5. Wien: Institut für Numismatik.

Schlumberger, Hans. 1997. *Goldmünzen Europas von 1800 bis Heute*. München: Battenberg Verlag.

Ugričić, Miodrag. 1967. *Novčani sistem Jugoslavije*. Beograd: Zavod za Izdavanje Udžbenika SR Srbije.

Vinaver, Vuk. 1970. *Pregled istorije novca u Jugoslovenskim zemljama (XVI-XVIII vek)*. Beograd: Izdanje Istorijskog Instituta.

Zegga, Nicola. 1925. Die Münze als Schmuck. *Wiener Zeitschrift für Volkskunde* 30(3–6): 40–44.

AJN Second Series 13 (2001) pp. 133–146

© 2002 The American Numismatic Society

A DIE STUDY OF SOME SILVER COINS OF SINKIANG, CHINA

(PLATES 7–8)   WARREN W. ESTY* AND DAVID SPENCER SMITH**

In an account that did much to open Chinese silver coinages to the Western world, Kann (1954) illustrated and assigned reference numbers to selected, conspicuous die varieties of Sinkiang silver coins, but otherwise merely mentioned the number of varieties in his collection. In a detailed account of Sinkiang silver and gold coins, Lin et al. (1990) described (in Chinese) numerous die varieties of silver issues. Dong (1992) provided excellent illustrations of Chinese coins, but illustrated few die varieties, while Dong and Jiang (1991) provided a similar account but focused entirely on Sinkiang issues. The *Standard Catalog of World Coins* (Krause and Mishler 2002) provides a good historical overview of Sinkiang coins in all metals. Until recently, few Sinkiang silver coin issues were available in sufficient numbers to permit any die analysis, but when their collector value was recognized, during 1980 and for a short time thereafter, substantial numbers of these coins, both copper and silver, were smuggled to the West from China, via Singapore and Hong Kong. This enterprise was subject to dire penalties and soon ceased. Furthermore, the more recent burgeoning of interest in

* Department of Mathematical Sciences, Montana State University, Bozeman, MT 59717-2400, USA (esty@math.montana.edu); ** Jesus College, Turl Street, Oxford OX1 3DW, England.

Chinese coins within China has not only reduced the legal export of coins but has been responsible for scholarly numismatic work within the country. Of particular value is the recent comprehensive account by Ye et al. (1998). Our article contributes to the study of Sinkiang silver coins a detailed die analysis of a small portion of the wide range of silver coinage of Sinkiang.

The region of extreme western China that was known in the nineteenth century as Chinese Turkistan remains culturally and ethnically very different from the rest of the country. It most recently became part of China in the eighteenth century during the reign of the Manchu Emperor Chien Lung, when it was named *Hsin Chiang,* the "New Dominion". This was anglicized to "Sinkiang", a name that was invariably used in the West in geographical and historical accounts until after 1949, when the designation of "Xinjiang-Uighur Autonomous Region" was imposed by the central government. We have retained the name "Sinkiang" in this account, since all coins considered here were produced prior to the communist regime. The indigenous people of Sinkiang are largely Muslim, derived from varied stock including Kazakhs, Kirghiz, Tajiks, Uzbeks, and most importantly the Uighur, a name now often used collectively for the Turkic peoples of Sinkiang. Formerly, Han Chinese accounted for only a small percentage of the population of Sinkiang, but in recent years the central government in Beijing has conducted a policy of forced resettlement of Han in Sinkiang, resulting in near parity at the time of writing, and marked dilution of the autochthonous Muslim culture and religion of Sinkiang.

The numismatic history of Sinkiang is brief but varied. Copper cash were cast in several Sinkiang mints from the eighteenth century, but silver coinage made a modest start only between 1865 and 1877, when the region was wrested from Chinese control by Yakub Beg, under whose rule many small 5-*fen* (half-*misqal*) coins were produced. On reincorporation of Sinkiang into the Chinese Empire on Yakub Beg's death in 1877, authorities of the Kuang Hsu Emperor continued to make 5-*fen* coins; production of higher denomination coins did not start until 1893, when the Kashgar mint was reopened.

Three aspects of Sinkiang's silver coinage may be mentioned to introduce the issues discussed here. First, until 1949, the year of the defeat of the Kuomintang by the communist forces, all Sinkiang silver coins were based on the *tael* (of ten *misqals*), while the rest of China adopted the lighter dollar. Second, the legend of Sinkiang silver coins is either Turki alone, or a bilingual use of Turki and Chinese. Since the latter was the language of a small minority of the people of Sinkiang, any surface inscribed in Turki is here designated the obverse, and the side with Chinese inscription, the reverse. Third, in recognition of the Muslim majority of Sinkiang, silver coins of the Empire cite the *Hijri* (AH) year; this and the corresponding AD year are given here.

In June 1982 one of the authors (DSS) was given the opportunity by Spink (London) to examine two groups of Sinkiang coins, obtained via Hong Kong. One group comprised 327 5-*misqal* coins, of which 311, representing six issues, were selected for this study. Sixteen coins represented eight additional issues (one to three specimens each) which were too small for statistical analysis. Four of these were issues of Kashgar: Kann-1045 (3), 1049 (1), 1055 (1), and 1065 (3). Four were from the Ürümchi mint: Kann-1205 (1), 1208 (2), 1217 (2), and 1221 (3). The second group comprised 119 specimens of the 1949 dollar. It is probable that each group constituted a hoard. The 5-*misqal* coins were consistently dull and uncleaned. The dollars were also uncleaned and most were discolored They appear to be complete as found. There is no reason to believe that they are anything other than a representative sample. These coins form the basis of the statistical analysis offered here. Reference numbers from Kann (1954), Krause and Mishler (2002), and Lin et al. (1990) are used.

SILVER RATION COINAGE

Among the last Sinkiang coins of the Empire were silver *taels* and fractionals of 5, 4, 2, and 1 *misqal*, with the value in Turki and Chinese on the obverse and a stylish and well engraved facing dragon on the reverse. Kann suggested that these undated issues were made "about 1905" but, according to Lin et al. (1990), they (and a few gold coins) were minted in Ürümchi from 1907 and were primarily used to pay Chinese soldiers stationed in Sinkiang—hence the term "ration coinage". Dong Wenchao (1992) adds that the mint was established at the Shuimogou Machinery Bureau, an ordnance factory, and that production of these coins ceased in 1911 at the outbreak of the revolution that overthrew the Manchu Empire. Lin et al. (1990) state that modern minting machinery was obtained in Ürümchi from Shanghai in 1910 and used to produce the 1-*tael* coins; however, the fabric of all these coins is similar, and it seems likely that all were produced with similar minting equipment. Of the five denominations, the half-*tael* (5-*misqal*) issues were produced in by far the greatest number. Kann categorized the 5-*misqal* issues thus:

(a) Reverse with dragon and clouds (Kann-1012);
(b) Reverse with dragon and clouds enclosed within beaded circle (Kann-1013);
(c) Reverse with 2 rosettes outside beaded circle; obverse with central rosette (Kann-1015).

Lin et al. (1990) grouped all three types together (type H 6 to H 6-32) and illustrated thirteen examples of (a), six of (b) and eleven of (c). It was already clear that numerous dies were used in minting these coins; Kann mentioned that his collection included "28 varieties" of the first type.

The group of 5-*misqal* coins that we studied included 89 examples of Kann-1012, 34 of Kann-1013, and 35 of Kann-1015. In each instance, the number of dots in the obverse circle, along with variations in the Chinese and Turki legends, permit unambiguous recognition of differing dies. On the reverse, all features of the design, for example the dragon and head appendages, flaming sacred pearl in the center of the design, and placement of clouds with respect to head and fore-limb digits, vary conspicuously from one die to the next. Examples of these three types are shown in Plate 7 (nos. 1a, 1b, 2a, 2b, 3a, 3b). In each instance, die differences are so obvious (Plate 7 nos. 1c, 1d) that the degree of wear on individual coins presents no obstacle to recognition.

The sequence of production of these types is unknown, likewise the reason for their variety. Production of each type was evidently a largely independent event; the first two types share a similar obverse design, but in the group examined only one obverse die for Kann-1012 (die *J* in Figure 1) is shared with Kann-1013.

KASHGAR AH 1321 AND 1322 5-*MISQAL* COINS

Lin *et al.* (1990) state that the Kashgar authorities first minted 5-, 3-, 2-, and 1-*misqal* coins in February of the nineteenth year of the Kuang Hsu Emperor—in AH 1310, or AD July 1892 to July 1893, following a limited trial issue to test acceptability of a new issue during the previous year. These innovative coins were produced in Kashgar until AH 1322 (1904). Similar coins were issued, briefly, in Aqsu from AH 1310 to 1312 (1893 to 1895) and later in the provincial capital Ürümchi from AH 1321 to 1325 (1903 to 1907). The reverse of these coins bears the top-to-bottom Chinese legend "Kuang Hsu Silver Coin" (Plate 7 nos. 4b, 5c), at first with just the denomination, later with the mint of origin added. The 5-*misqal* obverse did not change throughout the period of issuing: an elegant design of an outer wreath of paired leaves, linked by a bow at base and flanking a rosette at top, enclosing the Turki legend. For the 5-*misqal* Kashgar coins, the legend reads (from top) "misqal five [with the terminal '*lam*' of *misqal* enclosing the *hijri* year] Kashgar minted in".

In the group of coins examined here, 5-*misqal* issues of Kashgar dated AH 1321 (Plate 7 no. 4a) and 1322 (Plate 7 nos. 5a, 5b) were each represented by 51 specimens. This design ended with the AH 1322 issue; Lin et al. (1990) note that from AH 1323 (March 1905 to February 1906) Sinkiang followed the general trend in other provinces, issuing silver coins which included the imperial dragon on the reverse but with Turki and Chinese legend on the obverse (see below). No overlap of reverse dies occurred in these groups between coins dated AH 1321 and 1322. Dies were engraved *de novo*, and differing obverse and reverse dies are distinguished with ease (e.g., Plate 7 nos. 4a and 4b vs. 5a and 5b).

KASHGAR UNDATED (c. 1906) 5-*MISQAL* COINS

In AH 1324 (1906) the Kashgar mint commenced production of newly designed silver taels and fractionals, continuing until AH 1327 (1909) when the last Manchu Emperor, Hsuen Tung, ascended the throne on the death of his father. A rather common type (Kann-1128; Lin et al. type E 60 to E 60-10) was undated, for no obvious reason, and Lin et al. (1990) reasonably assign these to AH 1324 (1906). Unlike the military pay "ration coins", devoid of a clue to origin but with which this issue must have circulated, these Kashgar coins exhibit all the rustic charm of an issue entirely indigenous to this remote province of China (Plate 00 no. 6a). The obverse (Plate 7 no. 6b) bears a central Chinese legend within a beaded ring "Tai Ching silver coin", and outside top "Kashgar made" and at bottom "Siangping [a weight standard] five mace". The marginal Turki legend is also included on the obverse (from 2:00 to 4:00): "minted in Kashgar" and (8:00–10:00) "misqal five". The Reverse, bearing no legend, retains a wreath of paired leaves to left and alternating flowers and leaves to right, linked by a bow at bottom and flanking a rosette at top. Within this circled design lies a squat dragon with hypertrophied appendages and a minuscule flaming pearl (Plate 7 no. 6a): an idiosyncratic creature offering no allegiance whatsoever to the Han Chinese or to then capital, Peking. The sample consists of 51 pieces. As with all the issues in this article, all dies were engraved *de novo* and dies are readily distinguished.

THE 1949 DOLLAR

During the last stages of the Kuomintang (KMT) war against the communist forces in China, inflation in Sinkiang reached dramatic levels, as evidenced by the issuing early in 1949 of KMT bank notes of up to 6 billion dollars (Pick, 1995; S1797). Production of a silver dollar in Sinkiang in 1949 was an extraordinary attempt to stabilize the currency. It was also a departure from tradition—hitherto the *tael* was retained in this westernmost province of China while the rest of the country adopted the dollar (equivalent to c. 74% of the tael) for the provincial coinages emerging late in the nineteenth century. Kann (1953) regarded these 1949 coins as "essays", noting that "...political events and surrender of Sinkiang to the communistic regime made the actual circulation of [this] coin superfluous". For almost three decades, the rarity of the 1949 dollar in the West seemed to substantiate Kann's

view, and until 1980 specimens occasionally offered by dealers com-
manded a price of several hundred dollars. However, according to Lin
et al. (1990), Sinkiang adopted the silver standard, presumably as a
measure of desperation, on 20 May 1949. That the silver content was
somewhat debased (to 85% silver according to Dong) detracts little
from the boldness of the venture. However, the People's Liberation
Army entered the provincial capital, Ürümchi, on 20 October 1949,
thus defining a period of no more than five months when these dollars
may have been available.

Few examples escaped to the West at or soon after minting. Beginning in 1980, the extremely hazardous enterprise of smuggling Sinkiang
coins out of the People's Republic brought substantial numbers of the
1949 dollar to the West and the market price dropped to one tenth or
less of the previous price. The sensible response to access to silver coin
after a period of rampant inflation in 1949 had been hoarding, rather
than circulation, presumably accounting for the uncirculated groups
reaching the West three decades later. Analysis of this sample of 119
coins shows that, far from being an unissued "essay", the 1949 dollar
was an extensive issue.

The obverse (here designated as the side with the Turki inscription)
bears a central "1" with the Turki phonetic "dollar" beneath, with
"1949" at base and a marginal Turki legend: "made in the Sinkiang
Money-making Factory". The Chinese on the reverse is similar, with
"one yuan" in the center and with the addition of "the 38th year of
the Republic" at the base. The "factory" may have been in Kashgar
and/or Ürümchi: Kann does not suggest a mint, Lin et al. suggest only
"mint(s)" while Dong Wenchao (1992) states that the coins were made
in the provincial capital, Ürümchi.

Plate 8 nos. 7 and 8 illustrate an obverse and a reverse of this coin.
Both surfaces offer numerous features facilitating identification of dies.
On the obverse, the marginal Turki legend, with diacritical marks,
shows detailed die differences, together with the Turki "dollar" beneath
the numeral "1". On the reverse, key details of die engraving include (i)
the spurs at top end of the grain ears around the central Chinese value,
(ii) the buckle at base of the ears, and (iii) the marginal Chinese legend.
Different dies can be recognized with ease: almost every aspect of design varies from one die to the next, and each die was engraved *de*

novo, with no parts of the design introduced mechanically. To illustrate this point, fields showing the upper part of the design from four obverse dies, and of the lower portion from four reverse dies are illustrated in Plate 8 nos. 7a–d and 8a–d.

An additional type of this coin, while not relating to the present account, is of historical interest. A version of the 1949 dollar was produced with the reverse date "the 38th year of the Republic" replaced with "1949", probably by the communist authorities. These coins remain scarce.

THE DIES

The dies of all the coins were identified. The data are in Figure 1, where obverse dies are denoted by capital letters, reverse dies by lower-case letters, and the numbers of examples are noted on the line segments that represent die-pairs. Table 1 summarizes the die counts. The samples were large enough to permit deductions about the operation of the mint and about the numbers of dies involved.

In the diagrams, linked groups are put in linear order, as far as possible. The alphabetical order is somewhat arbitrary. Each linked group could be reversed left-to-right and still maintain the same links. Similarly, the groups themselves could be rearranged. The order of the unlinked groups has no meaning—they are simply arranged largest to smallest, except for K-1013, which is linked to K-1012; therefore the linked group in K-1013 is put first. The link in K-1012 is to obverse die *J*, which is odd because it is in the middle of a linked group. Therefore, K-1013 cannot be arranged strictly after K-1012. It is likely that at least some of K-1013 was struck before the striking of K-1012 was complete. Die wear and coin wear turn out to be of no help in choosing the precise order, which is of little interest anyway. The real interest of the linkage is that it illuminates the mint operation and the completeness of the sample.

Four of the seven issues can be put in strictly linear order which strongly suggests only dies being used in the prototypical manner—one die after another with each die used to exhaustion. The exceptions are all of a simple variety easily explained by occasional reuse of dies. For

K-1094 it only takes one die temporarily retired and then reused to explain the diagram.[1] Similarly, the diagram for K-1128 could be explained by the reuse of reverse die c.[2] The diagram for K-1090 and 1090A is more complicated, but can be easily explained with anvil dies used in strict succession merely by positing that sometimes two reverse dies were available and neither was used to exhaustion before the other was employed.[3]

Table 1 summarizes the numbers. It gives the number of coins in the sample and, for each of the obverses and reverses separately, the number of dies observed, the number of dies represented by exactly one coin (N_1) the number of dies represented by exactly two coins (N_2) the number of coins per die, and the associated estimates of the coverage and numbers of dies. The coverage is defined to be the fraction of the entire issue struck by dies represented in the sample. The coverage and the original number of dies are estimated both by a single "best guess" and a more-realistic 95% confidence interval.[4]

---

[1] It could be that all the obverse dies were used to exhaustion in the given alphabetical order and the reverse sequence is abchdefgh..., with the single reverse h reused. Or, it could have been that die C was used before B was retired, and then the use of B resumed. The so-called "die box" theory of reverse-die usage allows reverse dies to be used and put in a "die box" with other reverse dies during breaks. This would allow a different die to resume usage with the same anvil die and a reverse die to be reused later in the sequence. See Esty (1990) for the theory.

[2] Or, if obverse dies could be reused, the reuse of either B or C would explain it.

[3] The linkage could occur if reverse dies f and g were switched after a break and later dies h and i were switched. For example, the obverse dies could have been used to exhaustion in the given order, with f and g both being used, but not to exhaustion, with B. Then f and g are both available for use with C. Similarly, h and i are used with both E and F.

[4] These estimates use the methods in formulas J1, J3, H5, and C3 in Esty (1986). Let n be the sample size (number of coins) and d the number of dies observed. Then the estimate of the coverage is

$C = 1 - N_1/n$, which is formula J1. The coverage interval has endpoints

$C \pm (2/n)\sqrt{(N_1 + 2N_2 - N_1^2/n)}$, which is formula J3. The die-number point estimate is given by

$e = (d/C)(1 + N_1/(2d))$, which is H5, algebraically simplified. The interval has endpoints

$e + (2e/n)^2 \pm (2e/n)\sqrt{(2e)}$, which is C3 simplified.

Of course, the estimates assume the samples are random. Our samples probably

CONCLUSION

The sample was large enough to deduce that these silver issues of Sinkiang were usually struck in the prototypical manner with dies used to exhaustion in a single sequence, one after the other. The few exceptions can be explained by occasional reuse of a reverse die. Furthermore, the estimated coverages are so high (90% or above in 5 of the 7 issues) that most of the dies that were used are represented in the sample and most of the links were observed. Therefore, the data in Table 1 are sufficient to closely determine the numbers of dies employed.

REFERENCES

Dong Wenchao, ed. 1992. *An overview of China's gold and silver coins of past ages: the gold and silver coins and medals of modern China.* Beijing: China Finance Publishing House and Economic Information Agency.

Dong Qingxuan and Jiang Qixiang. 1991. *Xinjiang numismatics.* Hong Kong: Xinjiang Art and Photo Press and Educational and Cultural Press.

Esty, W. 1986. Estimation of the size of a coinage: a survey and comparison of methods. *Numismatic Chronicle* 146:185–215.

—. 1990. The theory of linkage. *Numismatic Chronicle* 150:205–221.

Kann, E. 1954. *Illustrated catalog of Chinese coins (gold, silver, nickel and aluminum).* Los Angeles.

Krause, C.L. and C. Mishler; C. R. Bruce, ed. 2002. *Standard catalog of world coins,* 29th ed. Iola, Wis: Krause Publications.

consist of coins from hoards. If they were hoards formed from coins that were minted together and stayed together after leaving the mint, the resulting bias could be substantial. Then the given numbers would overestimate the coverage and underestimate the number of dies. However, substantial bias seems unlikely because the numbers of coins minted from individual dies in Figure 1 suggest that coins minted together did not stay together to enter and bias our sample.

Lin, G. M., T.-W. Ma, and G.-M. Chen. *Illustrated catalogue of Sinkiang gold and silver coins*. Hong Kong.

Pick, A.; N. Shafer and C. R. Bruce II, eds. 1995. *Standard catalog of world paper money*, 7th ed., vol. 1. Iola, Wis: Krause Publications.

Ye S., Yu X., and Qian J. 1998. Qing Mingguo yinding, yinyuan, tongyuan. In: F. Ma, general editor, *Zhongguo lidai huobi daxi (Encyclopedia of the historical currencies of China)*. Shanghai: Shanghai Numismatic Society and Shanghai Museum.

Table 1

	Coins	Dies	N1	N2	Coins/Die	Estimate	95% Interval
5-*Misqal* no date, uncircled dragon, no rosettes (K-1012)							
Rev:	89	11	1	3	8.1	cov: 99%	93%–100%
						dies: 11.6	11.0–13.0
Obv:	89	20	6	5	4.4	cov: 93%	84%–100%
						dies: 24.7	21.0–28.9
5-*Misqal* no date, circled dragon, no rosettes (K-1013)							
Rev:	34	9	2	1	3.8	cov: 94%	82%–100%
						dies: 10.6	9.0–13.9
Obv:	34	4	0	2	8.5	cov: 100%	88%–100%
						dies: 4	4.0–4.7
5-*Misqal* no date, circled dragon, small rosettes (K-1015)							
Rev:	35	6	1	1	5.8	cov: 97%	87%–100%
						dies: 6.7	6.0–8.2
Obv:	35	5	2	0	7.0	cov: 94%	86%–100%
						dies: 6.4	5.2–7.8
5-*Misqal* Kashgar AH1321 (K-1090, 1090A)							
Rev:	51	16	5	3	3.2	cov: 90%	77%–100%
						dies: 20.5	16.0–26.3
Obv:	51	10	0	2	5.1	cov: 100%	92%–100%
						dies: 10.0	10.0–11.9
5-*Misqal* Kashgar AH1322 (K-1094)							
Rev:	52	24	13	6	2.2	cov: 75%	57%–93%
						dies: 40.7	29.0–57.2
Obv:	52	10	1	2	5.2	cov: 98%	89%–100%
						dies: 10.7	10.0–12.8
5-*Misqal* no date (K-1128)							
Rev:	51	21	7	5	2.4	cov: 86%	70%–100%
						dies: 28.4	21.2–38.0
Obv:	51	19	9	1	2.7	cov: 82%	70%–94%
						dies: 28.5	21.3–38.2
1949 base silver 1 yuan							
Rev:	119	25	3	4	4.8	cov: 97%	92%–100%
						dies: 27.2	24.0–30.8
Obv:	119	26	7	2	4.6	cov: 94%	88%–100%
						dies: 31.3	27.4–35.8

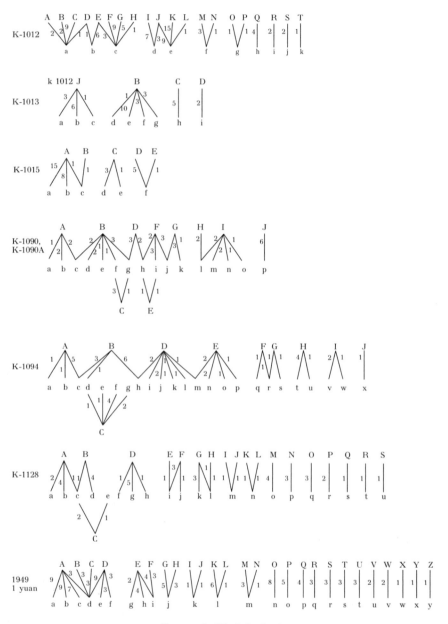

FIGURE 1. Die-link chart.

BOOK REVIEW

Kenneth Sheedy, Robert Carson and Alan Walmsley, *Pella in Jordan 1979–1990: The Coins*. Adapa Monograph Series 1. Sydney: Adapa, 2001. 183 pp., 15 pls. ISBN 0-9578890-0-3, AU $75.00.

This new volume describing the coin finds from the University of Sydney excavations at Jordanian Pella is a welcome addition to the small list of publications dealing with the coins from sites in Jordan. Indeed, it is the first full-scale numismatic report for any Jordanian site.

The book is divided into three major sections. An introductory section (pp. 1–14) gives a brief overview of the history of excavations at Pella under the College of Wooster, Ohio, and the University of Sydney and provides an historical and archaeological framework for understanding the coin finds. K. Sheedy points out that the importance of excavation coins often lies in the trends of production and loss that they reveal. These trends can be used to discern the economic and political history of the site even if only in "broad outline" (pp. 11–12). Discerning even the "broad outline" at Pella is somewhat complicated by the fact that at the time of writing there were few published comparanda from the surrounding region except for the coins from Gerasa and the coin collection of the Amman Museum.

The introduction is followed by a large section of commentary on the coins (pp. 15–66), which includes discussion of findspots and possible historical, economic, and archaeological interpretations. A chapter is provided for each of the main periods of coinage at Pella: Hellenistic (including Ptolemaic and Seleucid royal issues and autonomous city coins), Jewish (primarily the coinage of the Hasmonaean domination but also including two coins of Agrippa I), Roman Imperial (the Republic is not yet represented in the coin finds), Greek Imperial, Byzantine, and Islamic (including Arab-Byzantine issues).

In the chapter on Hellenistic coinage (pp. 15–25) Sheedy emphasizes the importance of the city mint at Akko Ptolemais as a supplying mint for Pella in the second and first centuries BC (pp. 22–24). Twelve coins from that city have been discovered, including two "municipal" pieces (the terminology follows that of O. Mørkholm) struck with the portrait of Antiochus IV. This discovery makes sense considering that Pella is located along a major route linked to Akko Ptolemais.

It is unfortunate that the authors of this work "submitted their texts for publication in 1994 and due to circumstances beyond their control, have been unable to update their work to take into account recent publications." For example, if the opportunity for revision had been available to them the importance of Akko might loom even greater. If Sheedy had been able to take into account recent work on Seleucid numismatics, he would have been able to add coin 1.007 with the types of Antiochus IV/Artemis and 1.008 with the types of Antiochus IV/Nike in biga to the list of Akko Ptolemais issues. The weight (2.35 g), diameter (15 mm), and serrated edge of the illegible coin 1.010 are also suggestive of the small seated Apollo (*SNG* Spaer 1108–1129) and veiled goddess bronzes (*SNG* Spaer 1130–1138, 1734–1737) produced by that mint under Antiochus IV and Demetrius I (see A. Spaer in Proceedings of the 8th International Congress of Numismatics [Paris, 1976], p. 139, and G. Bijovsky in *INJ* 13 [1994–99], pp. 39–45).

The chapter on Jewish coins from Pella (pp. 27–29) primarily deals with relating them to the destruction of the city by Hasmonaean Jewish forces in 83/2 BC, as mentioned by Josephus. Because the coins of Alexander Jannaeus appear in such quantity (17 coins) on the site, Sheedy, following Smith, suggests that perhaps the city was not physically destroyed, but that its Greek political and religious institutions were destroyed. He argues that a market could have continued to function under such circumstances.

R. Carson provides commentary (pp. 31–37) on the 849 Roman Imperial coins discovered at the site, most of which predictably date to the 4th and 5th centuries AD. In the early imperial period, Greek Imperials issued by local mints provided most of Pella's coinage. Only from the Constantinian period on does Roman Imperial coinage appear at Pella in quantity.

Sheedy discusses the Greek Imperials found at Pella (pp. 39–41). It comes as little surprise that the majority of the coinage uncovered on the site was supplied by the cities of the Decapolis, among which Pella was included. Coins from nearby mints at Bostra and Aelia Capitolina were also found, along with an issue of Tyre. The latter may represent the movement of Phoenician coinage into Jordan also documented at Gerasa (p. 40). It is tempting to see this movement as a continuation of a circulation pattern originating in the Hellenistic period. Three Hellenistic Tyrian civic issues (nos.1.040–042) and two Seleucid royal coins (nos.1.009, 1.011) from Tyre were found at Pella. What is most unusual is the fact that none of Pella's own Greek Imperials (produced in AD 81/2–82/3 and 117/8) have been discovered in the excavation.

In his commentary on the Byzantine coins (pp. 43–55) Sheedy discusses the remarkable finds of bronze folles, primarily from the mint of Constantinople, rather than the small and more easily lost denominations, suggesting a peculiarity of the local economy and the delivery of coinage from the imperial capital. Generally the finds, which include issues from Anastasius I (AD 491–518) to Constantine IV (AD 654–685), mirror those recovered at Gerasa and accurately reflect local circulation patterns, despite the relatively small sample (105 coins) from Pella.

The chapter on the Islamic coins (pp. 57–66) discusses the finds from the three major periods of Islamic occupation: Umayyad (AD 660–750), 'Abbasid (AD 750–969), and Mamluk (AD 1250–1517). Particularly interesting are the two Islamic hoards (Hoard 5 and Hoard 6) found in association with skeletons, apparently victims of the great earthquake of AD 749. In the discussion of the early Islamic periods, A. Walmsley points out that the different use of gold dinars and silver dirhams affected the areas in which they were lost on the site. The latter primarily appear in Area IX, which included the central market of Umayyad Pella, while the former are most commonly found in wealthy domestic contexts. The Mamluk coins, all dating to the fourteenth century, point to a period of economic prosperity in the later Islamic village of Fahl.

The coin catalogue (pp. 67–153) is very well organized, with each coin assigned a number to indicate the typological series to which it belongs and a number to identify the individual coin: for example,

coin 3.305 represents the 305th coin in the Roman Imperial series
(series 3 in the catalogue). Each coin is fully described, with information on weight, diameter, and die axes. Particularly valuable in the
catalogue are the Pella registration numbers, findspots, hoard numbers,
and indication of corrected identifications of coins previously published
in the *Pella in Jordan* final publication series. A separate Catalogue
Reference Card is provided as an aid to understanding the various
conventions and abbreviations used throughout the catalogue. Several
extremely useful concordances appear at the end of the volume (pp.
156–174), allowing the reader to search for individual coins by hoard,
mint, findspot, and Pella registration number.

The fifteen black-and-white plates included in the volume are well
produced and show what details remain on the excavation coins with
clarity. The only possible improvement might have been the inclusion
of all the coins listed in the catalogue, rather than the selection that
appears in the plates. The present reviewer would have liked to see
the uncertain Seleucid coins 1.009 and 1.025, and others would
certainly have been interested to see the other uncertain pieces that
appear throughout the catalogue. In ancient numismatics, and particularly in archaeological numismatics, it is often the group effort of
several sets of eyes that finally discovers the true identity of trouble-
some pieces. But of course, the cost of producing plates for all 1106
excavation coins would have been prohibitive.

Despite the inability of the authors to update their manuscripts from
1994, *Pella in Jordan: The Coins* is an extremely useful volume, adding
to our knowledge of coin finds and their contexts in Jordan. The book
strongly complements T. Marot's *Las monedas del Macellum de Gerasa
(Yaras, Jordania)* (Madrid, 1998), the other major publication of excavation finds from Jordanian sites. This reviewer hopes that numismatists and archaeologists at other sites in Jordan will be encouraged by
this work to produce similar volumes to further expand understanding
of the ancient economy and history of the region.

Oliver D. Hoover
American Numismatic Society

ACQUISITIONS FOR 2000 AND 2001 IN THE AMERICAN NUMISMATIC SOCIETY COLLECTION

(Plates 9–20)

Ute Wartenberg, Peter van Alfen,
Elena Stolyarik, Sebastian Heath,
Michael Bates, and Robert W. Hoge

Introduction

In 2000 and 2001, the cabinets of the American Numismatic Society grew by a substantial 5,600 objects, all of which were acquired through donations. Although not every donor could be mentioned below, the curators express their gratitude to all of them; the generosity of donors over the last 150 years is the true source of the Society's collection of an estimated one million objects. The recent donations have significantly improved parts of the collection, which in many places remains lacking in standard coins in mint condition suitable for exhibition purposes.

The recent donations include coins of almost all periods and from all over the world, medals, paper currency, counterfeit and reproduction dies, checks, and counterfeit coins. There are some valuable study collections such as the group of Central Asian coins and banknotes (donated by Edward Allworth), a collection of Indian gold coins (donated by Lawrence Brilliant), a number of items from the SS *Central America* (donated by Mr. and Mrs. Anthony Terranova), some exceptional Greek coins donated by Arnold-Peter Weiss. A particular rarity is the $5 series of 1890 with the number A1 (donated by Paul R. Wilson). The exceptional group of Greek and Roman coins, given by Jonathan H. Kagan, although registered for the year 2002, was given in 2000 and is accordingly included below.

Ute Wartenberg

Greek

In 2000 and 2001, the Greek Department received a number of impressive gifts which are described in more detail below. Jonathan Kagan gave 24 well-preserved coins of various types. Of Prof. Edward Allworth's large gift to the Society, thirteen Parthian and Bactrian issues went into the Greek collection. Dr. Arnold-Peter Weiss again donated a number of significant finds. No less important are the contributions given by Thomas Cederlind, Arthur Houghton, Martin Huth, Herman Miller, Thomas Tesoriero, Dr. Paul Peter Urone, and an anonymous donor. We thank them all for their generosity.

Calabria

*1. Tarentum, c. 365–355 (Plate 9 no. 1)
Acc. number: 2001.21.6 (anonymous donation)
Plated didrachm, 21 mm, 6.51 g, 4:00
Obv.: Naked horseman to r.; *kantharos* beneath horse
Rev.: Taras seated to l. astride dolphin; Θ beneath dolphin; ΤΑ-ΡΑΣ
Ref: Vlasto no. 457 (this coin); Fischer-Bossert (1999) Group 41
This coins joins twelve other plated examples of fourth-century Tarentine didrachms in the ANS collection.

Bruttium

*2. Caulonia, c. 500 (Plate 9 no. 2)
Acc. number: 2002.18.4 (gift of Jonathan Kagan)
AR stater, 31 mm, 8.17 g, 12:00
Obv.: ΚΑΥΛ; naked male advancing to r., with running figure on outstretched arm; in field r. a stag
Rev.: Same type, incuse
Ref: Noe (1958) nos. 1–4
This piece appears to be from the same dies as Noe nos. 1–4. As on many examples of this coinage, there are on the reverse a series of small rectangles in sequence which merge into the border and clearly are not part of the design schema. These likely do not represent any undertype but are marks left by the border design of the reverse die as the flan was pounded wafer-thin with a series of hammer blows.

*3. Croton, c. 380–340 (Plate 9 no. 3)
Acc. number: 2000.19.1
AE trikhalkon, 30 mm, 21.28 g, 11:00

Obv.: Head of Heracles r. wearing lion's skin headdress, **KPO** to r.
Rev.: Tripod, to r. **TPI**
Ref.: *SNG ANS* 3 no. 430

Sicily

*4. Catana, c. 430 (Plate 9 no. 4)
Acc. number: 2002.18.5 (gift of Jonathan Kagan)
AR drachm, 15 mm, 3.68 g, 12:00
Obv.: Head of Silenus facing
Rev.: Head of river god Amenanus to l.; **(KATA)NAIΩN**
Ref. *SNG ANS* 3 no. 1262
The ANS now possesses two examples of this coin. The new acquisition, a much better-preserved piece than the one already in the collection (1944.100.8360), was produced from different dies.

5. Motya, c. 420–396
Acc. number: 2000.9.1 (gift of Thomas Cederlind)
AR litra, 10 mm, 0.66 g, 12:00
Obv.: Female head facing
Rev.: Crab, below Punic legend: *mtv'*
Ref.: *SNG ANS* 4 no. 508

6. Naxos, c. 420–403
Acc. number: 2000.19.2
AE onkia, 11 mm, 1.32 g
Obv.: Bearded male to r., dot border
Rev.: Ivy leaf (off flan), one pellet; **NA**
Ref.: cf. Cahn (1944) no. 148

7. Segesta, c. 470–405
Acc. number: 2000.6.1 (gift of Paul Peter Urone)
AR tetradrachm, 30 mm, 16.64 g, 6:00
Obv.: Galloping quadriga to r., female charioteer; grasshopper in exergue
Rev.: Aegestes naked, standing to r., pilos hanging behind neck, chlamys about l. arm, stick in l. hand, dog behind
Ref.: Lederer (1910) no. 9

8. Syracuse, c. 425–413
Acc. number: 2002.18.6 (gift of Jonathan Kagan)
AR tetradrachm, 29 mm, 17.16 g, 10:00
Obv.: Female head to l., opposing dolphins; ΣΥΡΑ / ΚΟΣΙΟ / N
Rev.: Quadriga to l.; opposing dolphins in exergue
Ref.: Tudeer (1913) no. 5

Macedonia

9. Amphipolis, c. 370
Acc. number: 2002.18.7 (gift of Jonathan Kagan)
AR drachm, 15 mm, 3.48 g, 9:00
Obv.: Head of Apollo, three-quarter face
Rev.: ΑΜΦ / ΙΠΟ / ΛΙΤ / ΕΩΝ on raised frame, race torch within
Ref.: Lorber (1990) Type A

10. Alexander I or Bisaltai, c. 480 or later
Acc. number: 2002.18.8 (gift of Jonathan Kagan)
AR octodrachm, 32 mm, 28.21 g
Obv.: Naked warrior beside horse to r.
Rev.: Quadripartite incuse square
Ref. *SNG ANS* 8 no. 1.
Neither the attribution nor the date of this earliest anepigraphic
series is secure; see Troxell's comments in *SNG ANS* 8.

11. Alexander III, 325–310
Acc. number: 2000.7.134 (gift of Edward Allworth)
AE uncertain, 17 mm, 5.21 g, 11:00
Obv.: Head of Heracles to r. wearing lion-skin headress
Rev.: Bow in bowcase and club; star and delta below; ΒΑΣΙ
Ref.: Price (1991) no. 394

Thrace

12. Abdera, c. 411–386
Acc. number: 2002.18.9 (gift of Jonathan Kagan)
AR tetradrachm, 24 mm, 12.44 g, 12:00
Obv.: Seated griffin to l., ΑΒΔΗ above, cicada in l. field

Rev.: Heracles seated half-right on lion skin draped over rock; ΕΠΙ
ΦΙΛΑ / ΔΟΣ
Ref.: May (1966) no. 397

*13. Dikaia, c. 530–500 (Plate 9 no. 5)
Acc. number: 2000.14.1 (gift of Herman Miller)
AR stater, 19 mm, 9.96 g
Obv.: Head of bearded Heracles to r. in lion skin
Rev.: Rough incuse square
Ref.: May (1965) series A.

14. Maroneia, c. 386–347
Acc. number: 2002.18.10 (gift of Jonathan Kagan)
AR stater, 24 mm, 10.32 g, 12:00
Obv.: Horse to l.; underneath, dog to l.
Rev.: Incuse square with grapes, ΕΠΙ Κ / ΑΛΛ / ΙΚΡΑ / ΤΕΟΣ
Ref. Schönert-Geiss (1987) no. 489

15. Tomis, post-Lysimachus, c. 190–90
Acc. number: 2000.11.1 (gift of Thomas Tesoriero)
AV stater, 19 mm, 8.31 g, 12:00
Obv.: Head of deified Alexander to r., diadem with horns of Ammon
Rev.: Athena seated on throne to l., ΒΑΣΙΛΕΩS to l., ΛΥΣΙΜΑΞΟΥ
to l.; ΤΟ under throne, ΗΡΟ in l. field
Ref.: de Callataÿ (1997) p.141

Illyricum

16. Pelagia, c. 360–350
Acc. number: 2000.13.1 (gift of Arnold-Peter Weiss)
AR tetradrachm, 20 mm, 12.48 g
Obv.: Head of Apollo, laureate, r.
Rev.: "Macedonian" shield; inscription off flan
Ref.: May (1939) pl. X no. 1, p. 170 (obv. die of Daparria 1)

Locris

17. Locri Opuntii, c. 369–338
Acc. number: 2002.18.11 (gift of Jonathan Kagan)
AR, 22 mm, 12.25 g, 12:00

Obv.: Head of goddess (Persephone?) to l.
Rev.: Locrian Ajax armed to r., helmet below, snake on shield,
ΟΠΟΝΤΙ / ΩΝ
Ref.: *BMC Central Greece* series III
Same dies as ANS 1944.100.19590, but finer.

Attica

*18. Athens, c. 525–500 (Plate 9 no. 6)
Acc. number: 2000.13.2 (gift of Arnold-Peter Weiss)
AR tetradrachm, 24 mm, 16.51 g, 5:00
Obv.: Head of Athena, r.
Rev.: Owl to r., **ΑΘΕ** to l., olive spray to r. within incuse square
Ref.: Seltman (1924) group H, no. 296

Aegina

19. Aegina, c. 535–520
Acc. number: 2000.13.3 (gift of Arnold-Peter Weiss)
AR stater, 20 mm, 12.23 g
Obv.: Sea turtle
Rev.: Rough incuse square (pre-Union Jack)
Ref.: Beer (1980) period I

Elis

20. Elis, c. 421–365
Acc. number: 2002.18.12 (gift of Jonathan Kagan)
AR stater, 22 mm, 11.16 g, 1:00
Obv.: Round shield with raised rim, on which eagle to l. standing
on serpent
Rev.: **F** / **A**, fulmen
Ref.: Seltman (1921) no. 163
Same dies (Seltman BW/δε) as ANS 1944.100.37747, but finer.

Aegean Islands

21. Naxos, c. 500
Acc. number: 2002.18.13 (gift of Jonathan Kagan)
AR stater, 22 mm, 11.67 g

Obv.: Kantharos
Rev.: Quartered square incuse
Ref.: Nicolet-Pierre (1997) no. 36 (this coin)
In her catalogue, Nicolet-Pierre, who had not seen the coin, notes
the possibility of graffiti on the reverse. No marks are present.

Mysia

22. Cyzicus, c. 475
Acc. number: 2002.18.14 (gift of Jonathan Kagan)
EL stater, 20 mm, 16.02 g
Obv.: Corinthian helmet to l., tunny below
Rev.: Quartered square incuse
Ref.: Greenwell (1887) no. 36 = Fritze (1912) pl. II, no. 36

23. Cyzicus, c. 475
Acc. number: 2002.18.15 (gift of Jonathan Kagan)
EL hecte, 10 mm, 2.66 g
Obv.: Forepart of dog to l., head turned back; behind tunny
upwards
Rev.: Quartered square incuse
Ref.: Greenwell (1887) no. 139

Lesbos

24. Mytilene, c. 350–345
Acc. number: 2002.18.16 (gift of Jonathan Kagan)
EL hecte, 10 mm, 2.54 g, 11:00
Obv.: Head of Apollo to r. wearing oak wreath
Rev.: Head of woman (Artemis?) to r. within fine square border
Ref.: Bodenstedt (1981) Em. 95.

25. Lesbos, c. 550–440
Acc. number: 2002.18.20 (gift of Jonathan Kagan)
Billon stater, 20 mm, 14.50 g
Obv.: Two facing calves' heads
Rev.: Rough incuse square
Ref.: *BMC Troas* etc. p.154

Ionia

26. Phocaea, c. 521–478
Acc. number: 2002.18.17 (gift of Jonathan Kagan)
EL hecte, 10 mm, 2.57 g
Obv.: Two seals swimming to l.
Rev.: Incuse
Ref.: Bodenstedt (1981) Em. 46

27. Teos, c. 495–478
Acc. number: 2002.18.18 (gift of Jonathan Kagan)
AR stater, 20 mm, 12.30 g
Obv.: Seated griffin to r., THI
Rev.: Quartered square incuse
Ref.: same dies as Balcer (1968) no. 28

28. Teos, c. 495–478
Acc. number: 2002.18.19 (gift of Jonathan Kagan)
AR stater, 22 mm, 11.80 g
Obv.: Seated griffin to r., leaping dog to r. below, THIO
Rev.: Quartered square incuse
Ref.: same dies as Balcer (1968) no. 27

*29. Uncertain, c. 500 (Plate 9 no. 7)
Acc. number: 2002.18.21 (gift of Jonathan Kagan)
EL stater, 13.92 g
Obv.: Lactating lioness prowling to l., head facing
Rev.: Rectangular incuse, divided by narrow band
The one previously known example of this type, from the "Field in Western Thrace" hoard (*CH* 2, 1976, 1), was tentatively attributed to Acanthus by C. Lorber (*NFA* XVIII [1987], lot 95, and XXV [1990], lot 62). More recently (Sotheby's, Zurich, 27–28 Oct. 1993, lot 653), our coin, of the same dies as the Thracian example, was given an "uncertain" Ionian attribution. No reason for this shift in the attribution is provided, but it does nevertheless seem correct: the weight is congruent with the common "Milesian" EL standard, and the lactating lioness type, quite rare, has parallels from Asia Minor. While Lorber suggested parallels, none of those offered were admittedly close to this type. One coin not

noted in her overview is a Cyzicene stater (Fritze 1912: pl. III, no. 2), showing a lactating lioness in the same pose as that here, but with a fuller mane and tail turned up over the back. The fact that Cyzicus, known for borrowing motifs from mints in Ionia, reproduced this lioness should encourage us to look elsewhere in Ionia for its origins. In the Newell collection at the ANS, an unattributed and unpublished silver piece (1967.152.436; Plate 9 no. 8) shows again a lion(ess), in a similar pose, with a fuller mane, but not obviously lactating. The reverse of this coin, a winged boar protome within a dot-bordered incuse, is a well-known type from Archaic Samos and Clazomenai. However, an attribution for this coin also is problematic since the weight, c. 16.05 g, does not easily fit within the silver weight standards of the region for the sixth and fifth centuries, particularly those of Clazomenai and Samos. The "Phocaean" EL standard of 16.05–16.30 g corresponding to a three-drachm silver system (3 drachms = c. 16.00 g) is the most obvious candidate. However, tridrachms of this system, known only from Cos, are considerably less common than the didrachms and drachms (= siglos, 5.5 g) minted elsewhere, e.g., Antandros, Lesbos, and Colophon (Cahn 1970: 185, 1975: 68). There is little else besides the weight to suggest that the coin came from Cos. Besides the numismatic evidence, two gems published by Boardman (1968: nos. 433 and 442) also show lionesses (or panthers?), one of which is lactating, in the prowling, facing pose. Boardman places these types within an East Greek (i.e., Ionian) milieu. Even with this additional comparative material, it seems best at this point to leave the attributions for both coins, the EL stater and the AR tridrachm (?), open until more examples come to light.

Caria

30. Caunos, c. 490–470
Acc. number: 2001.21.4 (anonymous donation)
AR stater, 14 24 mm, 11.76 g
Obv.: Winged deity (Iris?) to l.
Rev.: Crude incuse
Ref.: Price and Waggoner, 1975, no. 669 (this coin); cf. Konuk, no. 1

31. Pixodaros, 340–336
Acc. number: 2002.18.22 (gift of Jonathan Kagan)
AR didrachm, 20 mm, 26.93 g, 12:00
Obv.: Facing head of Apollo
Rev.: Zeus Labraundos standing, ΠΙΞΩΔΑΡΟΥ
Ref.: Hurter (1998) p.153

32. Lindos, Rhodes, c. 500
Acc. number: 2000.13.4 (gift of Arnold-Peter Weiss)
AR stater, 20 mm, 12.62 g (n.b.: a portion of the coin has been
cut away)
Obv.: Head of lion to r. within square border, mouth agape, ΛΙ
above
Rev.: Incuse square halved.
Ref.: cf. Cahn (1957) A

Lycia

*33. Phaselis, c. 550–530 (Plate 9 no. 9)
Acc. number: 2002.18.23 (gift of Jonathan Kagan)
AR stater, 17 mm, 10.92 g
Obv.: Boar-shaped ship prow to l.
Rev.: Rhomboid incuse

*34. Phaselis, c. 550–530 (Plate 9 no. 10)
Acc. number: 2002.18.24 (gift of Jonathan Kagan)
AR stater, 17 mm, 10.83 g
Obv.: Boar-shaped ship prow to r.
Rev.: Rhomboid incuse
Nos. **33** and **34** are a Phaselian type that appeared only after
the publication of Heipp-Tamer's 1993 study. Other examples
have recently appeared in commerce: Triton II, 12/98, lots 447
and 448, CNG sale 47, 9/98, lot 506 and 507, where dates of
roughly 550–530 are given. Both the crude incuse and roughly
outlined boar-shaped prow of the obverse suggest that this series
is early, likely falling in line between Heipp-Tamer's no. 2 and
no. 3. This new series will be discussed in a forthcoming article
in *AJN*.

Pamphylia

35. Side, c. 460–430
Acc. number: 2002.18.25 (gift of Jonathan Kagan)
AR stater, 16 22 mm, 10.84 g, 9:00
Obv.: Pomegranate within cable border
Rev.: Head of Athena to r.
Ref.: Atlan (1967) nos. 14–16 (same reverse die as nos. 14 and 16
= Kraay 1969, no. 6)

Cappadocia

36. Cappadocia, Ariobarzanes I, 95–62
Acc. number: 2000.7.125 (gift of Edward Allworth)
AR drachm, 17 mm, 3.90 g, 11:00
Obv.: Diademed head of Ariobarzanes r.
Rev.: Athena standing l., Nike in r. hand, spear in l., monogram Ⱥ
to l.; ΒΑΣΙΛΕΣ ΑΡΙΟΒΑΡΖΑΝΟΥ ΦΙΛΟΡΩΜΑΙΟΥ
Ref.: *BMC Galatia* 21.

Syria

*37. Hierapolis-Bambyce, c. 340–325 (Plate 9 no. 11)
Acc. number: 2000.3.1 (gift of Martin Huth)
AR didrachm, 21 mm, 7.79 g, 11:00
Obv.: Facing female head with flowing hair (in the manner of Ci-
mon's Arethusa); Aramaic "... *tr*..." to r.
Rev.: Lion attacking stag to r., winged solar disk above
Neither Mildenberg (1999) nor Seyrig (1971) discuss this reverse
type. The iconography, as on many of the coins from this city,
relates to issues from Tarsus, while the winged solar disk places
the imagery firmly within a Persian context. Mildenberg suggested that some types with strong Persian characteristics, e.g., the
king in the chariot, were struck before Alexander, which may be
the case for this coin as well. One other highly unusual feature of
this coin is the inscription on the obverse: *tau* and *resh* are clearly
visible as are portions of other characters on either side of the
pair, which could be *'ayin*. If so, the full legend is likely to be
'tr'th (Atarateh = Atargatis), the primary goddess of the local cult

whose name is commonly found on the coins. However, on none of the published examples does her name appear alone in conjunction with the Arethusa-type obverse. On coins published by both Mildenberg (no. 1) and Seyrig (no. 4a), an abbreviated form of her name, along with the name of her consort, Hadad, appears on Arethusa-types: *hdd w'th* ("Hadad and Ateh").

38. Seleucus I, Seleucia ad Tigrim, c. 286/85
Acc. number: 2002.18.26 (gift of Jonathan Kagan)
AR tetradrachm, 26 mm, 16.11 g, 12:00
Obv.: Laureate head of Zeus to r., dot border
Rev.: **ΒΑΣΙΛΕΩΣ ΣΕΛΕΥΚΟΥ**, Athena in chariot drawn r. by four horned elephants, anchor above, pentalpha, theta
Ref.: *ESM* 1938 Series II, Type O

Palestine

39. Alexander III, Ake, 326–325
Acc. number: 2000.7.135 (gift of Edward Allworth)
AR tetradrachm, 25 mm, 16.16 g, 7:00
Obv.: Head of Heracles wearing lion's skin headdress to r.
Rev.: Zeus enthroned l. holding eagle and scepter; **ΑΛΕΞΑΝΔΡΟΥ**; Phoenician *'k* + numeral (= 21) below arm
Ref.: Price (1991) no. 3252

40. Judaea, Alexander Jannaeus, 103–76
Acc. number: 2000.7.132 (gift of Edward Allworth)
AE prutah, 14 mm, 2.31 g
Obv.: Pomegranate flanked by cornuacopiae
Rev.: Paleo-Hebrew inscription (*yhwn | tnhk | dwlwḥb | hyh*, "Yehonatan the High Priest and the Council of the Jews" surrounded by wreath
Ref.: *SNG ANS* 6 no. 112 (same reverse die?)

Parthia

41. Parthia, Darius?, 88–77
Acc. number: 2000.7.143
AE tetrachalkos, 16 mm, 2.82 g, 12:00

Obv.: Diademed and bearded king l., crowned by Nike from behind

Rev.: Horse prancing r.; inscription worn (ΒΑΣΙΛΕΩΣ ΜΕΓΑΛΟΥ ΑΡΣΑΚΟΥ ΦΙΛΟΠΑΤΟΡΟΣ ΕΥΕΡΓΕΤΟΥ ΕΠΙΦΑΝΟΥΣ ΦΙΛΛΗΝΟΣ)

Ref.: Sellwood (1980) type 36.19

42. Parthia, Phraates IV, 37–2
Acc. number: 2000.7.142 (gift of Edward Allworth)
AE lepton, 10 mm, 1.09 g, 12:00
Obv.: Diademed and bearded bust of king l.
Rev.: Athena standing l. holding spear and shield
Ref.: *SNG Cop* no. 143; Sellwood (1980) type 52.39

*43. Parthia, Artabanus II, Ecbatana, 10 BC–AD 38 (Plate 9 no. 12)
Acc. number: 2000.7.133 (gift of Edward Allworth)
AR drachm, 20 mm, 3.81 g, 12:00
Obv.: Diademed bust of king, dot border
Rev.: Parthian archer enthroned r. holding bow; monogram Ⱥ; ΒΑΣΙΛΕΩΣ ΒΑΣΙΛΕΩΝ ΑΡΣΑΚΟΥ ΕΥΕΡΓΕΤΟΥ ΔΙΚΑΙΟΝ ΕΠΙΦΑΝΟΥΣ ΦΙΛΕΛΛΗΝΟΣ
Ref.: Sellwood (1980) type 63.6

Bactria

44. Bactria, Eucratides I, 169–159
Acc. number: 2000.7.140 (gift of Edward Allworth)
AE, 20 mm square, 7.71 g, 12:00
Obv.: Helmeted head of Eucratides r., branch; ΒΑΣΙΛΕΩΣ ΜΕΓΑΛΟΥ ΕΥΚΡΑΤΙΔΟΥ
Rev.: Dioscuri on horseback riding r.; Kharoshti legend
Ref.: *SNG ANS Bactria* no. 556

45. Bactria, Menander I, 160–145
Acc. number: 2000.7.137
AR drachm, 16 mm, 2.09 g, 12:00
Obv.: Diademed bust of Menander wearing aegis and brandishing spear; ΒΑΣΙΛΕΩΣ ΣΩΤΗΡΟΣ ΜΕΝΑΝΔΡΟΥ

Rev.: Athena brandishing shield and thunderbolt r., monogram ⊀
to l.; Kharoshti legend
Ref.: *SNG ANS Bactria* no. 702

46. Bactria, Menander I, 160–145
Acc. number: 2000.7.136 (gift of Edward Allworth)
AR drachm, 17 mm, 2.49 g, 12:00
Obv.: Diademed bust of Menander wearing aegis and brandishing
spear; ΒΑΣΙΛΕΩΣ ΣΩΤΗΡΟΣ ΜΕΝΑΝΔΡΟΥ
Rev.: Athena brandishing shield and thunderbolt r., monogram ⋈
to l.; Kharoshti legend
Ref.: *SNG ANS Bactria* no. 802

47. Bactria, Antimachus II, 160–155
Acc. number: 2000.7.139 (gift of Edward Allworth)
AR drachm, 16 mm, 2.19 g, 12:00
Obv.: Nike standing l., holding palm branch; ΒΑΣΙΛΕΩΣ ΝΙΚΗΦΟ-
ΡΟΥ ΑΝΤΙΜΑΞΟΥ
Rev.: Horseman riding r.; monogram ⋈ to l.; Kharoshti legend
Ref.: *SNG ANS Bactria* no. 414

48. Bactria, Apollodotus I, 160–150
Acc. number: 2000.7.138 (gift of Edward Allworth)
AR drachm, 17 mm square, 2.36 g, 12:00
Obv.: Elephant r.; ΒΑΣΙΛΕΩΣ ΑΠΟΛΛΟΔΟΤΟΥ ΣΩΤΗΡΟΣ; mono-
gram: Ⱥ
Rev.: Humped bull r.; Kharoshti legend
Ref.: *SNG ANS Bactria* no. 303

49. Armenia, Tigranes II, 95–56
Acc. number: 2000.7.141 (gift of Edward Allworth)
AE, 19 mm, 5.26 g, 12:00
Obv.: Bust of king r. wearing Armenian tiara
Rev.: Tyche of Antioch seated r. on rock; Orontes swims below;
ΒΑΣΙΛΕΩS ΒΑΣΙΛΕΩΝ ΤΙΓΡΑΝΟΥ

Susiana

*50. Susiana, Kamniskires I, Elymais, 147–140 (Plate 9 no. 13)
Acc. Number: 2000.50.1 (gift of Arthur Houghton)

AR tetradrachm, 26 mm, 14.78 g, 3:00
Obv.: Diademed head r., monogram Ā to l.
Rev.: Apollo seated l. on omphalos testing arrow, holding bow;
(ΒΑΣΙΛΕΩΣ) ΚΑΜΝΙΣΚΙΡΟΥ ΝΙΚΕΦΟΡΟΥ
Ref.: Le Rider (1965) p. 75, pl. VIII

Carthage

*51. Carthage, c. 325 (Plate 9 no. 14)
Acc. number: 2002.18.27 (gift of Jonathan Kagan)
AR tetradrachm, 24 mm, 17.08 g, 6:00
Obv.: Female head to l.
Rev.: Leaping horse, palm tree behind
Ref.: Visonà (1998) no. 10

REFERENCES

Atlan, S. 1967. Sidenin milattan önce V. ve IV. yüzyıl sikkerleri üzer-
inde araştırmalar (Untersuchungen über die sidetischen Münzen des
V. und IV. Jahrhunderts v. Chr.). Ankara.

Balcer, J. M. 1968. The early silver coinage of Teos. *Revue Suisse de
Numismatique* 47:5–50.

Beer, L. B. 1980. *The coinage of Aegina: a chronological reappraisal
based on hoards and technical studies.* D. Phil. thesis, Oxford University.

Boardman, J. 1968. *Archaic Greek gems: schools and artists in the sixth
and early fifth centuries B.C.* Evanston: Northwestern University
Press.

Bodenstedt, F. 1981. *Die Elektronmünzen von Phokaia und Mytilene.*
Tübingen: Ernst Wasmuth.

Caccamo Caltabiano, M. *La monetazione di Messana.* Berlin: W. de
Gruyter.

Cahn, H. 1944. *Die Münzen der sizilischen Stadt Naxos.* Basel.

—. 1957. Die archaischen Silberstatere von Lindos. In: K. Schauen-
burg, ed., *Charites: Festschrift Ernst Langlotz,* pp. 18–26. Bonn:
Athenäum-Verlag.

—. 1970. *Knidos: die Münzen des sechsten und des fünften Jahrhunderts
v. Chr.* Berlin: W. de Gruyter.

—. 1975. *Kleine Schriften zur Münzkunde und Archäologie*. Basel: Archäologischer Verlag.

de Callataÿ, F. 1997. *L'histoire des guerres mithridatiques vue par les monnaies*. Louvain-la-Neuve: Séminaire de Numismatique Marcel Hoc.

Fischer-Bossert, W. 1999. *Chronologie die Didrachmenprägung von Tarent, 510–280 v. Chr.* Berlin: W. de Gruyter.

Fritze, H. von. 1912. Die Elektronprägung von Kyzikos. *Nomisma* 7.

Greenwell, W. 1887. The electrum coinage of Cyzicus. London: Reprint from *Numismatic Chronicle*.

Heipp-Tamer, C. 1993. *Die Münzprägung der lykischen Stadt Phaselis in griechischer Zeit*. Saarbrücken: Saarbrücker Druck und Verlag.

Hurter, S. 1998. The 'Pixadaros hoard': a summary. In: R. Ashton and S. Hurter, eds., *Studies in Greek numismatics in memory of Martin Jessop Price,* pp. 147–154. London: Spink.

Konuk, K. 1998. The early coinage of Kaunos. In: R. Ashton and S. Hurter, eds., *Studies in Greek numismatics in memory of Martin Jessop Price,* pp. 197–223. London: Spink.

Kraay, C. 1969. Notes on the mint of Side in the fifth century B.C. *Numismatic Chronicle* 9:15–20.

Lederer, P. 1910. *Tetradrachmenprägung von Segesta*. Munich.

Le Rider, G. 1965. Suse sous les Séleucides et les Parthes. Paris: Paul Geuthner.

Lorber, C. 1990. Amphipolis: the civic coinage in silver and gold. Los Angeles: Numismatic Fine Arts International.

May, J. M. F., C.M. Kraay and G.K. Jenkins, eds. 1966. *The coinage of Abdera (540–345 B.C.)*. London: Royal Numismatic Society.

May, J. M. F. 1939. *The coinage of Damastion and the lesser coinages of the Illyro-Paeonian region*. London: Oxford University Press.

—. 1965. The coinage of Dikaia-by-Abdera, c. 540/35–476-5 B.C. *Numismatic Chronicle* 5:1–25.

Mildenberg, L. 1999. A note on the coinage of Hieroplis-Bambyce. In: M. Amadry and S. Hurter, eds., *Travaux de numismatique grecque offerts à Georges Le Rider,* pp. 277–284. London: Spink.

Noe, S. P. 1958. *The coinage of Caulonia*. ANS Numismatic Studies 9. New York: American Numismatic Society.

Newell, E. T. 1938. *The coinage of the eastern Seleucid mints from Seleucus I to Antiochus III.* ANS Numismatic Studies 1. New York: American Numismatic Society.

Nicolet-Pierre, H. 1997. Naxos (Cyclades) archaïque, monnaie et histoire: la frappe des "Canthares", de la fin du VIe siècle. *Numismatica e Antichità Classica* 26:63–121.

Price, M. 1991. *The coinage in the name of Alexander the Great and Philip Arrhidaeus.* Zurich/London: Swiss Numismatic Society and British Museum Press.

Price, M. and N. Waggoner. 1975. *Archaic Greek coinage: the "Asyut" hoard.* London: V. C. Vecchi.

Schönert-Geiss, E. 1987. *Griechisches Münzwerk: die Münzprägung von Maroneia.* Berlin: Akademie-Verlag.

Sellwood, D. 1980. *An introduction to the coinage of Parthia,* 2nd ed. London: Spink and Son.

Seltman, C. T. 1921. *The temple coins of Olympia.* Cambridge: Bowes & Bowes.

—. 1924. *Athens: its history and coinage.* Cambridge: Cambridge University Press.

Seyrig, H. 1971. Monnaies hellénistiques. *Revue Numismatique* (6th ser.) 13:7–21.

Tudeer, L. O. Th. 1913. *Die Tetradrachmenprägung von Syrakus in der Periode der signierenden Künstler.* Berlin: W. Pormetter.

Visonà, P. 1998. Carthaginian Coinage in Perspective. *American Journal of Numismatics* 10:1–27.

Vlasto, M. P; compiled by O. E. Ravel. 1947. *Descriptive catalogue of the collection of Tarentine coins formed by M. P. Vlasto.* London: Spink and Son.

PETER VAN ALFEN

ROMAN, ROMAN PROVINCIAL, AND BYZANTINE

In 2000–2001 new coins were acquired by the Roman and Byzantine Department through several generous gifts. One of the rather rare types of the silver denarius of Julia Domna was donated by Herbert L. Kreindler (2000.4.1). Caroline Damsky donated an interesting selection of coins from the Roman Republic to the early period of the Byzantine Empire (2000.5.1–2000.5.31). An important donation from Richard Gordon McAlee included unpublished coins: a quadrans of Vespasian from Antioch (2000.12.1) and a bronze tetradrachm of Aurelian from the Alexandria mint (2000.12.2). The Society's collection of Roman tesserae benefited from the gift of two lead tokens (2000.26.1, 2000.26.2) donated by Oliver D. Hoover. A large selection of modern replicas of Roman dies and strikings made from them, produced by Peter Rosa, were donated by Wayne G. Sayles (2000.17.—; 2001.1.—).

ROMAN

1.   C. Serveilius M.f., 136 BC, Rome
Acc. number: 2000.5.4 (gift of Caroline H. Damsky)
AR denarius, 18 mm, 3.91 g, 6:00
Obv.: Helmeted head of Roma r., wearing necklace of pendants; behind wreath; border of dots; ✕ ROMA
Rev.: Dioscuri riding apart with spears reversed; border of dots; C SERVEILI·M·F
Ref.: Crawford 239.1; Sydenham 525

*2.   L. Lucretius Trio, 76 BC, Rome (Plate 10 no. 1)
Acc. number: 2000.5.2 (gift of Caroline H. Damsky)
AR denarius, 18 mm, 3.95 g, 5:00
Obv.: Laureate head of Neptune r. with trident over shoulder; behind, control-mark; border of dots
Rev.: Winged boy on dolphin speeding r.; L · LVCRETI / TRIO
Ref.: Crawford 390.2; Sydenham 784

*3.   Cn. (Cornelius) Lentulus, 76–75 BC, Spain? (Plate 10 no. 2)
Acc. number: 2000.5.1 (gift of Caroline H. Damsky)
AR denarius, 20 mm, 3.82 g, 6:00
Obv.: Genius Populi Romani bust r., scepter over shoulder; G·P·R
Rev.: Scepter, globe, and rudder; EX S·C LENT·CVR ✕ FL
Ref.: Crawford 393.1b; Sydenham 752a, Cornelia 55

4.   M. Claudius Marcellus, 50 BC, Rome
Acc. number: 2000.5.3 (gift of Caroline H. Damsky)
AR denarius, 17 mm, 3.64 g, 4:00

Obv.: Head of M. Claudius Marcellus r.; behind, triskeles; **MARCEL-LINVS**

Rev.: Male figure carrying trophy into temple; **MARCELLVS COS QVINQ**

Ref.: Crawford 439.1; Sydenham 1147

5. Drusus, 22–23 AD, Rome
   Acc. number: 2000.5.5 (gift of Caroline H. Damsky)
   AE dupondius, 29 mm, 14.93 g, 12:00
   Obv.: Bust of Pietas (Livilla?) diademed and veiled r.; **PIETAS**
   Rev.: **DRVSVS CAESAR TI AVGVSTI F TR POT ITER** surrounding **S·C**
   Ref.: *BMC* 98; *RIC* 43

6. Claudius, 49–50 AD, Lugdunum
   Acc. number: 2000.5.6 (gift of Caroline H. Damsky)
   AR denarius, 18 mm, 3.61 g, 11:00
   Obv.: Laureate head r.; **TI CLAVD CAESAR·AVG P M TR P·VIIII·IMP· XVI**
   Rev.: Nemesis walking r., preceded by a serpent; **PACI AVGVSTAE**
   Ref.: *BMC* 52; *RIC* 47

*7. Claudius, 41–50 AD, Rome (Plate 10 no. 3)
   Acc. number: 2000.5.7 (gift of Caroline H. Damsky)
   AE sestertius, 35 mm, 27.27 g, 7:00
   Obv.: Laureate head r.; **TI CLAVDIVS CAESAR AVG P M TR P IMP**
   Rev.: Triumphal arch surmounted by an equestrian statue r. between two trophies; **NERO CLAVDIVS DRVSVS GERMAN IMP/ S C**
   Ref.: *BMC* 121; *RIC* 98

8. Claudius, 41–50 AD, Rome
   Acc. number: 2000.5.8 (gift of Caroline H. Damsky)
   AE dupondius, 30 mm, 17.14 g, 6:00
   Obv.: Head of Claudius l.; **TI CLAVDIVS CAESAR AVG P M TR P IMP**
   Rev.: Ceres, veiled and draped, seated l. on ornamented throne, holding grain stalks in r. and transverse torch in l.; **CERES AVGVS-TA / S·C**
   Ref.: *BMC* 136; *RIC* 94

9. Antonia, 41–45 AD, Lugdunum
    Acc. number: 2000.5.9 (gift of Caroline H. Damsky)
    AR denarius, 18 mm, 3.65 g, 2:00
    Obv.: Bust draped r. wearing a wreath of grain stalks, hair in a long plait behind; **ANTONIA AVGVSTA**
    Rev.: Two long flaming torches linked by ribbon; **SACERDOS DIVI AVGVSTI**
    Ref.: *BMC* 114; *RIC* 68
    Same obv. die as Canessa, 28 June 1923 (Caruso), 174 (AV)

10. Vespasian, 77–78 AD, Rome
    Acc. number: 2000.5.10 (gift of Caroline H. Damsky)
    AR denarius, 18 mm, 3.16 g, 6:00
    Obv.: Laureate head l.; **IMP CAESAR VESPASIANVS AVG**
    Rev.: Prow r.; above, star of eight rays; **COS VIII**
    Ref.: *BMC* 211; *RIC* 108

*11. Vespasian, 74 AD, Antioch (Plate 10 no. 4)
    AE quadrans, 18 mm, 2.74 g, 6:00
    Acc. number: 2000.12.1 (gift of Richard Gordon McAlee)
    Obv.: Laureate head l.; **IMP VESP AVG**
    Rev.: Winged caduceus; **PON TR POT**
    Unpublished issue.
    Ref.: *BMC* 794v; RPC 1989 v

*12. Domitian under Vespasian, AD 71, Ephesus (Plate 10 no. 5)
    Acc. number: 2002.18.2
    AR denarius, 17.5 mm, 3.41 g, 6:00
    Obv.: Bust of Domitian r., cuirassed with aegis and draped, head bare; **DOMITIANVS CAESAR AVG F**
    Rev.: Female bust r., draped and turreted; **PACI ORB TERR AVG**; **ΕΦΕ** in exergue.
    Ref.: *RPC2* 849 (same dies as no. 3 from Vienna), *BMCRE* 474, *RIC* 350.

13. Vespasian Divus, 80–81 AD, Rome
    Acc. number: 2000.5.11 (gift of Caroline H. Damsky)
    AR denarius, 18 mm, 3.25 g, 6:00
    Obv.: Laureate head r.; **DIVVS AVGVSTVS VESPASIANVS**

Rev.: Quadriga l. with richly ornamented cart in form of temple; EX S C

Ref.: *BMC* 119; *RIC* 60

14. Titus and Vespasian Divus, 80–81 AD, Rome
    Acc. number: 2000.5.12 (gift of Caroline H. Damsky)
    AE sestertius, 33 mm, 22.90 mm, 6:00
    Obv.: Vespasian, holding scepter and Victory seated r. in a quadriga of elephants; DIVO / AVG / VESPAS / SPQR
    Rev.: IMP T CAES DIVI VESP F AVG PM TR P PP COS VIII surrounding S C
    Ref.: *BMC* 222; *RIC* 144

15. Titus/Drusus, 80–81 AD, Rome
    Acc. number: 2000.5.13 (gift of Caroline H. Damsky)
    AE as, 28 mm, 11.59 g, 6:00
    Obv.: Head of Drusus, bare, l.; DRVSVS CAESAR TI AVG F DIVI AVG N
    Rev.: IMP T CAES DIVI VESP F AVG REST surrounding S C
    Ref.: *BMC* 286; *RIC* 216
    Published in *CNR* 11, p. 4, 56

16. Titus/Germanicus, 80–81 AD, Rome
    Acc. number: 2000.5.14 (gift of Caroline H. Damsky)
    AE as, 28 mm, 10.42 g, 6:00
    Obv.: Head of Germanicus, bare, l.; GERMANICVS CAESAR TI AVG F DIVI AVG N
    Rev.: IMP T CAES DIVI VESP F AVG REST surrounding S C
    Ref.: *BMC* 293; *RIC* 228

17. Titus/Claudius, 80–81 AD, Rome
    Acc. number: 2000.5.15 (gift of Caroline H. Damsky)
    AE as, 28 mm, 10.58 g, 6:00
    Obv.: Head of Claudius, bare, l.; TI CLAVDIVS CAESAR AVG P M TR P IMP P P
    Rev.: Minerva, draped and helmeted, advancing r., brandishing javelin in r. hand and holding round shield in l.; IMP T VESP AVG REST / S C
    Ref.: *BMC* 300; *RIC* 241

18. Nerva, 97 AD, Rome
Acc. number: 2000.5.16 (gift of Caroline H. Damsky)
AE as, 27 mm, 11.04 g, 6:00
Obv.: Laureate head r.; IMP NERVA CAES AVG P M TR P II COS III
P P
Rev.: Fortuna standing l. holding rudder in r. and cornucopiae in
l.; FORTVNA AVGVST / S C
Ref.: *BMC* 143; *RIC* 98

19. Trajan, 103–111 AD, Rome
Acc. number: 2000.5.17 (gift of Caroline H. Damsky)
AR denarius, 18 mm, 3.00 g, 7:00
Obv.: Bust of Trajan, laureate, r., with drapery on l. shoulder,
front and back; IMP TRAIANO AVG GER DAC P M TR P
Rev.: Danuvius (the Danube), naked to waist, cloak floating out
behind, reclining l. on rocks, head r., placing r. hand on prow of
ship, l. elbow resting on rock; reeds over l. and r. arms; COS V P P
S P Q R OPTIMO PRINC; DANVVIVS in exergue
Ref.: *BMC* 395; *RIC* 100

20. Trajan, 106–111 AD, Rome
Acc. number: 2000.5.18 (gift of Caroline H. Damsky)
AE sestertius, 32 mm, 27.56 g, 6:00
Obv.: Bust of Trajan laureate r., with drapery on l. shoulder; IMP
CAES NERVAE TRAIANO AVG GER DAC P M TR P COS V P P
Rev.: Arabia draped, standing front, head l., holding branch in r.
hand over camel. l., half hidden behind her and bundle of canes
(?) over l. arm in l.; SPQR OPTIMO PRINCIPI; ARAB ADQVIS in
exergue; S C flanking figure
Ref.: *BMC* 877; *RIC* 466

21. Trajan, 115–116 AD, Rome
Acc. number: 2000.5.19 (gift of Caroline H. Damsky)
AE sestertius, 33 mm, 25.31 g, 6:00
Obv.: Bust of Trajan laureate r., draped; IMP CAES NER TRAIANO
OPTIMO AVG DAC GER DAC P M TR P COS VI P P

Rev.: Trajan, in military dress, seated r. on high platform on l.; by him stand two officers; in front of him stand an officer and four soldiers whom he is haranguing; IMPERATOR VIIII / S C
Ref.: *BMC* 1019; *RIC* 657

22. Hadrian, 124–128 AD, Rome
Acc. number: 2000.5.20 (gift of Caroline H. Damsky)
AR denarius, 19 mm, 3.46 g, 6:00
Obv.: Bust laureate r. with drapery on l. shoulder; HADRIANVS AVGVSTVS
Rev.: Hercules seated r. on cuirass holding club which rests on shield in r. and distaff in l.; COS III
Ref.: *BMC* 340; *RIC* 149

23. Hadrian, 134–138 AD, Rome
Acc. number: 2000.5.21 (gift of Caroline H. Damsky)
AE sestertius, 33 mm, 21.85 g, 6:00
Obv.: Bare head r.; HADRIANVS AVG COS III PP
Rev.: Pax seated l. on high-backed throne holding olive branch in r. and transverse scepter in l.; PAX AVG / S C
Ref.: *BMC* 1529; *RIC* 770
Same obverse die as *HCC* 546, which has same reverse type

*24. Hadrian, 128–132 AD, Sardis (Plate 10 no. 6)
Acc. number: 2000.5.22 (gift of Caroline H. Damsky)
AR cistophorus, 27 mm, 10.78 g, 6:00
Obv.: Bare head r.; HADRIANVS AVGVSTVS P P
Rev.: Cult image of Kore facing, grain stalks at l., grain stalk and poppy at r.; COS III
Ref.: *BMC* 1075, Metcalf 47
Obverse die is Metcalf 47.10; reverse die is unrecorded by Metcalf. The obverse is overstruck on a reverse of Augustus, undertype uncertain.

25. Antoninus Pius, 145–161 AD, Rome
Acc. number: 2000.5.23 (gift of Caroline H. Damsky)
AR denarius, 19 mm, 3.45 g, 7:00
Obv.: Laureate head r.; ANTONINVS AVG PIVS P P

Rev.: Winged thunderbolt lying horizontal on draped throne; COS IIII

Ref.: *BMC* 536

26. Antoninus Pius, 138 AD, Rome
    Acc. number: 2000.5.24 (gift of Caroline H Damsky)
    AE sestertius, 22 mm, 25.58 g, 5:00
    Obv.: Bare head r.; IMP T AELIVS CAESAR ANTONINVS
    Rev.: Pietas standing l., holding up r. hand over flaming altar and holding box of incense in l.; TRIB POT COS / PIETAS
    Ref.: *BMC* 1943; *RIC* 1083a

27. Antoninus Pius, 147–148 AD, Rome
    Acc. number: 2000.5.25 (gift of Caroline H. Damsky)
    AE sestertius, 32 mm, 26.70 g, 6:00
    Obv.: Laureate head r.; ANTONINVS AVG PIVS P P TR P XI
    Rev.: Annona standing l., holding grain stalks over modius in r. and anchor on ground in l.; ANNO-NA AVG / S C / COS IIII
    Ref.: *BMC* 1807; *RIC* 840

*28. Antoninus Pius, Alexandria, year 187 = AD 153/54 (Plate 10 no. 7)
    Acc. number: 2001.14.1
    AE obol, 19 mm, 3.10 g, 12:00
    Obv.: Agathodaemon r, crescent at left, start to right.
    Rev.: Uraeus r.; LI Z
    An apparently unpublished type.

29. Marcus Aurelius, 176–177 AD, Rome
    Acc. number: 2000.5.26 (gift of Caroline H. Damsky)
    AR denarius, 17 mm, 3.26 g, 12:00
    Obv.: Laureate head r.; M ANTONINVS AVG GERM SARM
    Rev.: Pile of arms: cuirass, hexagonal and oval shields, helmet, vexillum, carnyces, spears; TR P XXXI IMP VIII COS III P P / DE SARM
    Ref.: *BMC* 740; *RIC* 367

30. Faustina II, 161–176 AD, Rome
    Acc. number: 2000.5.27 (gift of Caroline H. Damsky)

AE sestertius, 32 mm, 25.53 g; 12:00

Obv.: Draped bust r.; **FAVSTINA AVGVSTA**

Rev.: Cybele seated r. on throne, resting l. on drum, between two lions; **MATRI MAGNAE / S C**

Ref.: *BMC* 932; *RIC* 16

31. Commodus, 190–191 AD, Rome
Acc. number: 2000.5.28 (gift of Caroline H. Damsky)
AR denarius, 16 mm, 2.50 g, 6:00
Obv.: Laureate head r.; **M COMM ANT P FEL AVG BRIT P P**
Rev.: Apollo laureate, in long robe to ankles, standing front, head r. holding plectrum in lowered r. hand and lyre, resting on column r., in l.; **APOL PAL P M TR P XVI COS VI**
Ref.: *BMC* 292; *RIC* 218

32. Commodus, 192 AD, Rome
Acc. number: 2000.5.29 (gift of Caroline H. Damsky)
AR denarius, 17 mm, 3.26 g, 6:00
Obv.: Laureate head r.; **L AEL AVREL COMM AVG P FEL**
Rev.: Fides Militum standing front, holding vertical standard and cornucopiae; star in r. field; **P M TR P XVII IMO VIII COS VII P P**
Ref.: *BMC* 317; *RIC* 233

*33. Julia Domna, 196–211 AD, Rome (Plate 10 no. 8)
Acc. number: 2000.4.1 (gift of Herbert L. Kreindler)
AR denarius, 18 mm, 3.27 g, 6:00
Obv.: Draped bust r.; **IVLIA AVGVSTA**
Rev.: Julia Domna standing l., sacrificing out of patera over flaming altar with r. and holding box with lid open in l.; to l., two standards set; **MATRI CASTRORVM**
Rare issue.
Ref.: *BMC* 164.57v

34. Geta, 203 AD, Rome
Acc. number: 2000.5.30 (gift of Caroline H. Damsky)
AR denarius, 19 mm, 3.54 g, 12:00
Obv.: Draped bust r.; **P SEPTIMIVS GETA CAES**
Rev.: Minerva standing front, head l., holding spear in l. and shield on ground in r.; **PONTIF COS**
Ref.: *BMC* 446; *RIC* 34b

*35. Pupienus, 238 AD, Rome (Plate 10 no. 9)
Acc. number: 2002.1 8.1 (gift of Jonathan Kagan)
AE sestertius, 29 mm, 18.98 g, 1:00
Obv.: Laureate, draped, and cuirassed bust r.; IMP CAES M CLOD PVPIENVS AVG
Rev.: Victory advancing l., holding wreath and palm; VICTORIA AVGG / S C
Ref.: *RIC* 23a

*36. Aurelian, 272/273 AD (Year 4), Alexandria (Plate 10 no. 10)
Acc. number: 2000.12.2 (gift of Richard Gordon McAlee)
AE tetradrachm, 20 mm, 6.92 g, 12:00
Obv.: Laureate bust r.; A K L ΔOM AYPEΛIANOC
Rev.: Eagle standing r., wreath in beak; L Δ
Unpublished issue.
Ref.: Dattari (1901) no. 5482; Milne (1927) no. 4390

*37. Lead token, second to third century AD (Plate 10 no. 11)
Acc. number: 2000.26.1 (gift of Oliver D. Hoover)
PB erotic tessera, 14 mm, 3.34 g, 3:00
Obv.: Male genitals
Rev.: Two-tined fork, tines r.
Ref.: Rostovtseff (1903a, 1903b, 1905); Kotansky (1979) p. 4; Buttrey (1973); Bateson (1991)

*38. Lead token, second to third century AD (Plate 10 no. 12)
Acc. number: 2000.26.2 (gift of Oliver D. Hoover)
PB tessera, 13 × 14 mm, 3.46 g, 12:00
Obv.: Victory advancing r. holding wreath in r. and palm in l.
Rev.: Wreath
Ref: Rostovtseff (1899) p. 295, t. VIII no. 9, (1903a) pp. 65, 88–89, 97, (1903b) no. 1913
According to M. Rostovtseff's classification this type has been classified as "uncertain tessarae", the function of which has not been determined

39. 168 replica dies of Roman coins by Peter Rosa
Acc. number: 2000.17.— (gift of Wayne G. Sayles)
Ref.: Sayles (2001)

40. 223 replicas of Roman coins by Peter Rosa
Acc. number: 2001.1.— (gift of Wayne G. Sayles)
Ref.: Sayles (2001)

ELENA STOLYARIK AND SEBASTIAN HEATH

ROMAN PROVINCIAL

The Society's collection of Roman provincial coins was most significantly enriched by Wayne Sayles' donation of 30 coins of Anazarbus, which was accompanied by a fine piece from Tarsus. Ziegler's 1993 die-study illuminated the detail of the former series and the Sayles gift nicely complements the coins already at the ANS. Caroline Damsky added four coins, including a very well preserved coin of Bizya struck under Philip I (no. 1) and a rare small denomination bronze of Aemilianus from Parium (no. 6). An anonymous donor added the Society's first coin of Asopus in the Peloponnese (no. 4), a bronze of Nero from Bargasa in Caria (no. 7), a coin of Anazarbus in Cilicia that required a very minor correction to *RPC2* (no. 13), and other interesting specimens. This same donation also included a coin previously in the Weber and Lockett collections (no. 8), the Lindgren collection (no. 10), and one from the Mabbott sale (no. 46). Finally, two Judean coins from the Allworth donation (nos. 47 and 48), which mainly consisted of Islamic coins, complete the additions for 2000 and 2001. Taken as a whole, Roman provincial coinage is a vast subject so that no single collection can be comprehensive. That said, the Society welcomes the opportunity to fill some of the gaps in its cabinet and is grateful to these donors for their generosity.

Thrace

*1. Bizya, Philip I (Plate 10 no. 13)
Acc. number: 2000.5.34 (gift of Caroline H. Damsky)
AE, 38 mm, 40.34 g, 7:00
Obv.: Laureate, draped, and cuirassed bust of Philip r.; AVT M IOVΛ ΦΙΛΛΙΠΟΣ AVΓ
Rev.: Man and woman reclining on couch, attendant with right hand on amphora at left, with tank hanging from branch above;

at right, forepart of prancing horse, shield above scene; BIZVH-
NΩN in exergue
Ref.: Jurukova no. 133

*2. Pautalia, Commodus (Plate 11 no. 1)
Acc. number: 2000.5.35 (gift of Caroline H. Damsky)
AE, 18 mm, 4.78 g, 7:00
Obv.: Laureate bust of Commodus r.; KAI KOMO ...
Rev.: Three-quarters view of tetrastyle temple, cult statue of As-
clepius within, single tree to each side; ΟΥΛΠΙΑΣ ΠΑΥΤΑΛΙΑ
Ref.: Price and Trell no. 102

Pontus

*3. Amasia, Caracalla, year 208 = 205/6 (Plate 11 no. 2)
Acc. number: 2000.5.33 (gift of Caroline H. Damsky)
AE, 30 mm, 15.12 g, 7:00
Obv.: Laureate, draped, and cuirassed bust of Caracalla r.;
...ΑΝΤΩΝΙΝΟC
Rev.: Tyche standing l. holding anchor in r. and cornucopiae in l.;
ΑΔ CEY ΑΝ[Τ ΑΜ]ΑCΙΑC ΜΗΤ ΝΕ ΠΡ Π / ΕΤ CΗ in field
Ref.: *RGA* T.1 f.1, p.65, no. 65 (2nd ed.). See *RPC2*, p. 237 for
calculating Amasia's era from 3/2 BC.

Lakonia

*4. Asopus, Caracalla (Plate 11 no. 3)
Acc. number: 2001.21.13 (anonymous donation)
AE, 23 mm, 5.27 g, 2:00
Obv.: Laureate, draped, and cuirassed bust of Caracalla r.; ...ΩΝΕ-
ΝΟΣ
Rev.: Tyche standing l., pouring out patera in extended right
hand, holding cornucopiae in left; ...CΩ ΠΕ ΤΗΩΝ
Ref.: Mionnet II. p. 225 no. 78; cf. Grunauer von Hoerschelmann
(1982).
This is the first coin of Asopus to enter the ANS collection.

Mysia

*5. Cyzicus, mid to late second century (Plate 11 no. 4)
Acc. number: 2001.21.7 (anonymous donation)

AE, 30 mm, 14.48 g, 6:00

Obv.: Diademed head of city-founder r.; **KYZIKOC**

Rev.: Flaming altar flanked by torches each with snake entwined; **KYZIKHNΩN NEOKOPΩ**

Ref.: von Fritze (1917) V.6 for obverse die, V.7e for reverse type.

*6. Parium, Aemilianus (Plate 11 no. 5)

Acc. number: 2000.5.36 (gift of Caroline H. Damsky)

AE, 22 mm, 4.27 g, 6:00

Obv.: Laureate and draped bust of Aemilianus r.; **IMP M AEM [AE]MI[L]IANVS**

Rev.: Eros standing l. extending r. hand over herm; **C G I H P**

Ref: *SNG vA Index Prägetabelle* 2 lists Parium among the cities that struck for Aemelianus and Dr. Weisser confirms that the two specimens in Berlin are of the same type as the ANS acquisition. The city also struck for Aemilianus' wife Cornelia Supera (e.g., *SNG Cop.* 4.302), and similar reverses are found on earlier coins such as those of Otacilia Severa (e.g., *SNG Cop.* 4.301).

Caria

*7. Bargasa, Nero (Plate 11 no. 6)

Acc. number: 2001.21.11 (anonymous donation)

AE24, 24 mm, 10.28 g, 11:00

Obv.: Draped bust of Nero r., bare; **NEPΩN KAIΣAP**

Rev.: Facing cult statue of Artemis with supports; **ΒΑΡΓΑΣΗNΩN**

Ref.: *RPC1* 2827

This is the larger of the two denominations that *RPC1* lists for the Neronian coins of Bargasa. Only one example is listed in *RPC1*; the ANS specimen is in somewhat better condition.

Lydia

8. Maeonia, Antonine

Acc. number: 2001.21.8 (anonymous donation)

AE, 22 mm, 7.05 g, 7:00

Obv.: Diademed head of Zeus l.; ...**ZEVC OΛVMΠ**

Rev.: Zeus seated l. on throne with patera in extended r. hand; ...**AΠΠA MAIONΩN**

Ref.: Weber 6834 (this coin). The tags that accompanied this donation indicate that this piece was included in lot 2911 of part XII of Glendining's sale of the Lockett collection in February of 1961. The individual coins of this multiple lot were not illustrated. The Weber catalog further indicates that this coin came from the Imhoof-Blumer collection in 1891.

Phrygia

9. Acmoneia, third century
    Acc. number: 2001.21.12 (anonymous donation)
    AE, 21 mm, 7.44 g, 6:00
    Obv.: Laureate and draped bust of Demos r.; ΔΗΜΟC
    Rev.: Eagle clasping thunderbolt r.; ΑΚΜΟΝΕΩΝ
    Ref.: *BMC Phrygia* 24

10. Ancyra, first to second century AD
    Acc. number: 42001.21.1 (anonymous donation)
    AE, 16 mm, 2.24 g, 7:00
    Obv.: Poppy with grain ears in border of dots
    Rev.: Anchor with rope
    Ref.: Lindgren *Asia Minor* A844B (this coin)

Cilicia

11. Anazarbus, Claudius, year 67 = AD 48/49
    Acc. number: 2000.8.1 (gift of Wayne Sayles)
    AE diassarion, 29 mm, 11.68 g, 12:00
    Obv.: Bare head of Germanicus(?) r.; ΓΕRΜΑΝΙΚΟC
    Rev.: Bust of Zeus Olybris r. before rocky hill with fortified acropolis; ...ΤѠΝ ΠΡΟC... / ΕΤΟΥC ΖΞ.
    Ref.: Ziegler 43, *RPC1* 4060
    RPC1 (p. 595) discusses the uncertain identification of the obverse portrait and favors Claudius' dead brother Germanicus over his son Britannicus.

12. Anazarbus, Domitian, year 112 = 93/4
    Acc. number: 2000.8.2 (gift of Wayne Sayles)
    AE assarion, 22 mm, 8.45 g, 11:00

Obv.: Laureate head of Domitian r.

Rev.: Elpis striding l.; KAICAPEΩN...; in field, ET O YC IB P.

Ref.: Ziegler 74, *RPC* 1748

*13. Anazarbus, Domitian and Domitia, year 112 = 93/4 (Plate 11 no. 7)

Acc. number: 2001.21.9 (anonymous donation)

AE assarion, 22 mm, 6.82 g, 12:00

Obv.: Laureate head of Domitian r.

Rev.: Draped bust of Domitia l.

Ref.: Zeigler 76, *RPC2* 1749, Sale Catalog Huston 134 (1994), lot 48 (this coin)

RPC2 lists "Huston 134.48 (1998)" as possibly the third example of its type 880 from Cyzicus. The sale catalogue Huston 134, which was published in 1994, does attribute its number 48 to Cyzicus but direct inspection of the coin shows it to be from the mint at Anazarbus. Despite the piece being quite worn and illegible, the engraving of Domitian's hair is sufficiently distinctive to make the identification certain.

*14. Anazarbus, Domitian and Domitia, year 112 = 93/4 (Plate 11 no. 8)

Acc. number: 2000.8.26 (gift of Wayne Sayles)

AE assarion, 22 mm, 7.09 g, 12:00

Obv.: Laureate head of Domitian r.; AYTO KAI ΘE YI ΔOMI TIA-NOC CE ΓEP

Rev.: Draped bust of Domitia l.; KAICAPEΩN ΔOMETIA CEBACTH; IB P in field;

Ref.: Ziegler 76, *RPC2* 1749

15. Anazarbus, Domitian, year 112 = 93/4

Acc. number: 2000.8.25 (gift of Wayne Sayles)

AE diassarion, 26 mm, 10.22 g, 12:00

Obv.: Laureate head of Domitian r., star behind; ...IANOΣ ΣE ΓEP

Rev.: Crossed cornucopiae, caduceus; KAICAPEΩN ΠP ANAZ...; E[T]OYC IB P above; border of dots

Ref.: Ziegler 79, *RPC2* 1747

16. Anazarbus, Domitian, year 113 = 94/5

Acc. number: 2000.8.27 (gift of Wayne Sayles)

AE diassarion, 22 mm, 14.39 g, 12:00

Obv.: Laureate head of Domitian r.; ...ΔOMITIAN...
Rev.: Veiled head of Tyche r.; ...ΠΡ ANA...
Ref.: Ziegler 87, *RPC2* 1754

17. Anazarbus, pseudo-autonomous, year 132 = AD 113/4
Acc. number: 2000.8.28 (gift of Wayne Sayles)
AE hemiassarion, 19 mm, 3.71 g, 12:00
Obv.: Veiled bust of Demeter r., poppy head and two grain stalks at right
Rev.: Veiled bust of Artemis Perasia r. with polos, torch at right; ET BΛP
Ref.: Ziegler 100

18. Anazarbus, pseudo-autonomous, year 132 = AD 113/4
Acc. number: 2000.8.29 (gift of Wayne Sayles)
AE hemiassarion, 16 mm, 4.12 g, 12:00
Obv.: Veiled bust of Demeter r., poppy head and two grain stalks at right
Rev.: Veiled bust of Artemis Perasia r. with polos, torch at right; ET BΛP
Ref.: Ziegler 100

19. Anazarbus, pseudo-autonomous, year 132 = AD 113/4
Acc. number: 2000.8.30 (gift of Wayne Sayles)
AE assarion, 22 mm, 8.26 g, 12:00
Obv.: Head of Zeus bearded r.; KAICAPEⲰN ... ANAZA...
Rev.: Veiled and turreted bust of Tyche r.
Ref.: Ziegler 103

20. Anazarbus, Marcus Aurelius and Lucius Verus, year 182 = 163/4
Acc. number: 2000.8.6 (gift of Wayne Sayles)
AE trihemiassarion, 22 mm, 10.80 g, 11:00
Obv.: Marcus Aurelius (left) and Lucius Verus (right) clasping right hands. Marcus holds scroll (?) in left hand.
Rev.: Dekastyle temple, star in pediment
Ref.: Ziegler 182

21. Anazarbus, Crispina, year 199 = 180/1
Acc. number: 2000.8.11 (gift of Wayne Sayles)
AE trihemiassarion, 23 mm, 9.38 g, 5:00

Obv.: Draped bust of Crispina r.; ΚΡΙCΠΕΙΝΑ CΕΒΑCΤΗ

Rev.: Tyche, turreted, seated r. on rock with river god Pyramos at feet; ΑΝΑΖΑΡΒ ΕⲰΝ ΘΥΡ

Ref.: Ziegler 234

22. Anazarbus, Elagabalus
Acc. number: 2000.8.22 (gift of Wayne Sayles)
AE trihemiassarion, 22 mm, 4.45 g, 12:00
Obv.: Radiate bust of Elagabalus r.; ... Μ ΑΥ ΑΝΤⲰΝΕΙΝΟC CΕ Β
Rev.: Dikaiasyne standing l., scales in extended right hand, spear in left; ΑΝΑΖΑΡΒ...
Ref.: Ziegler 365

23. Anazarbus, Severus Alexander, year 248 = 229/30
Acc. number: 2000.8.23 (gift of Wayne Sayles)
AE hexassarion, 32 mm, 21.53 g, 6:00
Obv.: Laureate, draped, and cuirassed bust of Alexander Severus r.; ΑΥΤ Κ Μ Α CΕ ΑΛΕΞΑΝΔΡΟC
Rev.: Two temples in three-quarters view; ΑΝΑΖ ΕΝΔΟΣ ΜΗΤΡΟ / Γ Β / ΕΤ ΗΜC
Ref.: Ziegler 542

24. Anazarbus, Gordian III
Acc. number: 2000.8.14 (gift of Wayne Sayles)
AE hexassarion, 33 mm, 25.04 g, 1:00
Obv.: Radiate, draped, and cuirassed bust of Gordian III r.
Rev.: Cross-legged figure seated l. on rock wearing pointed headgear
Ref.: Ziegler 702

25. Anazarbus, Gordian III, year 261 = 242/3
Acc. number: 2000.8.12 (gift of Wayne Sayles)
AE hexassarion, 34.5 mm, 23.56 g, 12:00
Obv.: Radiate, draped, and cuirassed bust of Gordian III r.; ΑΥΤ Κ Μ ΑΝΤⲰΝΙΟC ΓΟΡΔΙΑΝΟC CΕΒ
Rev.: Cross-legged figure seated l. on rock, wearing pointed headgear; ΑΝΑΖΑΡΒΟΝ ΕΝΔΟ Ϛ ΜΗΤΡΟ / G Β / ΕΤ ΑϞC
Ref: Ziegler 701

26. Anazarbus, Philip II as Caesar, year 263 = 244/5
Acc. number: 2000.8.9 (gift of Wayne Sayles)
AE triassarion, 25 mm, 6.52 g, 12:00
Obv.: Draped and cuirassed bust of Philip II r.; Μ ΙΟΥΛ ΦΙΛΙΠ-ΠΟΣ ΚΑΙCΑΡ
Rev.: Capricorn l. above globe; ...Ο...
Ref.: Ziegler 728
The one example of this coin that Ziegler lists has a die axis of 6.

27. Anazarbus, Herennia Etruscilla, year 268 = 249/50
Acc. number: 2000.8.8 (gift of Wayne Sayles)
AE triassarion, 33 mm, 12.58 g, 6:00
Obv.: Draped bust of Herennia Etruscilla r. in crescent.
Rev.: Crescent below seven stars; Γ Γ
Ref.: Ziegler 758

28. Anazarbus, Herennia Etruscilla, year 269 = 250/1
Acc. number: 2000.8.7 (gift of Wayne Sayles)
AE tetrassarion, 30 mm, 13.17 g, 6:00
Obv.: Diademed bust of Herennia Etruscilla r. with crescent; ...ΕΝΝΙΑΝ ΕΤΡΟVC... CΕ...
Rev.: Dionysos, holding thyrsus, seated l. on leopard r.; ΑΝΑΖΑΡΒ ΟΝ ΜΗΤΡ / Γ / Γ / ΕΤ ΙΕΡ ΟΛV / VΜ ΘΞC
Ref.: Ziegler 766

29. Anazarbus, Hostilian as Caesar, year 269 = 250/1
Acc. number: 2000.8.10 (gift of Wayne Sayles)
AE diassarion, 22 mm, 6.86 g, 12:00
Obv.: Draped bust of Hostilian r.; ...ΟV ΟC ΜΕC
Rev.: Apollo nude standing l., branch in right hand, lyre resting on altar to right; ...ΖΑΡΒΟ ...
Ref.: Ziegler 754

*30. Anazarbus, Volusian (Plate 11 no. 9)
Acc. number: 2000.8.24 (gift of Wayne Sayles)
AE diassarion, 21 mm, 6.38 g, 7:00
Obv.: Laureate bust of Volusian r.; ΑVΤ Κ ΟVΟΛΟCCΙΑΝΟC CΕ
Rev.: Apollo nude standing l., branch in right hand, lyre resting on altar to right; ...ΖΑΡΒΟ ΜΗΤΡΟ...

Ref.: Obverse die matches that of Ziegler 775, the reverse die is unrecorded but closest in composition to those of Ziegler 754 and 755, both struck for Hostilian.

31. Anazarbus, Volusian, year 270 = 251/2
Acc. number: 2000.8.21 (gift of Wayne Sayles)
AE diassarion, 20 mm, 5.6 g, 6:00
Obv.: Laureate bust of Volusian r.; AVT K OVOΛOCCI[A]NOC CE
Rev.: Apollo nude standing l., branch in right hand, lyre resting on altar in left; ANAZARBOV MHTP ET OC / A / M / K / Γ Γ;
Ref.: Ziegler 776

32. Anazarbus, Volusian , year 271 = 252/3
Acc. number: 2000.8.20 (gift of Wayne Sayles)
AE triassarion, 24 mm, 10.27 g, 12:00
Obv.: Radiate draped and cuirassed bust of Volusian r.
Rev.: Horse prancing r.; ANAZAPBOV MHTPOΠOΛ / A / M / K / Γ / Γ [E]T AOC
Ref.: Ziegler 797

33. Anazarbus, Valerian, year 272 = 253/4
Acc. number: 2000.8.16 (gift of Wayne Sayles)
AE diassarion, 22 mm, 7.34 g, 6:00
Obv.: Laureate, draped, and cuirassed bust of Valerian r.; AVT K OVAΛEPIANO[C]
Rev.: Apollo nude standing l., branch in right hand, lyre resting on altar in left; AN AZA PBOV ET BOC / A / M / K / Γ Γ
Ref.: Ziegler 803

34. Anazarbus, Valerian, year 272 = 253/4
Acc. number: 2000.8.15 (gift of Wayne Sayles)
AE triassarion, 25 mm, 10.97 g, 6:00
Obv.: Laureate, draped, and cuirassed bust of Valerian r.; AVT K OVAΛEPIANOC CE
Rev.: Prize urn with palm branch on table with twisted legs; ANA-ZAPB MHTPOΠOΛ / Γ Γ / A /.../ K / T / ET BOC
Ref.: Ziegler 808

*35. Anazarbus, Valerian, year 272 = 253/4 (Plate 11 no. 10)
Acc. number: 2000.8.13 (gift of Wayne Sayles)
AE tetrassarion, 29 mm, 15.11 g, 6:00
Obv.: Laureate, draped, and cuirassed bust of Valerian r.; AVT K
Π·ΛΙΚ·ΟΥΑΛΕΡΙΑΝΟC CE
Rev.: Dionysus reclining r. on panther, thyrsus in r. hand; ANA-
ZAPBOV / ET·BOC / T / ·AMK·
Ref.: Ziegler 828

36. Anazarbus, Valerian, year 272 = 253/254
Acc. number: 2000.8.5 (gift of Wayne Sayles)
AE tetrassarion, 28 mm, 11.39 g, 6:00
Obv.: Laureate, draped, and cuirassed bust of Valerian r.; ...VT
K·Π·ΛΙΚ·ΟΥΑΛΕΡΙΑΝΟC·CE
Rev.: Dionysus with raised right hand reclining right on leopard,
thyrsus in left hand; ANAZAPB OY MHTPO / Γ Γ / ET·B·O·C· /
·A·M·K·
Ref.: Ziegler 829

*37. Anazarbus, Valerian, year 272 = 253/4 (Plate 11 no. 11)
Acc. number: 2000.8.17 (gift of Wayne Sayles)
AE hexassarion, 29 mm, 13.48 g, 6:00
Obv.: Laureate bust r., cuirassed and draped; ...Π·ΛΙΚ·ΟΥΑΛΕΡΙΑ-
ΝΟC CE
Rev.: Valerian and Gallienus seated l. on curule chairs; AVT K
ΟΥΑΛΕΡΙΑΝ OC ANAZAPB / A / M / K / BOC / AVT ΓΑΛΛΙ HNOC
Ref.: Ziegler 832

38. Anazarbus, Valerian, year 272 = 253/4
Acc. number: 2000.8.3 (gift of Wayne Sayles)
AE hexassarion, 28 mm, 19.43 g, 6:00
Obv.: Laureate, draped, and cuirassed bust of Valerian r.; AVT K
Π ΛΙΚ ΟΥΑΛΕΡΙΑΝΟC CE
Rev.: Six prize urns in two rows, branch in center-top urn; ANA-
ZAPBOV MHTPOΠ / Γ Γ / ET BOC / A M K T
Ref.: Ziegler 834

39. Anazarbus, Valerian, year 272 = 253/4
Acc. number: 2000.8.18 (gift of Wayne Sayles)

AE hexassarion, 29 mm, 13.03 g, 6:00
Obv.: Laureate, draped, and cuirassed bust of Valerian r.; **AVT K Π ΛΙΚ ΟΥΑΛΕΡΙΑΝΟC CE**
Rev.: Six prize urns in two rows; **AN AZAPB OV / ET BOC / A M K**
Ref.: Ziegler 836

40. Anazarbus, Valerian, year 272 = 253/4
Acc. number: 2000.8.4 (gift of Wayne Sayles)
AE hexassarion, 30 mm, 14.87 g, 7:00
Obv.: Radiate, draped, and cuirassed bust of Valerian r.; **AVT· K·Π·ΛΙ·ΟΥΑΛΕΡΙΑΝΟC CE**
Rev.: Six prize urns in two rows, branch in center-top urn; **ANA-ZAPBOV ENΔOΞ MHT / Γ Γ / ET BOC / A M K**
Ref.: Ziegler 838

41. Anazarbus, Valerian
Acc. number: 2000.8.19 (gift of Wayne Sayles)
Triassarion, 23 mm, 9.52 g, 3:00
Obv.: Bust r., radiate and draped; **AVT K ΟΥΑΛΕΡΙΑΝΟC**
Rev.: Bust of Selene r. within crescent; **ANAZAPBOV MHTPOΠO / Γ Γ / A M K**
Ref.: Ziegler 816

42. Tarsus, Caracalla
Acc. number: 2000.8.31 (gift of Wayne Sayles)
AE, 34 mm, 19.64 g, 12:00
Obv.: Bust of Caracalla r., wearing crown and garments of demi-urgos; **AVT KAI M AVP CEVHPOC ANTΩNEINOC / Π Π**
Rev.: Elephant l. with ciliarch crown on back bearing the letters **OMAKKI**; **ANTΩNEINIANHC CEVHP AΔPIA**; **TAPCOV ΓB** in exergue
Ref.: *SNG Levante* Suppl. 1 no. 269 (same dies)

Syria

43. Zeugma, Antoninus Pius
Acc. number: 2001.21.2 (anonymous donation)
AE, 22 mm, 8.27 g, 12:00
Obv.: Laureate bust of Antoninus Pius r.

Rev.: Temple overlooking hill with two-level façade in foreground; ΖΕΥΓΜΑΤΕωΝ Α(?)
Ref.: *BMC Galatia* 1; Butcher (1998), third issue

44. Zeugma, Philip I
 Acc. number: 2001.21.3 (anonymous donation)
 AE30, 30 mm, 20.00 g, 6:00
 Obv.: Laureate, draped and cuirassed bust r.; ΑΥΤΟΚ ΚΑΙ Μ ΙΟΥΛΙ ΦΙΛΙΠΟC CEB
 Rev.: Tetrastyle temple overlooking wooded hill with two-level façade in foreground; small figure between central columns of temple; in exergue, capricorn l.; ΖΕΥΓΜΑΤΕΩΝ
 Ref.: *BMC Galatia* 29, Butcher (1998), eighth issue

45. Zeugma, Philip I
 Acc. number: 2000.21.5 (anonymous donation)
 AE30, 30 mm, 15.94 g, 12:00
 Obv.: Laureate, draped and cuirassed bust r.; illegible counter-mark near center, probably eagle with closed wings (Howgego 340); ΑΥΤΟΚ ΚΑΙ Μ ΙΟΥΛΙ ΦΙΛΙΠΟC CEB
 Rev.: Tetrastyle temple overlooking wooded hill with two-level façade in foreground; small figure between central columns of temple; in exergue, capricorn r.; ΖΕΥΓΜΑΤΕΩΝ
 Ref.: *BMC Galatia* 29var, Butcher (1998), eighth issue

46. Heliopolis, Philip II, AE13
 Acc. number: 2001.21.10 (anonymous donation)
 AE13, 13 mm, 3.87 g, 6:00
 Obv.: Bust r., paludamentum
 Rev.: Eagle; standards within wreath; COL [HE]L
 Ref.: Mabott 2614 (this coin); De Saulcy p. 15, 1; Mionnet V. p. 303, no. 129

Judaea

47. Herod the Great
 Acc. number: 2000.7.131 (gift of Edward Allworth)
 AE prutah 25 mm, 6.08 g, 12:00
 Obv.: Bowl on tripod; ΗΡωΔΟΥ ΒΑΣΙΛΕωΣ / Ⱶ / ✝

Rev.: Helmet with star or crest above, cheek guards and straps or couch below, flanked by palm branches.

Ref.: *AJC* 2, p. 235, 1. See Magness (2001) and Jacobson (2002) for recent discussions of this much debated type.

48. First revolt, year 3 = 68/9
Acc. number: 2000.7.130 (gift of Edward Allworth)
AE prutah, 20 mm, 2.76 g, 5:00
Obv.: Amphora with lid; paleo-hebrew legend *shnt...*
Rev.: Vine leaf on branch; paleo-hebrew legend *hrwt...*
Ref.: *AJC* 2, p. 261, 20

SEBASTIAN HEATH

BYZANTINE

*1. Phocas, Constantinople, AD 603–607 (Plate 11 no. 12)
Acc. number: 2000.5.31 (gift of Caroline H. Damsky)
AV solidus, 20 mm, 4.30 g, 7:00
Obv.: Crowned and draped bust facing, wearing cuirass, paludamentum, and crown without pendilia, with cross on circlet; in r., globus cruciger; O N FOCAS PERP AVG
Rev.: Angel facing, holding in r. hand long staff with Christogram at the top and in l. globus cruciger; VICTORIA AVCCΔ; CONOB in exergue
Pierced for suspension at 12:00 on reverse = 5:00 on obverse.
Ref.: *DOC* 5d

ELENA STOLYARIK

REFERENCES

Babelon, E., Th. Reinach, and W. Waddington. 1925. *Recueil général des monnaies grecques d'Asie Mineure,* t. I, fasc. 1, 2nd ed. Paris: Éditions Ernest Leroux.

Bateson, J. D. 1991. Roman spintriae in Hunter Coin Cabinet. In: *Ermanno A. Arslan studia dicata,* parte II, pp. 385–397. Glaux 7. Milano: Edizioni Ennere.

Burnett, A., M. Amandry, and I. Carradice. 1999. *Roman provincial coinage, vol. II: from Vespasian to Domitian (AD 69–96)*. London: British Museum Press.

Burnett, A, M. Amandry, and P. Ripollès. 1992. *Roman provincial coinage, vol. 1: from the death of Caesar to the death of Vitellius (44 BC–AD 69)*. London: British Museum Press.

Butcher. K. 1998. The mint at Zeugma. In: D. Kennedy, ed. *The twin towns of Zeugma on the Euphrates: rescue work and historical studies*, pp. 233–243. Journal of Roman Archaeology Supplementary Series 27. Portsmouth, RI: Journal of Roman Archaeology.

Buttrey, T. V. 1973. The spintriae as a historical source. *Numismatic Chronicle* 13:52–63.

Dattari, G. 1901. *Numi augg. alexandrini*. Cairo: Istituto Francese d'Archeologia Orientale.

De Saulcy, F. 1976 (Reprint). *Numismatique de la Terre Sainte*. Bologna: A. Forni.

Forrer, L. 1926. *The Weber collection, volume III, Part 1: Greek coins*. London: Spink & Son.

Franke, P., W. Leschorn, and A. Stylow. 1981. *Sylloge nummorum graecorum Deutschland: Sammlung v. Aulock. Index*. Berlin: Gebr. Mann Verlag.

Fritze, H. von. 1917. Die autonome Kupferprägung von Kyzikos. *Nomisma* 10:1–32.

Grunauer von Hoerschelmann, S. 1982/83. The Severan emissions of the Peloponnesus. *Israel Numismatic Journal* 6–7:39–46.

Head, B. 1906. *A catalogue of the Greek coins in the British Museum: catalogue of the Greek coins of Phrygia*. London: Trustees of the British Museum.

Jacobson, D. 2002. Herod the Great shows his true colors. *Near Eastern Archaeology* 64(3):100–105.

Jurokova, J. 1982. *Griechisches Münzwerk: die Münzprägung von Bizye*. Schriften zur Geschichte und Kultur Antike 18. Berlin: Akademie Verlag.

Kotansky, R. D. 1979. The Roman lead-tesserae: a survey of the research. *Collector's Journal of Ancient Art* 1(1):2–6.

Lindgren H. and F. Kovacs. 1985. *Ancient bronze coins of Asia Minor and Levant from the Lindgren collection*. San Mateo: Chrysopylon Publishers.

Magness, J. 2001. The cults of Isis and Kore at Samaria-Sebaste in the Hellenistic and Roman periods. *Harvard Theological Review* 94.2: 157–177.

Meshorer, Y. 1982. *Ancient Jewish coinage, vol. II: Herod the Great through Bar Cochba*. Dix Hills, NY: Amphora Books.

Milne, J. G. 1933. *Catalogue of Alexandrian coins in the Ashmolean Museum*. Oxford: Oxford University Press.

Mionnet, T. 1807. *Descriptions de médailles antiques, grecques et romaines, avec leur degré de rareté et leur estimation*. Paris: Imprimerie de Testu.

Price, M. and B. Trell. 1977. *Coins and their cities*. Detroit: Wayne State University Press.

Rostovtseff M. and M. Prou. 1899. Catalogue des plombs antiques de la Bibliothèque Nationale. *Revue Numismatique* (4th ser.) 3:199–219, 278–337, 417–460.

Rostovtseff, M. 1903a. *Rimskija svintsoviya tesseri*. St. Petersburg.

—. 1903b. *Tesserarum urbis Romae at suburbi plumbearum sylloge*. St. Petersburg: Académie Imperiale des Sciences.

—. 1905. *Römische Bleitesserae*. Leipzig.

Sayles, Wayne G. 2001. *Classical deception: counterfeits, forgeries and reproductions of ancient coins*. Iola, Wis.: Krause Publications.

Wroth, W. 1899. *A catalogue of Greek coins in the British Museum: catalogue of Greek coins of Galatia, Cappadocia, and Syria*. London: Trustees of the British Museum.

Ziegler, R. 1993. *Kaiser, Heer und städtisches Geld. Unterschungen zur Münzprägung von Anazarbos und anderer ostkilikischer Städte*. Ergänzungsbände zu den Tituli Asiae Minoris 16. Wien: Verlag der österreichischen Akademie der Wissenschaften.

ISLAMIC, SOUTH ASIAN, AND EAST ASIAN

Gifts to the Islamic, South Asian, and East Asian cabinets of the Society ranged from large collections of major importance down to small change, but all of them contribute to our goal of maintaining the most complete assemblage possible of the world's money. It is difficult to decide which of several gifts were the most important. The most valuable and spectacular of these major donations was surely Lawrence Brilliant's donation of 156 coins of India during the last millennium, including 152 gold pieces, three silver, and one copper. Many of these are of the greatest rarity or historical interest, ranging from twelfth-century Chauhan dinaras depicting the god Rama in a scene from the *Ramayana*, through the coins of the Sultans of Delhi and their contemporaries, of the Mughals and their successors, down to the last gold coin to be struck in India, some fifty years ago. All of these coins were listed in the Spink-Taisei "Skanda" auction of 1991. Their computer records include the Skanda catalogue reference, making them easy to find on the ANS web page.

The most colorful and novel of our large gifts was the Central Asia Collection of Professor Edward Allworth of Columbia University, with 1,033 items in all. The core of the gift is 466 bills and notes from the Caucasian and Central Asian territories of the Russian Empire and the U.S.S.R., as well as from Russia and the other post-Soviet successor states. The most interesting are the notes of the various entities of the Russian Revolutionary period, from 1917 to about 1924. These notes, often printed locally in emergency conditions, on silk or on paper of various kinds, using hand-made block printing, are valuable evidence for politics, society and culture during a murky period of twentieth-century history. The gift also includes 550 coins of Central Asia from ancient times to the present, with sixteenth-century Shaybanid material of special interest.

Henry Amin Awad continued his generosity to the Society with two donations, of Umayyad and other coins, and of Egyptian glass weights. The latter, along with Awad's earlier donations, are fully described in an article by former ANS staffer Katherina Eldada, "Glass Weights and Vessel Stamps," that has recently appeared in a new book honoring Dr. Awad, *Fustat Finds: Beads, Coins, Medical Instruments, Textiles, and Other Artifacts from the Awad Collection* (Cairo: American University in Cairo Press, 2002), which was edited by ANS Fellow and former Council Member Jere L. Bacharach. The book also contains an article by ANS Curator Michael Bates (with an alumna of our Graduate Seminar, Lidia Domaszewicz), "The Copper Coinage of Egypt in the Seventh Century", and several other articles and contributions made possible by Dr. Awad's many gifts to the ANS (starting in 1972) and to museums in Egypt.

Among other gifts are several from William B. Warden, who supported the Islamic and South Asia departments generously up to his unexpected death on 5 August 2000. As usual, he donated individual coins selected to fill gaps in the Society's collection, including Sasanian, Hephthalite, Arab-Sasanian, and Islamic coins. His brother Derek Warden continued Bill's support with a gift of Iranian material. Wayne Sayles gave a number of image-bearing coppers of the Artuqids and their neighbors in twelfth-century northern Mesopotamia, generally with a view to adding photogenic examples or rare variations for our holdings of this popular series. Jan Vagassky, through the mediation of John Aiello, donated a hoard of about a thousand late-fourteenth-century Mamluk Egyptian copper coins which awaits study by an interested specialist. We are also grateful to Mamie Gettys Atkinson, Jere Bacharach, Kevin Butcher, Solange Cheney, Adrienne Daly, Paul F. L. de Groot, the late Boris Demitrievich Kochnev, Garo Kurkman, Jinyun Liu, Kenneth M. MacKenzie, Leonard Gregory Mazzone, Emmett McDonald, William E. Metcalf, Wayne G. Sayles, and Robert W. Schaaf for interesting and important additions to our collection.

*1. Zubayrid caliphate, governor 'Abd al-'Azīz b. 'Abd Allāh b. 'Āmir; Iran, Sistan province, dated 66 Hijra (685–86) (Plate 12 no. 1)

Acc. number: 2001.9.2 (gift of Derek P. Warden)

AR drahm, 32 mm, 3.665 g, 9:00

Obv.: Image of Sasanian emperor, facing right; to left, '*pzt' GDH*, "may his glory increase"; to right, *apdlacyc y abdwla y amyran*; margin *bism Allāh al-'azīz*, "in the name of God the Glorious".

Rev.: Zoroastrian fire-altar with two attendants; to left, *šššst*, "66"; to right, *SK* (for "Sakastan"). Three counterstamps, one reading *jā'iz*, "current".

Ref.: *BMCArabSas* 192, Album 25; counterstamps Göbl 42 and 14 (twice)

This is the only coin issue attributable to this governor with certainty. There are also two rare issues of seven and eight years later naming someone with the same name and same father's name as this figure, but it is doubtful that they refer to the same person, especially since the caliphal dynasty had changed. The Arabic motto on this issue is a play on words. The governor's name is 'Abd al-'Azīz, "Slave of The Glorious" [*i.e.*, God], to which the inscription refers with *bism Allāh al-'Azīz*, "in the name of God The Glorious". This issue was lacking from our collection.

*2. Umayyad, anonymous, uncertain mint and date (Plate 12 no. 2)
Acc. number: 2000.32.2 (gift of William B. Warden)
AE fals, 23 mm, 1.132 g, 2:00
Obv.: Image of Sasanian emperor, full-face; to left *GDH* ("glory"); to right, *ḥwslwy*, "Khusraw". In margin, *bism Allāh rabbī*, "in the name of God my Lord"
Rev.: Goddess Anahit full-face, in tiara of flames; to left, *'pzt'*, "increase"; to right, *ḥwslwy*, "Khusraw"
Ref.: Curiel-Gyselen 143
The prototype for this interesting issue is a special coinage of the Sasanian emperor Khusrō II issued from about 611 to 627. The Arabic marginal inscription, however, was the numismatic slogan of Ziyād b. Abī Ṣufyān, governor of Basra from 665 and later of all Iran, until his death in 673 or 674. This fals was either issued officially during his governorate, or is a later concoction by a local or private minter. The issue is new to the ANS collection.

*3. Egypt, eighth century (Plate 12 no. 3)
Acc. number 2001.12.30 (gift of Henry Amin Awad)
Glass weight for 1/4 *raṭl* [pound], 40–47 mm, 86.94 g (chips missing)
Ref.: Balog, *Glass Weights, passim*
Although the validating stamp on the top is illegible, this is a glass weight for ordinary commodities issued by a special office in eighth-century Egypt. The trapezoidal form with a hole is intended to be used on a steelyard, which is a kind of balance with a pan for the commodity on one end and a bare shaft at the other end on which weights would be slipped until the balance was level. Specialists call these "ring weights." It is rare to find weights as nearly intact as this one. Mostly, broken pieces are found, indi-

cating that the weights were supposed to be destroyed when their validation was out of date. Normally the stamps name the current governor and his technical agent, and state the weight unit. The illegibility of this stamp may result from error by the maker, or might indicate a cheaper privately made substitute for the government issue.

*4. Abbasid caliphate, caliph al-Muqtadir with local ruler Subkarī, Iran, Fārs provincial mint (probably Shīrāz?), 296 Hijra (909) (Plate 12 no. 4)

Acc. number: 2000.33.2 (gift of William B. Warden)

AR dirham, 30 mm, 3.008 g, 6:00; pierced

Obv.: lā ilah illā

    Allāh waḥdahu

    lā sharīk lahu

    Subkarī

Inner margin: *bism Allāh ḍuriba hadhā'l-dirham bi-Fārs sana sitt wa-tis'īn wa-mi'atayn*

Outer margin: *lillāh al-amr min qabl wa-min ba'd wa-yawma'idh[in] yafraḥu al-mu'minūn bi-naṣr Allāh*

Rev.: Muḥammad

    rasūl

    Allāh

    al-Muqtadir billāh

Margin: *Muḥammad rasūl Allāh arsalahu bi'l-hudā wa-dīn al-ḥaqq li-yuẓhirahu 'alā al-dīn kullihi wa-law kariha al-mushrikūn*

Ref.: Stephen Album, *Checklist*, 1406

Subkari, named on this dirham, was a military commander for the Ṣaffārids, a southern Iranian dynasty in the second half of the ninth century. The Ṣaffārid of his time delegated all the administration to Subkarī, who finally, in 909, persuaded the other army commanders to give him formal as well as practical supremacy (although he remained within the caliphate, as shown by the caliph al-Muqtadir's name). He was, however, unable to hold on to power very long. Coins with his name were issued at the Fārs mint for three years, 296–98, and at 'Umān across the Gulf in 298. They are relatively scarce. None seems to have been published formally, and this is the first of Subkarī's coins in the ANS collection. The evidence for Subkarī and the coinage with his name was collected by Deborah Tor in her 1999 ANS Graduate Seminar paper "A Numismatic History of the First Saffarid Dynasty (247–297/861–911)" which was a useful resource for this note; it has since been published in *Numismatic Chronicle* (2002).

*5. 'Abbāsid caliphate, Qarākhānid rulers Naṣr b. 'Alī and Aḥmad b. 'Alī; Farghana province, mint Ūzkand, 394 Hijra (1003–04) (Plate 12 no. 5)
Acc. number: 2000.32.3 (gift of William B. Warden)
AR dirham, 25 mm, 2.795 g, 9:00.
Obv.: ('ayn)
> *lā ilah illā*
> *Allāh waḥdahu*
> *lā sharīk lahu*

Margin: *bism Allāh ḍuriba hadhā'l-dirham bi-Ūzkand sana arba' wa-tis'īn wa-thalathami'a*
Rev. lillāh
> *Muḥammad rasūl Allāh*
> *al-Qādir billāh Nāṣir al-Ḥaqq Khān*
> *al-Mu'ayyad al-'Adl Ilak*
> ["Nasr" in Uyghur script]

Margin: *Muḥammad rasūl Allāh arsalahu bi'l-hudā wa-din al-ḥaqq li-yuẓhirahu 'alā al-dīn kullihi wa-law kariha al-mushrikūn*
Ref: Mayer 104-05 variant; Album, *Checklist*, 3302
Although coins such as this are ordinarily classified as issues of the dynasts named upon them, they are in fact coins of the Abbasid caliphate, within which the local rulers were, in legal theory, merely provincial governors. The coin has all the standard religious inscriptions of the caliphate and names the caliph himself, al-Qādir. It also refers to the supreme Turkish Khan of the time, whose actual name was Aḥmad b. 'Alī but on the coin is designated "Who Makes the Truth Victorious, Khān"; and to the viceroy or Ilek of the western realm, Naṣr b. 'Alī, by his titles "The Supporter of Justice, Ilek". His name Naṣr is written in Uighur script, a derivation of Aramaic writing, written downward (like Chinese)

rather than right to left. The mint Ūzkand was Naṣr's capital, in Farghana. Naṣr evidently introduced a new dirham standard, not yet fully understood, but known after him for over a century as *mu'ayyadiyya 'adliyya* dirhams. This may be the first year of issue of such dirhams.

*6. Khwarazmian People's Soviet Republic, 1339 Hijri (1920–21) (Plate 12 no. 6)
Acc. number: 2000.7.441 (gift of Professor Edward Allworth)
5,000 ruble note, 145 x 111 mm
Obv.: Brown silk with stamped red design, overstamped with violet architectonic frame and black inscriptions
Rev.: Blank
Ref.: Pick S1085
Khwarazm or Khwarizm is the country of the Oxus (or Syr Darya) delta, isolated and clearly bounded by the Aral Sea to the north and the desert on the east and west. In modern times it was governed by the Khans of Khiva, its capital city. In the nineteenth century, the Russian Empire brought the country gradually under its control, until in 1873 the part east of the Oxus was annexed to Russia and the Khan, west of the Oxus, was forced to sign a treaty of obedience to the Czar. The Bolsheviks forced the abdication of the Khan and created a nominally independent soviet republic, still on the left bank only. In 1924, the eastern Russian territory was assigned to the Uzbek SSR, now Uzbekistan, while the western half of the country became part of the Turkmen SSR, now Turkmenistan.

*7. Khwarazmian People's Soviet Republic, 1340 Hijri (1921–22) (Plate 13 no. 1)
Acc. number: 2000.7.440 (gift of Professor Edward Allworth)
10,000 ruble note, 171 x 108 mm
Obv.: Gray paper block-printed with red, green, and black stamps
Rev.: Blank
Ref.: Pick S1094
The high denominations of this and the preceding note, issued in successive years, testify to the rampant inflation and the difficul-

ty of maintaining a stable currency in the chaos of revolutionary Russia.

*8. Chauhan kings, attributed to Vigraharaja IV (Sambhor & Ajmir in India, 1153–63) (Plate 13 no. 2)
Acc. number: 2000.2.3 (gift of Dr. Lawrence B. Brilliant)
AV dinara, 20 mm, 4.08 g, 12:00
Obv.: Rama, standing, holding bow
Rev.: *Srimad Vigraha Raja Deva*
Ref.: Skanda sale 170 (this coin)
This is the only numismatic representation of the god Rama.

*9. Governors of Bengal, 'Alī Mardān, probably Gawr mint, c. 1210–13 (Plate 13 no. 3)
Acc. number: 2000.2.5 (gift of Dr. Lawrence B. Brilliant)
AV fractional tanka, 17.5 mm, 2.25 g, 3:00
Obv.: Horseman with mace; circular inscription *Muḥammad rasūl Allāh...*
Rev.: *al-Sulṭān al-Mu'aẓẓam Rukn al-Dunyā wa'l-Dīn Abu'l-Muẓaffar 'Alī Mardān*
Ref.: Lowick 2 (same dies as ANS example) = Goron and Goenka p. 147 no. B7; Skanda sale 255 (this coin)
The horseman image was used on the very earliest Muslim coins of Bengal, issued in April 1206 with a verbal reference to the conquest, and therefore the image probably originated in celebration of that event. It became the standard type for some decades afterward. The new ANS coin may be the second recorded example of its issue.

*10. Delhi Sultan Muḥammad III, without mint name or date, c. 1327–29 (Plate 13 no. 4)
Acc. number: 2000.2.22 (gift of Dr. Lawrence B. Brilliant)
AV half tanka, 16 mm, 5.51 g, 3:00
Obv.: *Muḥammad b. Tughluq*
Rev.: *al-Rājī bi-raḥmat Allāh*
Ref.: Goren and Goenka p. 53 no. D355 (this coin); Skanda sale 291 (this coin)

This unique example of a half-tanka of Muḥammad III is undated, but the corresponding tanka was issued with dates from 727 to 729. The inscriptions, being briefer than normal, are more elegant than the usual cramped and distorted writing on coins of Muḥammad III. The epithet on the reverse is one of seven used by Muḥammad; it means "He Who Comes Back to the Mercy of God". The corresponding tanka was issued at the Delhi and Deogir mints.

11. Bengal sultans, A'zamshāh, 1389–96 (Plate 13 no. 5)
Acc. number: 2000.2.28 (gift of Dr. Lawrence B. Brilliant)
AV tanka, 25 mm, 10.78 g, 1:00
Obv.: al-Mu'ayyad bi-Ta'yīd al-Raḥmān Ghiyāth al-Dunyā wa'l-Dīn Abu'l-Muẓaffar A'zamshāh Ibn Sikandar Shāh Ibn Ilyās Shāh al-Sulṭān
Rev.: Yamīn Khalīfat Allāh Nāṣir Amīr al-Mu'minīn Ghawth al-Islām wa'l-Muslimīn khallada Allāh khilāfatahu
Ref.: Goron and Goenka p. 179 no. B237; Skanda sale 301 (this coin)
Although the example illustrated by Goron and Goenka is a mohur of 11.6 grams, this is a normal tanka of the mint. The small round countermark on the reverse is a "shroff's mark", the stamp of a moneychanger indicating that he had found the coin to be genuine.

12. Gujarat, Maḥmūd Shāh, mint Muḥammadābād 'urf Chāmpānīr, 902 Hijri (1496–97) (Plate 13 no. 6)
Acc. number 2000.2.31 (gift of Dr. Lawrence B. Brilliant)
AV mohur, 23 mm, 11.50 g, 3:00
Obv.: al-Wāthiq bi-Ta'yīd al-Raḥmān Naṣir al-Dunyā wa'l-Dīn Abu'l-Fath
Rev.: Maḥmūd Shāh al-Sulṭān khallada khilāfatuhu; in margin, ... Muḥammadābād 'urf Chāmpānīr 902 ... hilāliyya
Ref.: Goron and Goenka p. 368 no. G78 (this coin); Skanda sale 305 (this coin)
The ingenious obverse design of this impressive gold issue, with all the vertical letters alif and lām placed in parallel, was copied in India for centuries. The city of Champanir, Maḥmūd Shāh's capi-

tal, was given the honorary name Muḥammadābād, "Muhammad City", which is expressed on the coin as "Muḥammadābād known as Champānir".

*13. Niẓām Shahi kings of Aḥmadnagar, Murtaḍā Shah, 993 Hijra (1585) (Plate 13 no. 7)
Acc. number: 2000.2.38 (gift of Dr. Lawrence B. Brilliant)
AV pagoda or quarter tanka, 15 mm, 2.89 g, 1:00
Obv.: lā ilah illā Allāh Muḥammad rasūl Allāh ʿAlī walī Allāh
Rev.: Murtaḍa... Nagar ... 903 sana thalath wa-tisʿīn wa-tisaʿmiʾa
Ref.: Goron and Goenka p. 326 no. N1 (this coin); Skanda sale 315 (this coin)
This is the only known gold coin of the kings of Aḥmadnagar, who broke away from the sultanate of Kulbarga in 1490. The religious statement on the obverse shows Murtaḍā to have been a Shīʿī. The word Nagar, "city", identifies Aḥmadnagar on the coins of this kingdom.

*14. Kingdom of Kutch, Madanasinghji, 2004 Vikrama samvat era (1947–48) (Plate 13 no. 8)
Acc. number: 2000.2.96 (gift of Dr. Lawrence B. Brilliant)
AV rupee, 32.5 mm, 18.73 g, 12:00
Obv.: Mahor ek Kachchh Bhuj 2004; in margin, *maharaja dhiraj mirjan maharao Shri Madanasinhji Sivai Bahadur*
Rev.: Jaya Hind; in ribbon, *Bhuj*
Ref.: Krause-Mishler M8; Skanda sale 549 (this coin); Baronitschek p. 109 no. 28.14
The Kingdom of Kutch, one of the many autonomous states under British suzerainty before the establishment of the Republic of India in 1947, was located in the west, now in Gujarat. This coin is remarkable in a number of aspects. It is not a circulation issue, having been struck with obsolete rupee dies intended for the kingdom's silver coinage. It should not have been struck at all, since one of the first acts of the Republic was the prohibition of state coinage preparatory to the integration of the kingdoms and principalities into the states of the Republic. Nevertheless, it was struck, and it is the last gold coin, up to now, made in the Republic of India.

REFERENCES

Album, Stephen. 1998. *A checklist of Islamic coins*, 2nd ed. Santa Rosa, Calif.: Stephen Album.

Balog, Paul. 1976. *Umayyad, 'Ābbasid and Tūlūnid glass weights and vessel stamps*. ANS Numismatic Studies 13. New York: American Numismatic Society.

Bartonitschek, Norbert. 1995. *Das Geld von Kutch: Münzen, Papiergeld und Gebührenmarken des indischen Fürstenstaates*. Stolberg: Norbert Bartonitschek.

Curiel, Raoul and Rika Gyselen. 1984. *Une collection de monnaies de cuivre arabo-sasanides*. Studia Iranica, cahier 2. Paris: Association pour l'Avancement des Études Iraniennes.

Göbl, Robert. 1971 [1968]. *Sasanian numismatics* (rev. tr. of *Sasanidische Numismatik*). Braunschweig: Klinkhardt & Biermann.

Goron, Stan and J. P. Goenka. 2001. *The coins of the Indian sultanates, covering the area of present-day India, Pakistan and Bangladesh*. New Delhi: Munshiram Manoharlal Publishers.

Lowick, Nicholas. 1973. The horseman type of Bengal and the question of commemorative issues. *Journal of the Numismatic Society of India* 35:196–208.

Mayer, Tobias. 1998. *Sylloge numorum arabicorum Tübingen: Nord- und Ostzentralasien*, XV b *Mittelasien* II. Tübingen and Berlin: Ernst Wasmuth Verlag.

Pick, Albert. 1995. *Standard catalog of world paper money, I: specialized issues*, 7th ed. Iola, Wisc.: Krause Publications.

Skanda sale = Singapore Coin Auction Spink-Taisei catalogue 9 (20/2/1991): the Skanda collection of Indian gold coins.

Tor, Deborah. 2002. A numismatic history of the first Saffarid dynasty (247–297/861–911). *Numismatic Chronicle* (in press).

Walker, John. 1941. A catalogue of the Muhammadan coins in the British Museum: a catalogue of the Arab-Sassanian coins (Umaiyad governors in the East, Arab-Ephthalites, 'Abbāsid governors in Tabaristan and Bukhārā). London: British Museum.

MICHAEL BATES

MEDIEVAL, MODERN, UNITED STATES, LATIN AMERICA, AND MEDALS

It is gratifying to be able to note that the quantity of material received has, in some cases, been too large to describe item by item; therefore, this introduction must generalize for the most part, leaving only a selection of pieces—including several of particular interest—to illustrate the gifts. All of the accessions are nevertheless most appreciated.

The only Medieval accessions were part of a group of coins of France and the Low Countries donated by Mark and Lottie Salton in memory of Felix Schlessinger. These pieces, all gold, include an écu neuf of Charles VII (1436–1461) from the mint of St. Lô; a St. André de Ville-neuve-lès-Avignon écu au soleil of Louis XII (1498–1514); an écu du Dauphiné of Francis I (1515–1547) minted at Crémieu; and two Brabantine issues of the Habsburg emperor Charles V (1506–1555): a half real and a florin, both of the Antwerp mint.

The Salton donation also constituted a fine addition to the cabinet of modern issues. The French portion includes three interesting coins of Louis XIV (1643–1715). These are gold louis from the mints of Nantes, Tours, and Bordeaux. A final French gold coin in the gift is a Parisian 1864 5-franc piece of Napoleon III (1852–1870). Another piece included is an Austrian Netherlands 1749 silver ducaton of the empress Maria Theresa (1740–1780), from the Antwerp mint. The remaining four coins are all issues of the Kingdom of the Netherlands from the Utrecht mint: gold ducats of 1830 and 1841 and silver gulden of 1923 and 1931.

The modern cabinet expanded further as the result of other generous gifts. Of particular note for future reference is the gift of about a thousand mid-1970s Italian "miniassegni", an extensive collection of these elusive and ephemeral notes formed on-site at the time by the donor, Sidney W. Harl. Another important addition to the modern cabinet came from John Aiello, who contributed about 350 miscellaneous recent issues of world coinage and paper money. Dr. Ute Wartenberg donated examples of the five German 2001 ten-coin mint sets. Other donors of individual modern coins included Oliver D. Hoover, Sebastian Heath, Leonard Gregory Mazzone, and Sra. Katalin Uzdi.

The only accessions to the Latin American cabinet were in the form
of 31 counterfeits from Horace P. Flatt, two recent Venezuelan issues
from an anonymous donor, two Brazilian commemorative notes from
the Banco Central of Brazil, and two early Mexican 4-reales pieces
from Richard H. Ponterio. These latter are a significant addition to
this part of the ANS collection (they feature the assayer/mint combinations of R and M, Nesmith 74; and Mo and G, unlisted in Nesmith).

The United States portion of the cabinet benefitted from a variety
of interesting gifts. Probably the most valuable of these was the donation, by Paul R. Wilson, of two superb U.S. Treasury ("Coin") notes of
Series 1890: a $1 bill with serial no. A55* and a $5 bill with serial no.
A1*! Historically, the most evocative pieces received are undoubtedly
a group of coins recovered from the famous 1857 shipwreck of the SS
Central America, donated by Mr. and Mrs. Anthony Terranova. These
include a somewhat burnt and bent 1852 $10 gold piece from the US
Assay Office for Gold, a US $20 gold piece with a corroded base-metal
coin still adhering to it, a Moffat & Co. 1850 $5 gold piece, and US $5
half eagles of 1843, 1844-O, 1845-D, and 1852-C.

From James H. Blind came a group of twentieth-century half dollars, quarter dollars, and a dime, as well as fourteen nice Liberty
Seated half dimes, ranging in date from 1839 to 1872. The significance
of this latter group is underscored by the fact that many portions of
the collection have not heretofore been upgraded by the addition of
known varieties. In keeping with older collector traditions, previous
donations often featured single examples of dates of the different denominations. The US cabinet, in particular, is consequently still weak
in many important varieties. Along these lines, the dollar collection
was improved by a gift of a mint-state 1882-S Morgan silver dollar,
by Leo Boisvert.

Other miscellaneous enhancements to the US collection came from
Stephen Album, Dr. Michael L. Bates, Catherine E. Bullowa-Moore,
Michael Capen, the Chicago Coin Club, George Cuhaj, Jonathan Kagan, Roger deWardt Lane, Vanessa Samet, Anthony Terranova, Dr.
Ute Wartenberg, and an anonymous donor. In the form of replica dies
made by Peter Rosa and some strikings from them, Wayne G. Sayles
contributed materials relating to several departments, including the US
section.

The Society's cabinet of medallic works increased in a number of areas. Contributors of various recent commemorative issues included the Canadian Portrait Academy, the China Numismatic Society (Yao Shuomin, Editor), the Gateway Coin Club of Merced, California, the Indian Coin Society (Prashant P. Kulkarni, President), Stephen Mirabella, Edward C. Olsson, Madelyn O'Neil, Milton B. Pfeffer, Robert W. Shippee, Dr. Ralph R. Sonnenschein, and Dr. Ute Wartenberg.

Paul F. L. de Groot presented thirteen works by contemporary Netherlands medallic sculptors. Mr. and Mrs. Kenneth L. Edlow gave the impressive large cast Edlow birthday commemorative medallion by Jeanne Stevens-Sollman, President of the American Medallic Sculpture Association. Daniel M. Friedenberg donated a spectacular collection of about 600 medallic works by Jewish artists and of Jewish subject matter, including a splendid suite of the beautiful architectural medals by the mid-nineteenth-century Belgian master-engraver Jacques Wiener. Sebastian Heath gave an attractive eighteenth-century French piece. Gustaaf T. M. Hellegers presented two modern Netherlands medallic sculptures; Jonathan Kagan, a Napoleonic silver medal; and Marion Roller, her own Brookgreen Gardens medal. Donald Oresman presented 97 miscellaneous American medals of the nineteenth and twentieth centuries and Dr. Ira Rezak, an outstanding collection of 240 Russian and Soviet medals. Dr. Stephen K. Scher donated two modern medallic sculptures, by British Art Medal Society members Nicola Moss and Bogomil Nikolov.

A fine donation from Paul Franklin, Jr., included an important die by famed American medallic sculptor James Earle Fraser. It is an obverse prepared for the 1901 Buffalo Pan-American Exposition "Special Award of Honor", a commemorative presentation piece celebrating the achievements and participation of Augustus Saint-Gaudens. The well-preserved but previously undocumented work was accompanied by an original small plaster model, a negative galvano, two matching positive plaster models and a bronze cast, as well as five uniface trial strikes (in gold, "German silver", copper, and two in lead) from the die.

*1.   France, Charles VII, St. Lô mint (Plate 14 no. 1)
Acc. number: 2000.15.5 (donated by Mark and Lottie Salton in memory of Felix Schlessinger)

AV écu aux couronelles *dit* écu neuf, second period, sixth or seventh emission, 1450–1461, 28 mm, 3.334 g

Ref.: Lafaurie 510f.; Duplessy 511E and F

This piece is noteworthy as the first St. Lô specimen in the cabinet for this reign. As is the case with most of the mints which struck coinage during Charles' sixth and seventh emissions (from 18 May 1450 and 16 June 1455)—designated by a lozenge within a coronet as the initial mark—it is not possible to differentiate coinage into the two groups. The St. Lô mint denoted its output by means of a mint mark consisting of a *point secret* beneath the nineteenth letter of the legend on both obverse and reverse. Opening at the end of 1449, it commenced striking during the fifth emission (dating from 10 January 1448). Like the third emission, the fifth utilized a coronet with a dot within it as its initial mark; however, the earliest St. Lô pieces carried a fleur-de-lis initial mark, which was characteristic of the fourth emission at all the other mints. The Salton coin represents the first St. Lô emission issued in conformity with the national coinage.

*2. France, Louis XII, St. André de Villeneuve-lès-Avignon mint (Plate 14 no. 2)

Acc. number: 2000.15.6 (donated by Mark and Lottie Salton in memory of Felix Schlessinger)

AV écu d'or au soleil, first emission, c. 1498–1507, 30 mm, 3.378 g

Ref.: Lafaurie 592; Duplessy 647

*3. France, Francis I, Crémieu mint, first type (Plate 14 no. 3)

2000.15.7 (donated by Mark and Lottie Salton in memory of Felix Schlessinger)

AV écu d'or du Dauphiné, first emission, c. 1515–1528, 28 mm, 3.306 g

Ref.: Lafaurie 645; Duplessy 782

*4. Brabant, Charles V, Antwerp mint (Plate 14 no. 4)

Acc. number: 2000.15.1 (donated by Mark and Lottie Salton in memory of Felix Schlessinger)

AV demi réal d'or, 25 mm, 3.450 g

Ref.: Delmonte 99

*5.   Brabant, Charles V, Antwerp mint (Plate 14 no. 5)
Acc. number: 2000.15.2 (donated by Mark and Lottie Salton in memory of Felix Schlessinger)
AV florin carolus d'or, 22 mm, 2.927 g
Ref.: Delmonte 101

*6.   France, Louis XIV, Nantes mint (Plate 14 no. 6)
Acc. number: 2000.15.9 (donated by Mark and Lottie Salton in memory of Felix Schlessinger)
AV louis d'or aux quatre L, 1694-T, 24 mm, 6.653 g
Ref.: Gadoury 252; KM 302.14
The coin is overstruck on a Paris mint (A), 1691-dated louis d'or à l'écu.

*7.   France, Louis XIV, Tours mint (Plate 14 no. 7)
2000.15.8 (donated by Mark and Lottie Salton in memory of Felix Schlessinger)
AV louis d'or aux quatre L, 1694-E, 24 mm, 6.579 g
Ref.: Gadoury 252; KM 302.7
The coin is overstruck on a Paris mint (A), 1690-dated louis d'or à l'écu.

*8.   France, Louis XIV, Bordeaux mint, (Plate 14 no. 8)
2000.15.10 (donated by Mark and Lottie Salton in memory of Felix Schlessinger)
AV louis d'or aux insignes, 1704-K, 27 mm, 6.640 g
Ref.: Gadoury 254; KM 365.10
A poignant memento of Louis XIV's financial manipulations, this coin was overstruck on a 1694-dated example of the issue "aux quatre L" previously overstruck on a louis d'or à l'écu; note the flan cracks due to hardening from multiple striking without annealing.

*9.   Italy, miniassegni series, Banca Popolare de Bergamo, Brescia (Plate 15 no. 1)
Acc. number: 2001.34.1 (donated by Sidney W. Harl)
100 lire, 9 December 1976, 116 × 64 mm, serial no. A/0504670
Ref.: Not in Bobba or Mancini

*10. Italy, miniassegni series, Cassa di Risparmio di Jesi, Ancona (Plate 15 no. 2)
Acc. number: 2001.34.2 (donated by Sidney W. Harl)
150 lire, 18 January 1977; 128 × 55 mm; serial no. 062074
Ref.: Not in Bobba or Mancini

*11. Italy, miniassegni series, Banco Ambrosiano, Milano (Plate 16 no. 1)
Acc. number: 2001.34.3 (donated by Sidney W. Harl)
100 lire, 16 December 1976, 117 x 55 mm, serial no. 3416
Ref.: Not in Bobba or Mancini

*12. Italy, miniassegni series, Banca di Trento e Bolzano, Trento, Atesina Società Automobilistica, Trento (Plate 16 no. 2)
Acc. number: 2001.34.4 (donated by Sidney W. Harl)
50 lire, 18 February 1977, 115 × 63 mm, serial no. 4538605
Ref.: Not in Bobba or Mancini

*13. Italy, miniassegni series, Republic of San Marino, Cassa di Risparmio della Repubblica di San Marino (Plate 17 no. 1)
Acc. number: 2001.34.5 (donated by Sidney W. Harl)
150 lire, 5 April 1976, 159 × 69 mm, serial no. 174061
Ref.: Bobba (1977) p. 121.

*14. Italy, Miniassegni series, Banco S. Paolo, Brescia (Plate 17 no. 2)
Acc. number: 2001.34.6 (donated by Sidney W. Harl)
200 lire, 15 November 1976; 120 × 60 mm; serial no. 200014714
Ref.: Mancini (1976) p. 10.

*15. Mexico, Charles I and Johana, late series, c. 1542–1545 (Plate 17 no. 3)
Acc. number: 2000.20.1 (donated by Richard H. Ponterio)
AR 4 reales, Assayer G (Juan Gutiérrez), 33 mm, 13.626 g
Obv.: Crowned Spanish Habsburg arms, with o/M to l. and **G** to r.; **CHAROLVS:ET:IOHANA:REGES**
Rev.: Two crowned pillars above waves; across field divided by the pillars, **PLV SUL TRA/ 4; +HISPANIARVM:ET: IM[sic] DIARVM**
Ref.: Not in Nesmith (cf. 54, with obverse design 15, legend CH4; the reverse is of design B, legend unrecorded).

*16. Mexico, Charles I and Johana, late series, c. 1543 (Plate 17 no. 4)
Acc. number: 2000.20.2 (donated by Richard H. Ponterio)
AR 4 reales, Assayer R (Francisco del Rincón), 32 mm, 12.701 g
Obv.: Crowned Spanish Habsburg arms, with **R** to l. and **M** to r.;
CAROLVS·ET·IOHANA·REGES
Rev.: Two crowned pillars above waves; across field divided by
the pillars, **PLV SUL TRA/ 4**; **+HISPANIARVM·ET·INDIARVM**
Ref.: Nesmith 74 (obverse design 16, legend 24; reverse design C1,
legend 1).
Nesmith noted four examples of this late series R-M 4 reales, with
three different reverse legend varieties.

*17. United States, California, US Assay Office of Gold, San Francisco
(Plate 18 no. 1)
Acc. number: 2001.3.1 (donated by Mr. and Mrs. Anthony Terra-
nova)
AV $10, 1852, 28 mm, 16.910 g
Ref.: Breen 7718
Salvaged from the wreck of SS *Central America*; somewhat burnt
and bent as a result of the shipwreck.

*18. United States, San Francisco mint (Plate 18 no. 2)
Acc. number: 2001.3.2 (donated by Mr. and Mrs. Anthony Terra-
nova)
AV $20 (1854–1857), 33 mm, 36.306 g
With a badly corroded foreign base-metal coin adhering and obs-
curing the date. Salvaged from the wreck of SS *Central America*.

*19. United States, California, Moffat & Co., San Francisco (Plate 18
no. 3)
Acc. number: 2001.3.3 (donated by Mr. and Mrs. Anthony Terra-
nova)
AV $5, 1850, 21.5 mm, 8.108 g
Ref.: Breen 7785
Salvaged from the wreck of SS *Central America*.

*20. United States (Plate 18 no. 4)
Acc. number: 2001.3.6 (donated by Mr. and Mrs. Anthony Terranova)

AV $5, 1845-D, 21.5 mm, 8.219 g
Ref.: Breen 6558
Salvaged from the wreck of SS *Central America.*

*21. United States (Plate 18 no. 5)
Acc. number: 2001.3.4 (donated by Mr. and Mrs. Anthony Terra-
nova)
AV $5, 1852-C, 21.5 mm, 8.268 g
Ref.: Breen 6599
Salvaged from the wreck of SS *Central America.*

*22. United States, Treasury Note, Series 1890 (Plate 18 no. 6)
Acc. number: 2001.4.1 (donated by Paul R. Wilson)
1 dollar, 190 × 80 mm, serial no. A55*
Ref.: Friedberg 347

*23. United States, Treasury Note, Series 1890 (Plate 18 no. 7)
Acc. number: 2001.4.2 (donated by Paul R. Wilson)
5 dollars, 190 × 80 mm, serial no. A1*
Ref.: Friedberg 359

*24. United States, electrotype replica of "Excelsior" copper, 1781
(Plate 19 no. 1)
Acc. number: 2000.30.1 (donated by Wayne G. Sayles)
One of the well-known copies produced by Peter Rosa as "Bec-
ker".

*25. Italy (under French occupation), Milan mint, 1805 (Plate 19
no. 2)
2002.18.3 (donated by Jonathan Kagan)
AR struck coronation medal of emperor Napoleon I as King of
Italy, 42 mm
Ref.: Bramsen 420
This attractive classical piece by the talented Milanese mint master
and engraver Luigi Manfredini (1771–1840) shows an incorrect date
for Bonaparte's coronation: 23 May 1805 (in actuality, the date of
the decree was 26 May—so much for pre-planning!); the issue was
represented in the cabinet heretofore by a bronze example only.

*26. Belgium, Jacques Wiener (1815–1899) (Plate 19 no. 3)
Acc. number: 2000.1.9 (donated by Daniel M. Friedenberg)
AE struck medal, 59 mm, "Cathedrale de Reims", 1859;
Ref.: Bouhy 24; Van Hoydonck 170
Wiener's "Most Remarkable Buildings of Europe" series of 41 monumental medals is among the most ambitious (and breathtaking!) in all of numismatics.

*27. United States, James Earle Fraser (1876–1953) (Plate 19 no. 4)
Acc. number: 2001.42.1 (donated by Paul Franklin, Jr.)
Steel obverse die for 44-mm medal (smaller version of the actual award medal), "Pan-American Exposition, Special Medal of Honor Created for Augustus Saint-Gaudens", 1901
Ref.: Cf. Baxter 107
This medal was commissioned for presentation to Fraser's illustrious mentor, Augustus Saint-Gaudens, in appreciation for his participation in the ill-fated venue at Buffalo, New York, in the summer of 1901 (President McKinley was shot in the exposition's Music Pavilion). A work of art by Fraser depicting a wonderful, classic portrait Saint-Gaudens, this example of die-cutting ranks among the finest in American medallic sculpture. Of special interest, the Franklin die was cut in a size much smaller than that used to strike the recorded versions of the medal (44 mm as opposed to 91 mm). One uniface example of this die's output is presently known (apart from the five trial strikes included in this donation), in the collection of ANS member Gene Hynds.

*28. United States, Jeanne Stevens-Sollman (Plate 20 no. 1)
Acc. number: 2001.44.1 (donated by Mr. and Mrs. Kenneth L. Edlow)
AE cast medallion, 230 mm, Kenneth L. Edlow 60th birthday commemorative, 2001, with accompanying 100-year-old walnut presentation box; cast by Aesthetic Materials, of State College, Pennsylvania.
One of an edition of eight, the work was actually produced by the process of sintering—kiln-firing powdered bronze in a mold to just the point where the metal will flow and form a molecular bond. Long used in industry for precision casting, sintered-bronze

foundry-work has recently been made available to artists by Dr. Randall M. German and Julian Thomas, at Pennsylvania State University. This impressive medallion was the first double-sided work so cast by Aesthetic Materials.

*29. Great Britain, Bogomil Nikolov (Plate 20 no. 2)
Acc. number: 2000.25.1 (donated by Dr. Stephen K. Scher)
AE cast medallion, 110 mm, "Acta est Fabula", 1989

REFERENCES

Baxter, Barbara A. 1987. *The Beaux-Arts medal in America*. New York: American Numismatic Society.

Bobba, Cesare. 1977. *Catalogo nazionale dei miniassegni con valutazioni*. Asti: Bobba Numismatico.

Bouhy, Victor. 1883. Jacques Wiener, graveur en medailles, et son œuvre. *Revue Belge de Numismatique* (1883):5–175.

Bramsen, L. 1904–11. *Médaillier Napoléon le Grand, ou, description des médailles, clichés, repoussés, et médailles-décorations relatives aux affaires de la France pendant le consulat et l'empire*. Paris: A. Picard.

Breen, Walter. 1988. *Walter Breen's complete encyclopedia of U.S. and colonial coins*. New York: Doubleday.

Delmonte, A. 1964. *Le Bénélux d'or: répertoire du monnayage d'or des territoires composant les anciennes Pays-Bas*. Amsterdam: Jacques Schulman.

Duplessy, Jean. 1988–89. *Les monnaies françaises royales de Hugues Capet à Louis XVI (987–1793)*. Paris: Maison Platt.

Friedberg, Arthur L. and Ira S. Friedberg. 2001. *Paper money of the United States: a complete guide with valuations*, 16th ed. Clifton, N.J.: Coin & Currency Institute.

Gadoury, Victor. 1986. *Monnaies royales françaises, 1610–1792*. Monte-Carlo: V. Gadoury.

van Hoydonck, Emiel. 1971. *Jacques Wiener (1815–1899): médailles [et] jetons*. (Belgium): E. van Hoydonck.

Krause, Chester L. and Clifford Mishler. 2000. *2001 standard catalog of world coins*. Iola, Wis.: Krause Publications.

Lafaurie, Jean. 1951. *Les monnaies des rois de France*. Paris: É. Bourgey.

Mancini, Libero. 1976. *Catalogo dei miniassegni*. Bologna: L. Mancini.

Nesmith, Robert I. 1955. *Coinage of the first mint of the Americas at Mexico City, 1536–1572*. Numismatic Notes and Monographs 131, New York: American Numismatic Society.

Robert W. Hoge

PLATES

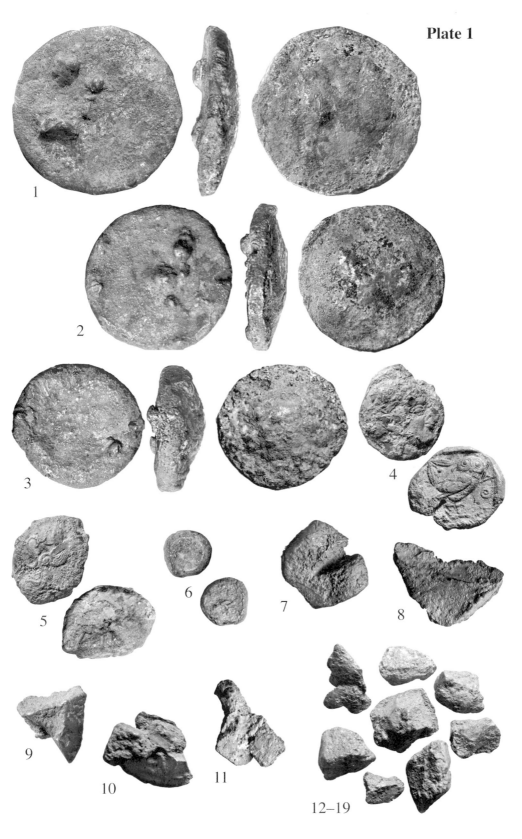

Plate 1

1

2

3

4

5

6

7

8

9

10

11

12–19

Silver Bullion from Egypt

Plate 2

1

(2x)

2

(2x)

3

(2x)

4

5

6

7

8

9

10

Scythians in the West Pontic Area

Plate 3

1

2

3

(2x)

(2x)

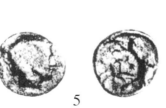

4

5

6

Scythians in the West Pontic Area

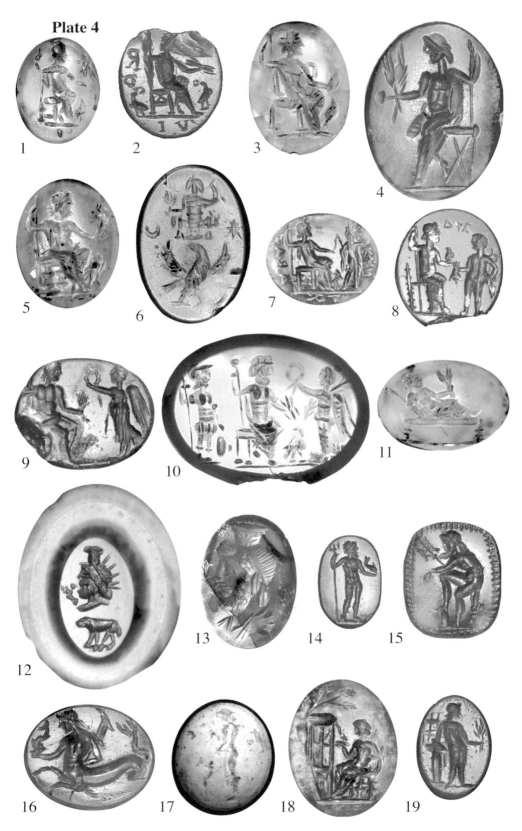

Plate 4

1

2

3

4

5

6

7

8

9

10

11

12

13

14

15

16

17

18

19

Engraved Gems with Gods and Heroes

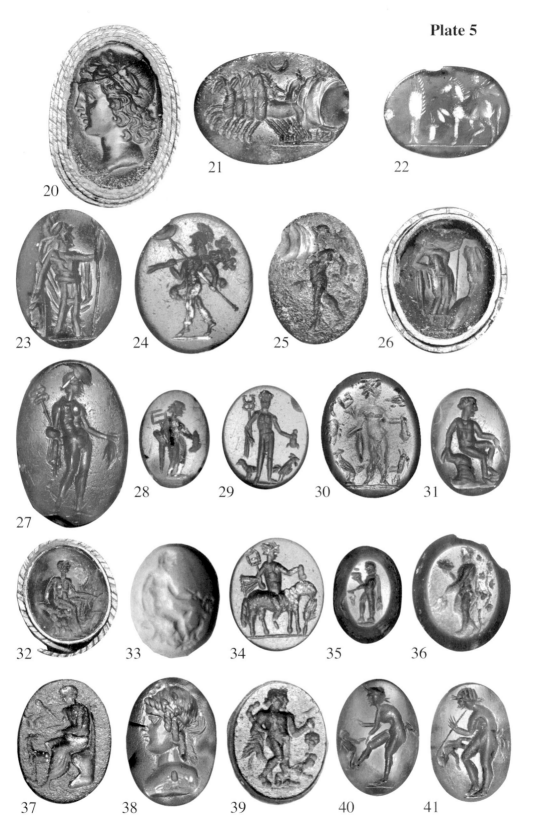

Plate 5

Engraved Gems with Gods and Heroes

Plate 6

Engraved Gems with Gods and Heroes

Sixth-Century Tremissis

Plate 7

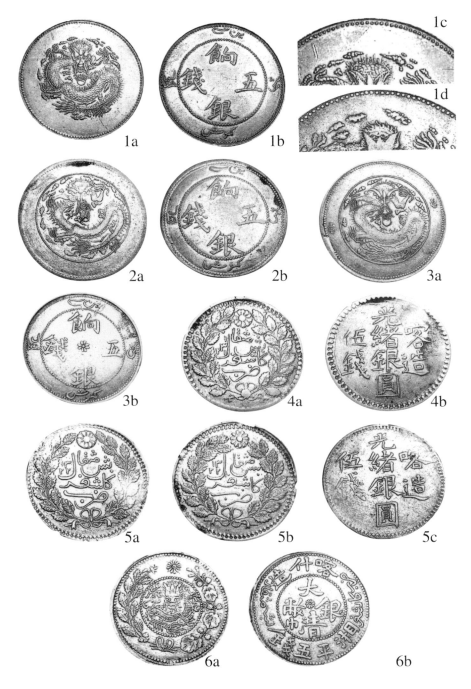

A die study of silver coins of Sinkiang, China

Plate 8

A die study of silver coins of Sinkiang, China

Greek

Plate 9

Acquisitions for 2000 and 2001

Plate 10

Roman

1

2

3

4

5

6

7

8

9

10

11

12

Roman Provincial

13

Acquisitions for 2000 and 2001

Roman Provincial

Plate 11

Byzantine

Acquisitions for 2000 and 2001

Plate 12

Islamic

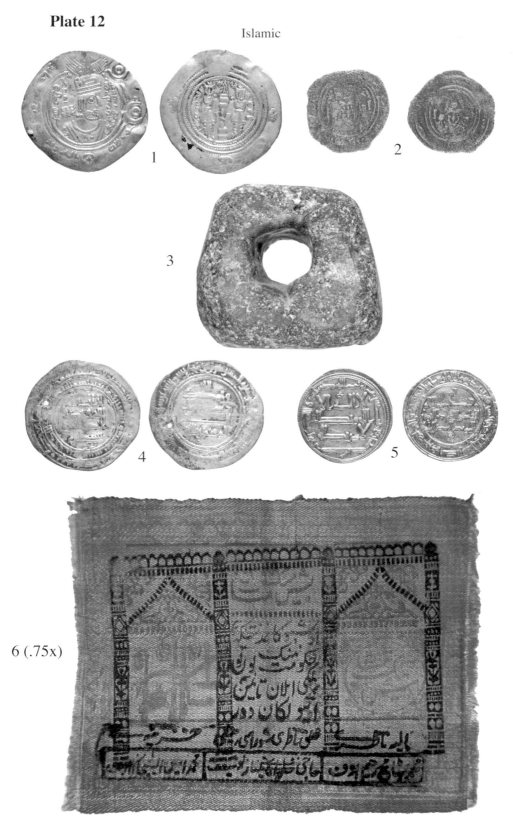

1

2

3

4

5

6 (.75x)

Acquisitions for 2000 and 2001

Plate 13

Islamic

1 (.75x)

South Asian

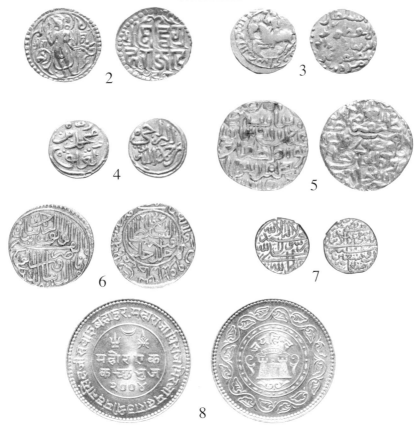

2

3

4

5

6

7

8

Acquisitions for 2000 and 2001

Plate 14

Medieval

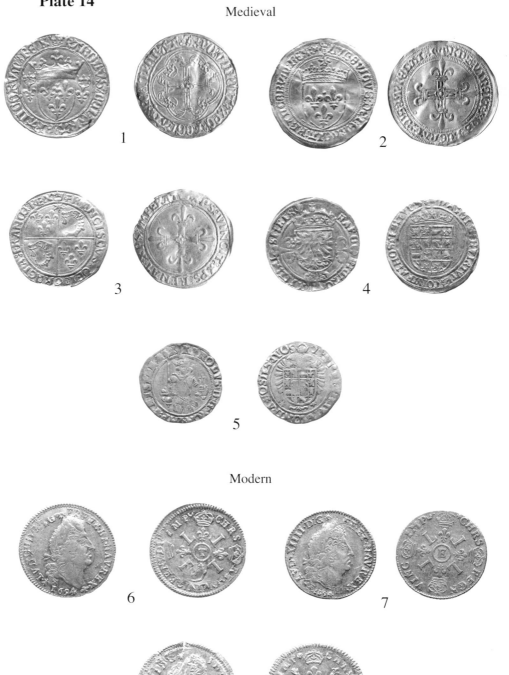

1

2

3

4

5

Modern

6

7

8

Acquisitions for 2000 and 2001

1 (.75x)

2 (.75x)

Plate 16

Modern

1 (.75x)

2 (.75x)

Acquisitions for 2000 and 2001

Plate 17

Modern

1 (.75x)

2 (.75x)

Latin America

3

4

Acquisitions for 2000 and 2001

Plate 18

United States

1

2

3

4

5

6 (.66x)

7 (.66x)

Acquisitions for 2000 and 2001

Plate 19

United States

Medals

Acquisitions for 2000 and 2001

Plate 20

Medals

1 (.33x)

2 (.50x)

Acquisitions for 2000 and 2001